The Graven Image

ARCHAEOLOGY, CULTURE, AND SOCIETY

Ian Hodder and Robert Preucel, Series Editors

A complete list of books in the series
is available from the publisher.

The Graven Image

Representation in Babylonia and Assyria

Zainab Bahrani

PENN

UNIVERSITY OF PENNSYLVANIA PRESS

Philadelphia

10 9 8 7 6 5 4 3 2 1

Published by
University of Pennsylvania Press
Philadelphia, Pennsylvania 19104-4011

Library of Congress Cataloging-in-Publication Data
Bahrani, Zainab, 1962–
   The graven image : representation in Babylonia and Assyria / Zainab Bahrani.
      p.   cm. — (Archaeology, culture, and society)
   Includes bibliographical references and index.
   ISBN 0-8122-3648-3 (cloth : alk. paper)
      1. Aesthetics, Oriental. 2. Art, Assyro-Babylonian. 3. Aesthetics, Oriental—Historiography.
4. Art, Assyro-Babylonian—Historiography. I. Title. II. Series.
BH102.B34 2003
302.2'0935—dc21   2003047322

To Kenan with love

Contents

Illustrations

Introduction

THE GRAVEN IMAGE is an inquiry into the concept of representation in the ancient Near East. The book is concerned specifically with the Assyro-Babylonian practice of combining writing and visual representation for the production of images as a form of essential presence or for what might be described as conjuring presence in an image. An essential presence in an image means that the image takes the place of the real or that what is conceived of as a real essence is present in and through the image. Yet this presence is not a matter of a simple substitution. This practice is the main historical thesis of the book. At the same time, the study is also concerned with the parallel practice of image making in academic discourse. It means to make allusion likewise to our own reconstructions of the identity of past peoples and cultures through a process of writing and representation. Historical writing and archaeological practice are modes of presencing—that is, they are modes of making present distant and past societies. As such, they can be described as representations of culture. The book is therefore a study of representations, both ours and that of a distant Mesopotamian past. It is also a study of how past and present come to be woven together, and how to some extent we continue to re-create that past and have an effect on it, in a continuous reciprocal relationship. Therefore, this book is an investigation into the relationship between creation and representation. I have chosen this theme not only as a means of engaging with questions of representationality currently under discussion in both the humanities and the social sciences but also because as an area of philosophical enquiry this relationship was of foremost concern in antiquity.

The book is intended as a theoretical investigation of image making and concepts of signification (both visual and verbal) in a civilization where such notions developed quite apart from post-Greek metaphysics and ideas of representation as mimesis, or close copy. It is thus an aesthetic tradition that opens unique avenues to a rethinking of art historical and critical conceptions of the nature of representation itself—conceptions that have viewed image making primarily in terms of the mimetic activity of depicting the real or natural world around us. Studies of ancient Near

Eastern art have focused, on the one hand, on chronological develop-ments of style or iconography or, on the other hand, on political patron-age and ideology. *The Graven Image* diverges from both of these scholarly traditions in considering Near Eastern representation at the level of onto-logical meaning and function. Through this analysis of the ontology of representation, other aspects of image making and image uses become clarified. Thus, the book focuses on topics such as the treatment of im-ages in battles, the inscription of curses on portraiture, and the relation-ship of the image of the king to the king's organic body. These are conceptions of representation, and practices and rituals involving images that, despite being a rich source of information for the social function of images in Near Eastern societies, have been mostly neglected until now, due to a number of scholarly biases that will be discussed here.

Another set of issues that concern art history and archaeology in general emerges from historiography and focuses on the place of language and interpretation in the production of historical narratives. Assyrian art in particular also is taken as an opening into an investigation of the back-ground of the discipline of art history and its discursive representations of origins, civilization, and the other. Art historians specializing in areas other than antiquity, therefore, do not necessarily need to read this book primarily as a source of empirical information for Assyrian and Babylonian culture but for the interrogation of the problematic of representation—both our representations (how we write history and produce meaning re-garding past or alien cultures and systems of belief) as well as one of the main objects of art historical study—image making. In this way I hope to release Near Eastern art from its simple comparative and teleological posi-tion in the discipline of art history, a position that I will argue has had a great deal to do with the interpretation of Mesopotamia and its artifacts.

A standard factual statement made repeatedly in art history and in ar-chaeology is that civilization can be said to have begun in the Near East. How or why this is the case is not often considered. But this statement cannot be made if we do not adhere to a notion of civilization as one uni-versal whole, an entity that develops through time in a sequential order, nor can this statement be made without an unproblematic concept of be-ginning or origin. For this reason the ancient Near East, and Mesopotamia in particular, is an area of study worth pursuing for the investigation of some of the most essential historical topoi. Origins, in theology, in narra-tive, or in history, can be divine, mythical, and privileged. They also can be chaotic or savage and primitive. The origin of civilization is a primordial place, existing at the very beginning. It is a historical boundary—and even a liminal "in between" area, bridging what is considered real historical time and prehistory. A return to Mesopotamia, so to speak, has much to offer. As a point of origin for what we have come to call history or civilization, the ancient Near East's position, at the limits of this referential structure, can become a rich place from which to analyze a number of fundamental disciplinary concepts.

Throughout the book I will move between the past and the present. I look at the present and the recent past in order to investigate Assyrian and Babylonian culture, because it is through this modern context that it has been defined. Thus, a large part of the book's pages are devoted to addressing what ancient Mesopotamia has come to be in Western discourse. I return to Akkadian texts and reexamine cuneiform as a system of script in order to reach what I feel is a better understanding of the ancient Near Eastern notion of representation. As a result, the book is not written in the form of a seamless narrative but as a series of essays that confront a number of unexamined theoretical assumptions and propose rereading Assyro-Babylonian art practices from a new theoretical position.

At the basis of my argument is the theoretical stance—common to the thinking of postprocessual archaeology, poststructuralist, deconstructivist, and postcolonial scholarship—that our capacity to access the past is complicated both by the problematic nature of the documentation that forms the original context we retrieve and by our own present subject positions, or how we retrieve the past. In other words, the original context is not simply formed by data, found by the scholar. It also is produced through an entire set of interpretive decisions and assumptions that are often left unstated. This is not an approach that claims the past has no real existence beyond our interpretations but one that looks into the way a scholarly text organizes itself as a form of knowledge and acknowledges that historical narratives are necessarily invested with the values of the present. These become particularly important factors to acknowledge when the object of investigation has been the paradigmatic hostile other of the tradition in which we work.

The essays begin with challenging the position of the ancient Near East within the constructed narrative of universal history and continue to question the unstated assumptions that underlie the standard interpretations of Assyro-Babylonian concepts of representation and art objects. The material is not amassed in the exhaustive manner of traditional archaeological studies, nor is it arranged in a standard or familiar art historical method. Nevertheless, it is an intentional arrangement in which a number of issues are brought together on theoretical rather than empirical grounds. Likewise, my aim has not been to record every known Assyrian portrayal or reference to image making in the standard monograph method but to gain a better understanding of these concepts by considering questions of representation outside the limits of the visual arts. Rather than attempting a survey of all such practices in the Assyro-Babylonian tradition, I have focused on certain issues that seem to span art, philosophy, and political practice—in Near Eastern antiquity as well as today.

One of the main points of the book is that Mesopotamia, as we know it, is a sort of discursive map. Maps are cartographic representations that are said to coincide exactly, even scientifically, with the real mapped space. We are well aware that the map is merely a schematic indication, but the map asserts itself as real because it is a representation based on scientific knowledge and reason. The discursive map of Mesopotamia is in many ways a simulacrum, a simulation rather than a close mimetic copy of the real. This book therefore takes up a series of concepts for consideration as the assemblage forming Mesopotamia. Before turning to the Mesopotamian practices of image making, our own textual representations of Mesopotamia are addressed in the first three chapters.

The first chapter considers the ethnohistorical disciplinary structures that formed the background for the study of ancient Near Eastern art and architecture, instigated in the mid-nineteenth century. Art history was a discipline enfolded with race, notions of racial evolution, linguistics, and ethnography as well as a political theory of progress that saw the natural destiny of civilization in Europe. A critical reassessment of the structure of the discipline and its global system of knowledge cannot be properly understood outside the context of the European enterprise of colonialism. The second chapter considers how the name *Mesopotamia* established this simulacral cartographic space as historically factual. The structuring horizons of space and time allowed a construction of a "Mesopotamia" as the infancy of world civilization in order to facilitate a historical narrative with its ideal outcome in the modern West. *Mesopotamia* is a colonial term, and its continued usage has numerous political implications that must be brought to light. However, I should like to point out that in unmasking the term *Mesopotamia,* and examining the latent Orientalist epistemology it brings with it, I am not calling for an outright ban on the usage of the word in scholarship. What I do emphasize instead is the necessity of becoming aware of the invention of such terminology, its place in the mythohistorical tradition of the West, and the taxonomy of which it is part. My aim, therefore, is to show the links between European intellectual practices of the nineteenth century and the power and authority of imperialism. For my own purposes, I have opted to use terms such as *Assyro-Babylonian* or simply *Babylonian* when referring to ontology, theology, and so on. I use the term *Babylonian* to refer to what is now central and southern Iraq. This is the area in which much of the scholarly thinking was developed in antiquity, and this Babylonian scholarship became incorporated into the Assyrian tradition of northern Iraq and Syria as well.

Chapter 3 considers two oppositions. The first is between subject and object of study in art history and archaeology. This opposition is a rarely questioned division upon which all that qualifies as valid and objective interpretation hinges. In this chapter, I argue that the subject position of the scholar of antiquity is not separable from the object of study presented in the text. Historical truths are mediated by, among other things, the relationship of the historian to the past. Because the art historian or archaeologist is in the position of translator or mediator of culture, that position can be defined as one of an ethnographer, depending on ethnographic authority for the representation of culture. The notion of a problematic context applies to our own roles as scholars and not simply to a separate object of study. The second division that I examine here is the fictional binary opposition of perceptual/conceptual representation, or sign/symbol, as equivalent to West/other in aesthetic discourse. This framework has not only influenced our reading of ancient non-Western aesthetics and arts. It is a framework that requires the East to be, as Hegel describes it, the realm of the symbol (1975:303). Although they may seem not to belong in the same chapter, in my view the two oppositions are related because perceptualism or mimesis remains a point of reference in art history.

The four chapters that follow comprise a second unit in Part 2. They present a main thesis of the book: in the Assyro-Babylonian tradition, representation, far from aspiring to mimesis, is conceived of as being part of the real. This section discusses how representation in Mesopotamia had the power of creating the real and in fact was thought to create the real.

Chapters 4 and 5 are an explication and theorization of the Assyro-Babylonian notion of representation in both script and images. Chapter 4 focuses on the cuneiform script, defining it as a pluridimensional system of writing and demonstrating its intimate connection to magic and divination in Assyro-Babylonian thought. Chapter 5 shifts this focus to *ṣalmu*, the Akkadian word for image, which I define as a system of visual representation, arguing that it is not to be separated from the verbal system of the script nor to be directly equated to the European concept of image.

Chapter 6 looks particularly at the related practices of assailing images and image theft as a means of demonstrating how representation was thought to control, or have an effect on, what is represented. It is the first discussion of the Assyro-Babylonian practice of substitution by image and the very real power with which images were invested in Mesopotamian antiquity. This practice and the belief in substitution were heavily dependent upon the combination word-image as a mode of creating a real and valid presence. In contrast to other studies that have looked at texts as parallel sources of information, next to the image, and considered these in the context of political ideology or propaganda alone, this chapter insists on the text as an integral part of the image, an aspect that makes it function as a representation.

Chapter 7 takes a canonical work of art, the so-called "altar of Tukulti-Ninurta," and reconsiders it from the point of view of this word-image dialectic, distinctive of Mesopotamian concepts of representation, in which it was thought that every sign was involved in a limitless process of semiosis.

I have written this book with more than one specialist discipline in mind, bridging the disciplinary divide in writing wherever possible. I use the language of semiology and of deconstruction that is familiar to art historians but not to the majority of ancient Near Eastern scholars. I will therefore attempt to clarify terms or theoretical concepts that may seem obvious to an art historical readership but not to all archaeologists or Near Eastern scholars. At the same time, I will make use of well-known Assyriological terms and historical references that will need to be explained to the art historian who is not familiar with the Near East, and I will beg the patience of Near Eastern scholars in those sections. My line of argument is that much of what has been separated on professional and epistemological grounds often can be better understood if viewed according to a broader frame of reference. While I use the languages of semiology and deconstruction, I have not applied a semiotic model to the ancient texts and images. Instead, these theories have been more important for my discussions of the similarities and differences between a Western tradition of metaphysics and ancient Near Eastern thought. The limitations of the semiological vocabulary became clear to me in the earliest stages of this project, and those limitations became a means of revealing the deficiencies and difficulties of universalized semiotic models.

A few words about the style of writing are perhaps also necessary here. In his groundbreaking book, *Metahistory* published in 1973, Hayden White first argued that the way we write history—our rhetoric and tropes—creates our object of study to a great extent. They are not neutral objective words but descriptive and significatory in themselves. In her 1990 essay "Past Looking," Michael Ann Holly has made a similar argument with regard to art historical writing. Since then, many art historians have also taken up the question of the place of the gaze in our contemplation of the works we study and the histories we write. Since the end of the 1970s, this psychoanalytic theoretical notion of the gaze, stemming from the writings of Jacques Lacan, has emerged as a primary term for thinking through perception. Its use has not been limited to art history and other visual disciplines but has had an effect on a significant sector of the humanities and social sciences. The importance of the gaze as a concept is that it allows for a theorization of the relationship between vision-looking and power. The gaze, then, is not simply a glance or a look but a look that structures and controls. I further believe that our limits of observation as historians and critics become even more problematic when the object of observation is both an alien and a temporally distant culture. And in this case it is an alien culture that is in the paradigmatic position of hostile other to the classical and biblical traditions that form the basis of the Western humanist tradition. In my previous work I have already argued that ethnographic concerns regarding observation must also be taken into account in art history, because our relationship to the object of study cannot be neatly separated out of our descriptions. As Michael Ann Holly puts it, "We may be talking about an artifact, but we are also talking about ourselves" (1990:390). In this way Holly and several other art historians have reconsidered the relationship between observer and object of observation. What is remarkable to my thinking is that this movement between observer and observed seems to have been particularly well understood by the ancient Mesopotamians, and on many different levels, some of which will be presented in this study.

In effect there are two primary subjects that form the focus of this book and structure its main critical points. The first is historiographic and explicitly political, and the second is concerned with the concept of mimesis: the relationship of representation and the real. In my mind the two are linked because historical writing depends on mimesis in order to function as truth. Art historical writing very often concerns itself with describing verbally the visual representations of others. In other words, we as art historians often concern ourselves with describing how other cultures at differing times and places conceived of the relationship that makes up mimesis: the extent to which their representations come to resemble the real, or conversely, how they deny this resemblance through abstraction or symbolism. As a result of the concern with mimesis, a third subject emerges in this book, and that is the conception of this universal real that we posit as an integral part of mimetic copies. Here I will consider representation and realism as aesthetic genres as well as review their epistemological status in art historical discourse.

A number of terms reappear throughout the text: *likeness, similitude, representation, resemblance*. These terms are not meant to be interchangeable. Each is chosen to convey a particular nuance of images and image making. The term *real*, as I have used it, refers to the psychoanalytic designation, especially via the work of Jacques Lacan, of the brute real world to which we have no unmediated access but can only approach by means of the system of the signification of which we are part. If the relationship between representation and the real is not necessarily always the same, as will be seen here, and cannot be accessed by a universalized notion of mimesis, then the real as an identifiable realm is also problematic, especially when we are dealing with an ancient non-Western culture such as that of Assyria. My study is therefore also of an ontotheological domain that allows the representation to function. Philosophical concepts are at times necessary in order to come to terms with basic a priori concepts with which we approach antiquity. In this context my strong philosophical dependance on the writings of Jacques Derrida will be obvious to those familiar with his work. I think this dependence is justified, given Derrida's own interest in cuneiform script and his adoption of the term *grammatology* from the work of the Assyriologist Ignatius Gelb.

In Derrida's critical philosophy, language suggests a metaphysical presence that simultaneously entails absence (see Chapter 3). This philosophy is one that I have found useful for critical analysis of disciplinary practices and for unmasking a priori and universalized notions that are transposed unproblematically to Mesopotamia. I have also found Derrida's deconstruction useful for thinking about Assyro-Babylonian representational practices and cuneiform script. What struck me when I first began to read the work of Derrida was the similarity between some Derridian notions and Assyro-Babylonian logic. So, rather than imposing a Derridian model onto the Assyro-Babylonian material (as I might be accused of doing), I have simply tried to point out the similarity of Derridian anti-Platonism to Assyro-Babylonian logic as well as show the places where they differ. The similarities should come as no surprise, given Derrida's interest in Gelb's work and his own research into systems of writing, which has focused on those scripts that are not entirely phonetic.

In terms of historiography, deconstruction enables the unmasking of the epistemological claims of historical and archaeological representations in order to show how they are no less determined by the workings of power—by language and by ontotheological concepts—than the Assyrian representations that are the object of study here. In adopting deconstruction as a form of disciplinary or textual critique, I have not, in any way, attempted to maintain an apolitical view. Rather than leaving the political stance or position unspoken or latent in the text, I have set out to make it explicit where possible. Nor have I attempted to adhere to or confine myself within the boundaries of a definable deconstructive theoretical approach or its language. I have made use of critical terms and concepts as needed, following what Gayatri Spivak refers to as theoretical bricolage (Spivak 1974:xix). Some critical terms are borrowed from recent continental philosophy while other terms, such as *metonymy* and *synecdoche,* are derived from very traditional literary criticism stemming from the ancient Greeks. Likewise, I have used words or phrases to express certain concepts, such as *Being-in-the world,* from Western European philosophical writing. I have found the writings of the French philosopher Gilles Deleuze, his call for horizontal thinking, and his interrogation of the concepts of difference and repetition particularly valuable for stepping outside the constraints of the categories of traditional Western metaphysics in order to rethink some Assyro-Babylonian philosophical notions. Jean Baudrillard's writings on simulation and representation have likewise been an impetus in my rethinking of Mesopotamian concepts of representation. In the field of ancient Near Eastern studies, my greatest intellectual debt is perhaps to the brilliant work of Jean Bottéro. His name turns up often throughout this book, especially in relation to the system of the cuneiform script, and many of the ideas I present here have developed as a direct result of studying Bottéro's work. All of these works have been catalysts rather than models, however, as I hope will be obvious in a reading of the book since I will stress the limitations of even postmodern theories of representation when applied to the Assyro-Babylonian record.

My use of contemporary critical theory is therefore not unidirection-
ally applied to Near Eastern antiquity. I have found some Western theories useful for attempting to understand ancient Eastern art practices, but
at the same time these ancient practices have emerged as a means of his-
toricizing contemporary theories of representation. In other words, there
are many places in this study where I come to question contemporary
critical theories on the basis of the ancient Assyro-Babylonian material.
The Mesopotamian record itself, being a tradition that is unlike that developed in later Western philosophy, has led me to see the limitations of
recent theoretical approaches that have been unable to break free of traditional notions of metaphysics.

Although I often make use of the language of European criticism
and philosophy, it is important to stress that the theoretical base for this
study is neither simply Eastern nor Western, being dependent on the writings of both Euro-American and Third World scholars. I would also argue
that a labeling of all postmodern theories in the academy as "Western" is
misleading and might even be defined as intellectual imperialism, considering the groundbreaking work of numerous non-European contemporary theorists such as Edward Said, Gayatri Spivak, and Jacques Derrida.
Above all, however, my study is based on the Assyro-Babylonian record
itself. While I discuss the problematic of narrating the past and interpreting the ancient texts and images, for me, the ancient record itself remains
the place to which I return for knowledge of the past. This return to the
ancient texts and images is important because in arguing against the
Western tradition's representations of Mesopotamia, I base my theory on
the Assyro-Babylonian textual and archaeological record. While I have attempted to read this record critically, the problematic of reconstructing
the past, discussed above, will also apply to my own interpretations.

This study might be considered a postcolonial view in that it investi-
gates art history's historical context in the period of European imperial
expansion and questions the epistemological grounds of the discipline
and its interpretive practices on this basis. And it is perhaps a postcolonial
critique because it attempts to disengage Near Eastern history from colonial narrative. Canonical art history, it is argued, is (among other things) a
colonial narrative. It is a cultural discipline of empire. The imperialist past
of Oriental studies, of ethnography, and of aesthetics are brought to the
fore because they are part of the disciplinary structure upon which art history stands. As Homi Bhabha (1994) has made clear, postcolonial works
are written, both by necessity and by definition, from a hybrid place. This

hybridity exists not simply between East and West, or First and Third Worlds, as some scholarship has attempted to make it more recently, but as a critical and discursive hybridity of subject/object and disciplinary fields. My discussion is sometimes interrogative and sometimes polemical, and at times both. It is meant to be read as an antagonism to discursive structures that have formulated traditional interpretations rather than at particular instances of their articulation by individual scholars. And while countercentrist discourse indeed has the effect of reaffirming the center by continuing to respond to its authority, I feel that at this point in time, unless the discourse of the center is confronted, there can be no space for the voice of counterhegemonic critiques.

In his introduction to *Black Skin, White Masks* (1967b) Frantz Fanon wrote that his book should have been written years before but that he could not have written it at the time he first intended because its truths had been like a fire then. For reasons similar to Fanon's, I too have waited a long time to present this work. I would therefore like to say at the outset that my interest in this subject has never been purely academic, and my scholarly orientation itself derives from my position of exteriority. In "On National Culture," a paper delivered at the second Congress of Black Writers and Artists in Rome in 1959, Fanon stressed that far from having been merely concerned with its present moment, "colonialism turns to the past of the oppressed people, and distorts, disfigures, and destroys it" (Fanon 1963:210). Ancient history and archaeology continue to be areas of scholarship that are inseparable from geopolitical issues, even if these issues are not the same as the ones that had been of foremost concern to Fanon. Numerous preconceptions regarding the Middle East and Middle Eastern antiquity have gone into the construction of Mesopotamia, and Orientalism continues to operate with its stereotypes of violence, fanaticism, despotism, sloth, and hypersexuality. While I do not intend this study as the liberation of the only "true" Mesopotamian past, at the same time I do hope to dismantle a fabricated conception of this Mesopotamia. As a result, mine is a reclaiming of that past, not in the sense of nationalist historical identity, however, but as discursive territory. There are no studies of Near Eastern antiquity written from a position outside the European tradition. Those written in the Middle East, for the most part, repeat Western paradigms because the field of Near Eastern archaeology is a European field of knowledge, instituted into the Middle East and North Africa under colonial rule. To rethink its basic paradigmatic structures seems the obvious thing to do. However, if I am intolerant of what

I see as a Eurocentric and colonial discursive heritage, I have even less tolerance for nationalist manifestos that proclaim direct ethnic links to the past, using history and archaeological monuments as statements of racial purity or instruments of repression. I hope that mine will be an intervention that calls into question both polarities, each of which represents authority through the sign of history, and allows cultures to remain fixed in their colonial status.

In attempting to rethink Near Eastern art from outside the Western tradition of mimesis and to return it to its own cultural context, I have found that for the Assyrians and Babylonians, ontology and semantics were inseparable. To them, things in the world—words and images—had a continuous influence on one another. They could never be separated according to the ontological categories in which we believe. I hope that in demonstrating how another culture, at another time and place, was able to conceive of the world, of artifice and reality, in a way so unlike that which we have assumed to be universal, I am able at the same time to show that it is both relevant to contemporary critical thinking and endlessly fascinating.

I

The Aesthetic and the Epistemic: Race, Culture, and Antiquity

> The Symbol, in the meaning of the word used here,
> constitutes the beginning of art, alike in its essential
> nature and its historical appearance, and is therefore to
> be considered only, as it were, as the threshold of art. It
> belongs especially to the East and only after all sorts of
> transitions, metamorphoses, and intermediaries does it
> carry us over into the genuine actuality of the Ideal as
> the classical form of art.
> —Georg Wilhelm Friedrich Hegel (1975:303)

> They picked out promising adolescents; they branded
> them, as with a red hot iron, with the principles of
> Western culture; they stuffed their mouths full with
> high-sounding phrases, grand glutinous words that
> stuck to the teeth. After a short stay in the mother
> country they were sent home, whitewashed. These
> walking lies had nothing left to say to their brothers;
> they only echoed. From Paris, from London, from
> Amsterdam we would utter the words "Parthenon!
> Brotherhood!" and somewhere in Africa or Asia lips
> would open ". . . thenon! . . . therhood!" It was the
> golden age.
> —Jean-Paul Sartre (1963:7)

IN 1992 W. J. T. Mitchell wrote an article titled "Postcolonial Culture, Postimperial Criticism." In this essay he points to how the traditional cultural exports of Western empires—literature, history, philosophy, and the fine arts—tended to move in one direction only, from colonizer to colonized, and how these cultural exports supported the authority of the imperial center. Culture was transported to the colonized "natives" in order to "civilize" them and to serve "as a continual reminder of where civilization was really located—in the imperial center." In describing postmodern criticism, Mitchell continues to explain that today the most important new literature comes from the colonies and the most provocative criticism comes from the imperial centers that once dominated them. Contemporary criticism, unlike the traditional exports of colonialism, he suggests, subverts the imperial authority; it lacks the authoritarian force of traditional imperial culture. Mitchell concludes the article by drawing a parallel between the waning empire of the United States today and Athens in the age of Pericles: "Only after Athens lost its navy did it become in fact what Pericles had, at the height of its power, hoped for it to be—'the School of Hellas.' Perhaps American higher education can aspire to such a role in the next century—a world school for intelligent, peaceful, and productive decolonization. The idea of a 'university' might then well live up to its name" (Mitchell 1992:479).

Mitchell's emphasis on the importance of cultural exports for political purposes is one that particularly needs to be borne in mind by art history. Like literature, works of visual art from the "non-Western" world are considered today to be the bearers of a certain amount of aesthetic value. That which determines the value of such art, or identifies it as art in the first place, continues to be the criticism of the imperial centers that once dominated these areas. Whereas contemporary literary criticism indeed very often subverts the traditional authority of Western empires, a similar subversion has yet to take place in the case of art history and criticism. In the past twenty years a number of art historians have argued for an investigation of the foundation of the discipline and its critical practices, a reconsideration of what made art history possible in the first place. In this chapter I would like to take this investigation further, in order to consider art history's rise as an institutionalized discipline in the historical period of European imperialism, and to think about the possible effects of this aspect of its historical background. In other words I would like to consider art history's relationship to colonial discourse. I do not mean to suggest here that art history's agenda or subtext was simply and primarily in the service of colonialism or the imperial enterprise. Rather, I propose that just as art historians have begun to consider relationships of art history to other disciplines such as anthropology, sociology, or philosophy, the formation of the art historical enterprise—its practices and assumptions, its taxonomies and categorizations, and particularly its historical chartings—needs to be brought to light and considered within the larger sociopolitical background of late–eighteenth- and nineteenth-century Europe. Discourse analysis from a political perspective, which has become fairly common in the academy today, has not had an impact on art history. An approach referred to as postcolonial art history has been developed in the last ten years, but (with a few exceptions) it has not been concerned with colonial discourse analysis. Instead, postcolonial art history has come to mean the formal study of works of art produced during periods of colonialism, whether ancient or modern. Such investigations are perhaps necessary. However, to limit art historical investigations of colonialism's relation to the arts to this approach is to miss the main, original postcolonial polemic, which defines colonial discourse as a powerful and pervasive apparatus for the production of knowledge (Said 1978; Spivak 1985).

Today, global art history remains strongly grounded in theories of culture and civilization established during the height of European imperialism despite arguments set forth by a number of critical art historians (Preziosi 1989, 1998; Bal and Bryson 1991; Moxey 1994). This is certainly the case with regard to the methodological approaches utilized for the analysis of non-European traditions in the Middle East and North Africa that are perceived as the sources of European civilization. The areas and times designated by the subdisciplinary term *ancient Near East* seem to fall outside the realm of colonial criticism or politics. Most scholars, whether art historians, archaeologists, or cultural critics of the modern period, see Near Eastern history as an esoteric antiquarian field unrelated to the workings of power through knowledge and only a marginal area in canonical art history. The study of Near Eastern art is thus considered to be unlike the study of African art and cultures or those of the pre-Colombian Americas. It is now commonly accepted in art history that approaches to the latter cultures are compromised by factors of politics, racism, or ideology. On the other hand, the interpretation of the aesthetic production of the Middle East (or Near East, as it is otherwise known) is generally assumed to be unproblematic, without similar imbrication in racial and political issues, because it is an area that has always been allowed its place at the borders of the canon. The art of Near Eastern antiquity, however, has never been simply a marginal area in art history. In the first section of this book I will attempt to demonstrate that far from being a peripheral field, it was a necessary component of the development of a concept of a recognizable aesthetic in European aesthetic discourse. In Hegel's words, it is the threshold of art because the East is the realm of the symbol.

Orientalism

The idea of representation is a theatrical one: the Orient is the stage on which the whole East is confined.
—*Edward W. Said (1978:63)*

Since the publication of Edward Said's *Orientalism* in 1978, a vast body of writing has appeared that is concerned with the discourse of imperialism, with the role that the arts and sciences played in the production of knowledge and as a tool of imperial power. Although colonial discourse analysis, or postcolonial criticism, as it is otherwise known, was initiated as an academic subdiscipline within literary and cultural studies, it quickly spread throughout the humanities and social sciences. In *Orientalism*, Said describes how the identity of modern Europe had been constituted to a large extent by means of its relation to the Orient and how an expansive discourse worked to sustain the image of the Orient, to Orientalize it for European consumption. It was this critique of how cultures constitute themselves by means of a relation with an other that became the point of departure for an entire field of study, in the humanities and social sciences, that concerns itself with the main Saidian issue of the representation of alien cultures through systematic discourse and its relation to very real and pragmatic political interests. The issue of representation and how it works to sustain imperial authority then became a focus of counterhegemonic critiques in the decades following the first publication of *Orientalism*.

A main thesis of this book is that since the discipline of art history developed during the period of European expansion, it came to rely upon, as well as be utilized by, the imperialist endeavor. Consequently, aesthetic discourse today continues to be a site for the play of alterity. In other words, I maintain that the epistemology of separation and difference of Western/non-Western art and aesthetics was originally necessary for the functioning of the discipline, for a notion of a telos in the civilized West, and for building the borders of Western self against barbaric other. I would like to point out here that in using the term *West* I mean to refer to a Eurocentric identity created by late–eighteenth- and nineteenth-century Western European discourse. The term is not intended to refer to a geographically or racially identifiable entity but rather to the European-constructed image of its own culture. The naturalization of a European concept of the aesthetic, I will propose, required the inscription of the history of the other into a hierarchical historical narrative of the progress of civilization. This concept of the aesthetic, like the contemporaneously developed notions of culture and civilization as racially definable entities, became a useful, perhaps even an indispensable, device of imperialist ideology. It is not my argument that art history was a direct result of the political imperatives of imperialism but rather, as is the case with anthropology, the two endeavors were interdependent, each being in the service of the other. Perhaps there are many reasons for art history's rise to the status of a discipline beginning in the late eighteenth century, but here I will be concerned with tracing its place within the grid of knowledge that structured the world according to the imagination of Europe. Art historical writing, like ethnography, is an enunciation of cultural difference. In what follows I present an oppositional historiographic account that aims to trace the role of European art history and archaeology in the production of colonial knowledge.

The development of the aesthetic as a separable philosophical category and its necessity for the ideology of modern Europe has been cogently argued by Terry Eagleton. Eagleton contends that the aesthetic question was assigned a particularly high priority in eighteenth- and nineteenth-century European philosophy and that "the construction of the modern notion of the aesthetic artefact is thus inseparable from the construction of the dominant ideological forms of modern class-society, and indeed from a whole new form of human subjectivity appropriate to that social order" (Eagleton 1990:3). Eagleton's assessment of the necessity of the concept of the aesthetic for the creation of an identity and for the internal structuring of modern European society can be expanded to take into account its necessity for the structuring of the world beyond Europe—and further, how the description of world aesthetics became indispensable for the creation of national and racial identities, whether that identity was the European self or its conception of the other. In other words, Eagleton's point can be taken further in order to define more clearly the link between this aesthetic realm and colonial expansion. Since the cultural is the site of the self-styled civilizing mission of colonialism, the event of the syncretism of art and history should not be neatly separated from the related geopolitical imperatives of empire. Therefore, I will attempt to outline briefly some of the links between concepts of culture, race, and historical monuments as they developed in the late eighteenth and nineteenth centuries. Since this is a vast area of study that not even several volumes could exhaust, my survey is no more than a sketch of the discursive realm out of which the scholarly discipline of Near Eastern history and archaeology emerged.

Particularly in the nineteenth century, the visual arts and aesthetics were used as defining factors of race in that a work of art was said to reflect not only aesthetic cultural values but also inherent levels of morality that expressed themselves in the artistic capabilities of "man." European cultural identity was formulated and valorized in art historical writing in comparison to the arts of colonized lands, much in the same way that colonial literature compared colonized to colonizer and the contemporary disciplines of ethnography and anthropology analyzed scientifically the colonized subject. Yet, even though the global history of art became a means of categorizing others through aesthetic production, as Donald Preziosi (1998) has already suggested, the epistemological basis of the discipline and its discursive practices have rarely been questioned by art historians of non-European traditions, even in the past twenty years of reassessments of the field of art history. There has been surprisingly little theoretical concern with the representation of other cultures by art historical discourse, a concern that ought to be at the heart of a postcolonial critique but that has not been taken up by the majority of self-styled postcolonial art historical works.

In her review of the exhibition titled "Orientalism: The Near East in French Painting, 1800–1880," Linda Nochlin, initiated a new approach to viewing Orientalist paintings produced during the height of European imperialism in the East. Here, Nochlin argued that to disregard the political context and moralizing messages regarding the East inherent in these works of art is to miss their significance. In the same review she was also resolute in her criticism of the discipline of art history and its "refusal to proceed in anything but a celebratory mode" (1983:189) Her groundbreaking work paved the way for a number of studies in this area that adopted a similar approach, which for the first time was willing to see such European pictorial images as something other than objective, truthful documentations of the Arab world. European fantasies regarding the eroticism, decadence, and mystery of the Orient, a vaguely defined entity, were now being taken into account in assessments of this genre of painting. In addition, significant art historical work followed in the area of spectacle. Public displays such as those in museum collections, the Universal Expositions, and the Crystal Palace in London are events and spaces in which the construction of what was Oriental took place and was made available for the Western audience at home (Breckenridge 1989; T. Mitchell 1989; Kinney and Çelik 1990; Çelik 1992). Such critiques, however, while addressing all manner of visual images and representations produced by Europeans in the nineteenth century, have been confined to the visual, to the way artists in the Western tradition portray the foreign world. Surely these lines of inquiry should also be applied to art historical descriptions of aesthetics and styles, and the images that they form of alien cultures. Despite the enormous methodological changes that have taken place in the discipline of art history in the past years, there has been a lack of discussion of the *discursive* representation of other cultures by means of aesthetic categorizations and descriptions—in other words, representation in the broader sense, originally defined by Michel Foucault as formed by discourses of power (Foucault 1970, 1972). Such representation is a constructed image or abstraction that becomes reified to the point of naturalization through particular practices.

Visual display and representation are certainly spaces for the discursive operations of power. But textual representations, among which are those of academic writing, are also such sites (Said 1978; Clifford and Marcus 1986; Fabian 1990; Taussig 1993). Foucault was not so much concerned with the way in which power was concretely exercised through particular techniques by a state apparatus. Instead, he focused on how the effects of power are at play in discursive regimes. The importance of this work is that he posed the question of power and its relation to discourse, thereby opening up the area of discourse analysis. In *The Order of Things* Foucault explained that while his earlier history of madness and civilization was a history of the other, *The Order of Things* is a history of the same. In his history of madness he was thus "investigating the way in which culture can determine in a massive, general form the difference that limits it" through internal others who are "at once interior and foreign," whereas in the history of the order imposed on things, he is dealing with a history of the same, of Europe's own internal order (Foucault 1970:xxiv). Said's interest and focus on the order imposed through discourse is similarly an interest in how culture constitutes itself by means of comparison to the alien or the foreign other beyond its borders. The importance of *Orientalism*, therefore, is that whereas colonial history had been studied empirically, Said opened an entirely new method of its study by describing the discursive operations of colonialism, demonstrating the link between imperialism and the forms of cultural knowledge developed at the same time. It is therefore a Foucauldian study that describes how Orientalism (the disciplinary field of Eastern expertise) developed as a discursive formation. Said's main point is that cultural knowledge was complicit in the success of European imperialism. Hegemony, he argued, is in fact achieved by masking the relationship between the world of ideas and scholarship on the one hand and the world of politics and power on the other (1978:136).

A fundamental concept of colonial discourse analysis is that the business of "knowing" other people was a major tool in underpinning imperial domination (Said 1978:32). Knowing subordinate cultures and representing them through that knowledge, and subsequently exporting to them that knowledge about their subordinate position, *was* the civilizing mission of imperialism. In 1959 Frantz Fanon, writing in a colonized Algeria, had already said:

> When we consider the efforts made to carry out the cultural estrangement so characteristic of the colonial epoch, we realize that nothing has been left to chance and that the total result looked for by colonial domination was indeed to convince the natives that colonialism came to lighten their darkness. The effect consciously sought by colonialism was to drive into the natives' heads the idea that if the settlers were to leave, they would at once fall back into barbarism, degradation, and bestiality. (1963:210–11)

Thirty-five years later, in *Culture and Imperialism*, Edward Said discussed the issue of how imperialism was able to gain local consent by convincing a sector of the indigenous population that to emulate European culture was to achieve cultural advancement (1993:262). The concepts of "culture" and of "civilization" were formulated through the humanities and social sciences, beginning in the eighteenth, but particularly in the nineteenth century in Europe (and to a lesser degree later on in the United States). The study of the lands of the colonized and their categorization within a system of civilization and its progress were explicitly linked to the justification of imperialist aims in the writings of scholars of the Orient such as Ernest Renan:

> The regeneration of the inferior or degenerate races by the superior races is part of the providential order of things for hominids. With us, the common man is nearly always a déclassé nobleman, his heavy hand is better suited to handling the sword than the menial tool. Rather than work, he chooses to fight, that is, he returns to his first estate. *Regere imperio populos*, that is our vocation. Pour forth this all-consuming activity onto countries which, like China, are crying aloud for for-

eign conquest. Turn the adventurers who disturb European society into a *ver sacrum*, a horde like those of the Franks, the Lombards, or the Normans, and every man will be in his right role. Nature has made a race of workers, the Chinese race, who have wonderful manual dexterity and almost no sense of honour; govern them with justice, levying from them, in return for the blessing of such a government, an ample allowance for the conquering race, and they will be satisfied; a race of tillers of the soil, the Negro; treat him with kindness and humanity, and all will be as it should; a race of masters and soldiers, the European race. (1871:390)

The rise of professional scholarship regarding the world beyond Europe, and the ordering of this knowledge into academic disciplines, was bound up with the development of racial theory. This theory not only permeated all areas of academic thinking of its time but actually formed the basis of its divisions and organization, working as a scientific logical framework of "world culture" (Said 1978:227). To say that concepts of culture and race were complicit in the nineteenth century is not new. Said, and many after him, charted the complicity of academic knowledge regarding race and culture with the history of European colonialism (Said 1978, 1993; Bernal 1987:220; Todorov 1993:90–170; Young 1995:64; van der Veer 2001). Yet the extent to which the concept of the aesthetic and the development of an art history became an integral part of this organization is still underestimated by art historians and archaeologists today. In the field of ancient history and archaeology, Martin Bernal's *Black Athena*, published in 1987, attempted to record the racist and anti-Semitic background of the discipline of classical archaeology. Bernal argues that the alleged objectivity of classics, as a field unrelated to politics, can be shown to be determined by racism and Eurocentrism. Although Bernal's argument is marred by a number of problems (due to the fact that the author's approach to the ancient data is often uncritical and inaccurate as well as his desire to see Egyptian and Syro-Palestinian antiquity as a proto-European past), the book's broader premise, its critique of the formation of the academic discipline within the context of German ideology, is not usually contested.[1]

Orientalism as defined by Said is a discourse of the other; its main mission is the representation of the other: "It is a distribution of geopolitical awareness into aesthetic, scholarly, economic, sociological, historical and philological texts" (Said 1978:12). Art history, for the most part, has rejected this critique without much theoretical discussion. Postcolonial art history seems to disregard the now numerous debates regarding the complexity and ambivalence of colonial discourse. The most notable among these is perhaps Homi Bhabha's thorough confrontation of these issues in which he defined his use of the concepts of hybridity and ambivalence. These two theoretical concepts, formulated by Bhabha in relation to Said's distinction between "latent and manifest Orientalism" (Said 1978:201–25; Bhabha 1983, 1994), were soon taken up by numerous critics and writers, and have become fairly standard in colonial discourse analysis. In a series of articles, Bhabha problematized Said's monolithic notion of a discourse of imperialism by arguing in theoretical terms that incorporated an expanded psychoanalytic critique into Said's approach in which he had already relied upon the work of Sigmund Freud (Freud 1959) for his definition of latent and manifest Orientalism. The result is Bhabha's characterization of colonial discourse as a conflictual discourse in which the workings of unconscious desire cannot be separated from the manifest conscious production of knowledge (Bhabha 1983:194–211). It is this resulting ambivalence that Bhabha uses as a strategy of subversion. Bhabha sees ambivalence as an inherent part of the dialogic situation of colonialism: "The colonial presence is always ambivalent, split between its appearance as original and authoritative, and its articulation as repetition and difference" (Bhabha 1994:107). Colonial authority is thus not univocal. It is "agonistic rather than antagonistic." By using these terms, he also refers back to Frantz Fanon's point that colonialism is "a continual agony rather than a total disappearance of the preexisting culture" (Fanon 1967a:44; Bhabha 1994:108). The effect of colonial power is not a simple repression or denigration of native tradition but the production of what Bhabha defines as hybridization. For Bhabha, it is this very locus of interaction, the "hybrid displacing space," that can also be used for resistance against dominant discourse.

My concern with the art historical community's response to (or reformulation of) postcolonial theory, and my discussion of it here, may seem unnecessary in view of the growing numbers of art and architectural history books with the word *Orientalism* or *Postcolonial* in the title, but a perusal of a few recent art historical publications will show that the aim of such books is often to dismiss, rather than to engage with, the issues brought up by critics of Eurocentric discourse, such as Said or Bhabha, and to present the colonial situation as either beneficial to the colonized or inevitably infusing the local culture with the West in ways that make indigenous identity or indigenous production simply a result of an encounter with the West (for example, MacKenzie 1995; Crinson 1996). This self-styled postcolonial art history can therefore be described as an inversion, or a co-option, of the critiques of colonialism that were developed in adjacent disciplines. Postcolonial art history has come to stress the impossibility of accessing indigenous cultures. Agency itself thus becomes categorized as the realm of the Western subject. Such scholarship also presents a dichotomy whereby the critique of Orientalism takes a monolithic and reductive view of Western representations of the colonized world and of the processes of Orientalism, whereas if one would see them as dynamic or protean phenomena, then one will immediately see that Orientalism is in fact a rather positive thing (for example, MacKenzie 1995:208). This approach presupposes that dynamism is to be automatically equated with objectivity, or with a positive viewpoint, whereas much postcolonial scholarship (in the twenty-five years since the publication of Said's *Orientalism*) has argued that it was this heterogeneity and the ability to subsume various forms of representation that enabled the success of colonial discourse.[2] There has also been an ongoing internal debate about the utility of the notion "postcolonial" among practitioners of a colonial discourse analysis. Some (McClintock 1992; Shohat 1992; Dirlik 1994) have argued that postcolonial theory brings with it a level of political ambiguity, that it blurs distinctions between colonizers and colonized, and that it therefore dissolves the possibility of a politics of resistance because it is celebratory of the so-called end of colonialism. Others (Spivak 1987; Bhabha 1994; S. Hall 1996) maintain that postcolonial theory allows for a practice of cultural analysis that contests the Eurocentric tradition from within.

Rather than being developed into a theoretical position or a dialogue, the same twin criticisms of "monolithic and occidentalist" with regard to postcolonial criticism have now become a means of forging ahead without engaging with the issues at hand. Such attacks have reduced the book *Orientalism*, and the critique of Orientalism in general, to the traditional static sign of Orient itself: monolithic and yet given to extremes. Alternatively, some scholars make reference to *Orientalism* in a way that one architectural historian has likened to a superficial ornamental display, bearing no relation to structure (Monk 1993:32–34). Such a dismissive approach, which only engages with postcolonial critiques on the most superficial level, may be read as an indication of the general desire to maintain claims of the autonomy of the aesthetic. A main objective in all of this seems to be that the visual arts must remain a privileged field, beyond the realm of dominant culture or state politics. Many art historians and critics still prefer to locate subversion in the arts rather than see the arts or art historical writing as in any way being implicated by the political agendas of mainstream, or hegemonic, culture. Artists are, after all, those rebels who instigate social change by challenging societal constraints and by transgressing all manner of taboos. This is the avant-garde notion of a separate realm of art, a realm where the marginal and oppressed elements of society can express themselves. It is therefore carefully guarded from hegemonic culture as the site of the subversion of that culture. As Hal Foster points out, "There is the assumption that the site of artistic transformation is the site of political transformation" (1995:302). Foster warns of the dangers in such a belief because it locates truth in alterity and because of its realist assumptions of artists as inside the marginal or subaltern space. But it is important to see also that such claims reify the notion of an aesthetic realm, uncontaminated by hegemonic culture, an aesthetic realm that includes within its borders art historical writing. In separating out this aesthetic realm as a privileged field, which is either completely isolated from ideology or has only a transgressive relationship to it, art history effectively closes the space to the subaltern critique.

While the historiography of the discipline has certainly been questioned with regard to class, gender, and even internal racial issues, especially within U.S. society today, the uses of the alien other in the narration of a history of art has yet to be considered.[3] Art and aesthetics of the areas outside the Euro-American tradition are perhaps included in some discussions in a separate-but-equal conception of cultural diversity. However, what the latter methodological approach seems to overlook is that alterity is a relationship. It is not the alien thing itself in a separate, uncontaminated realm of investigation. This error of replacing the alien with alterity is in fact an example of how representation can come to take the place of the thing represented. Alterity is not even a simple duality of self/other. It is a complex and multifaceted perceptual relationship that works on many levels, some of which I will take up in the following chapters.

Edward Said and a number of scholars working in areas other than art history or archaeology have pointed out that the two indivisible foundations of imperial authority are knowledge and power (Said 1978:32) and that modern colonialism was constructed upon a vastly increased power of representation that made possible an unprecedented fixing and policing of boundaries and an unprecedented power of portraying what lay outside (T. Mitchell 1988). A comprehensive imperial system categorized and represented to the European audience the colonized as different in race, language, and social customs in order to gain approval of the imperial project at home. But an important aspect of all of this is that the system was also consequently utilized in order to manufacture consent in the lands of the colonized, as was pointed out originally by such critics of colonialism as Frantz Fanon. If the natives were persuaded to know themselves as inferior, the civilizing mission to export European culture and values could continue. This manufacture of consent worked through state apparatuses like education, and particularly through fields or disciplines such as anthropology or history, but also through the representation of the native in literature, film, advertising, and the fine arts. Art history and archaeology are disciplines that came to be instituted in the universities of the Middle East and North Africa during the days of colonialism. The curriculum and books utilized stressed the unilinear development of culture as having its origins in Egypt, Mesopotamia, and India but culminating in Western modernity. The organizing of geography and history into a process whereby the rest of the world and its cultures could be consigned to places definable as primitive or premodern in comparison to Western modernity put Europe at the center of space and time (Preziosi 1998). It was indeed a colonization of time itself (Fabian 1983). Economic and political control was thus supported by objective scholarly knowledge or scientific observations and became an ideological regulator of the colonial subject.

In the colonial world, freedom, civilization, and progress were continuously defined against the despotism, savagery, and inertia of colonized lands. Colonialism presented the world in terms of spatial opposition, of geographic difference, and the autonomy of aesthetics played an important role in the establishment of this difference as one of the autonomy of man, an autonomy that was, of course, expressed in the political liberty provided by the West. Colonial discourse analysis, and the work of subaltern critics, demonstrates that history is not a disinterested project. It is what Gayatri Chakravorty Spivak calls "a process of epistemic violence" (Spivak 1985:130) in which particular discursive practices narrativize a representation into reality. Colonial historical accounts were written from the perspective of the colonizing power. The intention of subaltern criticism or postcolonial criticism is to interrupt the hegemonic narrative (which may or may not have a reality beyond the narrative). The purpose, however, is not to replace that narrative with the "real" image from the perspective of the colonized or subaltern but, as Spivak suggests, to write another narrative, in turn, of "the worlding of the Third World" (132).

Spivak's important point is that because such a production of knowledge continues today in our pedagogical systems, our academic disciplines continue to perpetuate these practices and thus to participate in neocolonialism.

The conception of a realm of aesthetics as a separate realm of the developmental behavior of man came to be fully articulated in the nineteenth century. This realm, which was thought to reflect varying degrees of a universal morality, was an integral part of the episteme of modern colonialism. For this endeavor, Greek antiquity was repeatedly used as the paradigmatic moment of the victory of the autonomy of the humanist and aesthetic realm, a moment that naturally belonged to the West. This ideal was thus repeatedly juxtaposed to "less developed" cultures that chronologically both succeeded and preceded ancient Greek civilization. These societies were defined as lacking a similar level of moral development, due to their political systems, and their lack of individual liberty and autonomy was described as having a direct result on their aesthetic artifacts.

Hellenism and Barbarism

> *First of all, look at the facts of the case. Western nations as soon as they emerge into history show the beginnings of those capacities for self government . . . having merits of their own . . . You may look through the whole history of the Orientals in what is called, broadly speaking, the East, and you never find traces of self-government.*
>
> —*Arthur James Balfour, speech to the House of Commons, June 13, 1910 (quoted in Said 1978:32–33).*

Mitchell's indispensable criticism of the neoconservative academic right's equation of American Western universal humanist values, quoted at the beginning of this chapter, is concluded by recourse to the allegory of classical antiquity. Part of the privileged position of aesthetic discourse, as a realm untainted by geopolitical power interests, is manifest in the equation of an ideal Western culture with the classical ideal, which has become so routine as to be considered an equation beyond the realm of power interests. Yet, ironically the traditional cultural exports of Western empires—literature, history, philosophy, and the fine arts—all relied heavily on the concept of the Greek classical ideal for their very foundation and legitimation of cultural superiority. Colonial discourse's invariable assumption of moral superiority was both explicitly and implicitly fortified by the classical and, in this art historical writing and archaeological descriptions, played a major role.

The ideal School of Hellas, held up as a model for the twenty-first-century American university, is exemplified in Plato's academy. According to Plato's teachings in the *Republic*, education is a necessary part of the ideal state, a state that he saw as being governed according to transcendental moral values. In Plato's system, education, *paedia*, is inseparable from the state and from morality, and this education is made up of *grammata* (mental learning), *gymnastike* (physical exercise), and *mousika* (all the arts). *Arete*, excellence or virtue arrived at through this educational system, was associated with an absolute morality, and this system of education as the foundation of the ideal state and the virtuous citizen was unique in antiquity and a sign of Greekness. It was Athens's prominent role in the Graeco-Persian wars that made it the School of Hellas. The main Athenian concern at that time was to establish the cultural superiority of the Greeks in comparison to the Orient and the political superiority of Athens over the Greek states (Morris 1992).

Thus, the conscious self-fashioning of a Western identity as being different from the East first occurred in the writings of the ancient Greeks. Geography and history as particular areas of knowledge began to emerge in sixth century B.C. Ionia; while the philosophers Thales and Anaximander of Miletus began an inquiry into the structure of the physical world, research into the origins and difference in human societies also had its inception at this time. It was also during this period that the conflict between Greeks and Persians began, and this conflict was to have a major impact in the self-fashioning of the Hellene (Morris 1992; E. Hall 1989). Consequently, it was a main factor in the later Western perspective on the Orient. Herodotus of Halicarnassus, who was named the Father of History by Cicero, declared in the opening statement of his *Histories* that his purpose was to establish the difference between Greeks and Barbarians. Herodotus saw Greeks and Near Easterners as inhabiting two different worlds that were diametrically opposed. In Greece individual freedom prevailed while in the Near East all decisions regarding the community were in the hands of the despot. There, absolute rulers always reigned over decadently luxurious courts. The bipolarity of civilized Greek/Barbarian appeared repeatedly in fifth-century writing in the form of rhetoric, in literature, including drama, and also provided one of the most prominent themes for the visual arts of this period. Numerous sculptural monuments employed the theme of the *agon* in which a Greek is in battle with a foreigner, either real or mythological, and large-scale sculptural narratives made use of stories that depict the valorous Greeks defeating the alien or the beastly. Traditional legends were transformed to reflect this conflict. Literature, commemorative monuments and paintings, and historical narratives all had the main aim of defining the virtue of the Hellene (Morris 1992).

Plato is said to have declared that he was grateful to fortune for making him a man, not a beast, a woman, or a barbarian. It was also he who held up the hatred of the foreign as a defining factor of Greekness, of the Greek identity:

> Such was the natural nobility of this city, so sound and healthy was the spirit of freedom among us, and the instinctive dislike of the barbarian, because we are pure Hellenes, having no admixture of barbarism in us. For we are not like many others, descendants of Pelops or Cadmus or Aegyptus or Danaus, who are by nature barbarians, and by custom Hellenes, but we are pure Hellenes, uncontaminated by any foreign element, and therefore the hatred of the foreign has passed unadulterated into the lifeblood of the city. (Plato 1892:245d)

This differentiation between Greek and Barbarian was applied to the production of visual arts and architecture as it was to all other aspects of cultural identity. And Plato, describing the monuments of Egypt in the fifth century B.C., had already made use of some of the most common stock phrases of what was to become the art historical tradition when he said:

"If you look you will find that things that were painted or carved there ten thousand years ago—I do not just mean 'ages ago,' but actually ten thousand years—are in no respect finer or worse than modern products, but were executed with the same skill" (Plato 1960:656; quoted in Schäfer 1974:349).

It was particularly during the fifth century B.C. that the image of Greece as a unified entity was developed, and this identity was portrayed as having been directly related to the defeat of the barbaric. Pausanias described how in the paintings that surrounded the Phidian statue of Zeus at Olympia, the representation of Salamis was placed with the figure of Hellas (Pausanias 1977:5.11.6). This association between a decisive battle, in which the Greeks were victorious against an invading force, and a Greek identity does not stand on its own. A great deal of writing and imagery from precisely this same period attests to the fact that a conscious distinction between what it meant to be a Hellene and what it was to be a barbarian from the East. The message of Greece was that qualities innate to the Greek (and especially the Athenian) character and culture is what made political victory inevitable (Morris 1992:362).

The difference between Greece and Persia, between democracy and monarchy were discussed at great length by writers such as Herodotus (*Histories*. 3.80–82), and the difference in political system was not only what was thought to underlie the difference in culture but was in itself a reflection of the innate nature of the barbarian. Herodotus said that it was people's natural habitat and particular ethnic character that accounted for their success or defeat at the hands of the Persians (Heinimann 1945; Immerwahr 1966:306–23). Democracy/nondemocracy, geography, and biology were thought to determine man's culture and destiny (Heinimann 1945; Immerwahr 1966; Morris 1992). After Herodotus, the distinction was given a more scientific grounding in the Hippokratic essay, *On Airs, Waters and Places*, where Europe and Asia were compared and their moral and natural differences were equated (E. Hall 1989:133–43; Morris 1992:366).

What is remarkable here is not that ancient Greek intellectuals writing at a time when Greece was under the oppressive shadow of an Eastern imperial power should wish to define themselves as unique and as the only society with individual freedom. It is the fact that the words of Plato, Herodotus, and numerous other ancient Greeks are echoed repeatedly in current academic writing and that rather than seeing that there was a particular need for such rhetoric in Greek antiquity, the ancient differentiations are quoted as historical facts. Thus, Sir John Boardman uses these very same differentiations, explaining that "the conservative character of the arts of many of the peoples with whom the Greeks dealt must in no small measure have been due to differences in society and patronage. An absolute ruler in full control of the wealth of his lands and its distribution could determine absolutely what should be done by craftsmen whose skills were monopolized by the court."[4]

In the *Republic*, Plato described what he himself defined as an ideal state, a state to which the Greeks should aspire. Classical scholarship, on the other hand, very often mythologizes ancient Greece as that very same ideal state. Thus, the fact that the most celebrated period of the flourishing of the visual arts and architecture in ancient Greece was fifth-century Athens—a city ruled by the very powerful, and even despotic, personality of Pericles, who, seemingly, diverted the funds of the Delian league in order to rebuild the Athenian Akropolis in as ostentatious a manner as possible—is not thought to be irreconcilable with this claim of Greek

artistic freedom. And even the *tyrannoi* of the preceding century are described by Boardman as not being "in our terms necessarily tyrannical"
because, in his view, they did not have absolute authority, unlike the
rulers of Egypt and Assyria. After comparing the political systems, Boardman concludes that "herein lies the seed for change and development in
the arts (of Greece)" (1994:14–16). Therefore, in the traditional view of
classical scholarship, the reason that Eastern arts are inferior to those of
ancient Greece is a direct result of their despotic political system. This
type of interpretation is not simply an idiosyncrasy of nineteenth-century
classical scholarship. It continues intact in much of the scholarly work
produced today.

The self-fashioning of the Hellene in opposition to the Barbarian was
a necessary political device in the struggle against Persian dominance in
antiquity, but the opposition of Greek/Barbarian was revived in Western
European writing of the late eighteenth century, the period of the bur-
geoning colonial interest in the East. Just as the ancient Greeks expressed
the opposition both literally and through the use of analogies by representing man/beast or mythological struggles in art in order to allude to
the Greek struggle against the Persian, so European culture came to use
this opposition as a paradigm for the difference between East and West.
And just as Herodotus traced the conflict between Greeks and Persians to
that older European/Asian war between Greeks and Trojans, so modern
Europe traced its irreconcilable difference from Asia by returning to the
fifth century B.C. Thus, the Ottoman rule over Greece was seen as an extension of that ancient conflict. The Greek war of independence from the
Ottoman empire was seen by historians of the romantic period as more or
less a replay of the Graeco-Persian wars, and that conflict was part of all
European people's history. John Stuart Mill, writing in the mid-nineteenth
century, aptly said that for the British, "the battle of Marathon, as an
event in English history, is more important than the battle of Hastings"
(quoted in Turner 1981:188; Spivey 1996:123). Along with the allegorical
parallel between the fifth century B.C. and the Greek struggle for independence from Ottoman rule, an entire series of binary opposites between East and West, which had already existed in eighteenth-century
thought, became even more standardized by the middle of the nineteenth
century. Thus, democracy/despotism was simply a characteristic opposition of West/East that could be further demonstrated through the related pairings of individual personality/anonymous rabble, science/
magic, rationality/mysticism, progress/stagnation, and so on. As Mario

Liverani points out, these oppositions did not deny the *ex oriente lux* paradigm of the origins of European civilization in the Middle East, which will be discussed in further detail below. Rather, they came to underscore it as a previous and lower step in the progressive formation of European advanced culture.[5]

During the period of the Italian Renaissance some interest in ancient Greece arose; a number of Greek texts were collected and translated for libraries of intellectuals such as Francesco Petrarca (A.D. 1303–74), who called for the study and appreciation of the literary achievements of the European past. However, the classical antiquity that formed the basis for the Renaissance was primarily Roman antiquity and the Latin literatures it produced. Very few Western European scholars knew Greek, and it was not until the latter part of the fifteenth century that the teaching of the Greek language by Byzantine scholars in Italy began. Greece became an area of intense focus only in the eighteenth century. It was then that Greek antiquity was looked to for concepts of ideal statehood by new political movements, and at the same time, collectors in Northern Europe began to compete for Greek monuments to bring home (Usher 1988; Jenkins 1992; Shanks 1996). This new rage of collecting led to the writing of learned volumes on the arts and architecture of antiquity, and the most influential study of this kind was Johann Joachim Winckelmann's *The History of Ancient Art*, published in 1764. In this ambitious tome Winckelmann set out to compare the arts of ancient Greece to those of other societies with the main purpose of showing how Greek art is superior to the arts of other ancient cultures. The writings of Winckelmann were of paramount importance in establishing the accepted masterpieces of ancient art, and it was this book, written for a cultivated audience of connoisseurs, that was to become the first comparative art historical text, establishing the model for the new discipline of art history. *The History of Ancient Art* is celebrated as the first text of modern art history because it departed in its approach from a focus on individual personalities and concerned itself instead with entire national identities and cultures. In this comparison Winckelmann's preference for all things Greek, as is well known, led him to see all else as inferior to classical sculpture. His idealization and, one can even say, adoration of Greek art was picked up by connoisseurs and antiquarians, and his writings came to be widely paraphrased or quoted in English and French travel books and treatises on art. At the same time, treatises on art began to rely on Winckelmann's concept of the ideal. This ideal was defined as a quality applicable to the assessment of works of art from any historical period or geographical region; however, this ideal, according to Winckelmann, could only be realized by Greek artists (A. Potts 1994). For Winckelmann, it was not only the political system that determined the arts. Like the ancient Greeks, he also believed that the weather, geography, and qualities inherent in the race of the people who lived in each society were factors that made their art inferior to the Greek. In this climatic and topographical determinism, Winckelmann viewed artistic output much in the same way that Montesquieu viewed political systems, and the two areas of government and aesthetics were thus seen as reflective of racially and topographically determined characteristics. Winckelmann attributed the beauty of Greek art to the individual liberty provided by the political system. In this view he was influenced by the third earl of Shaftesbury (A.D. 1671–1713), who wrote *Characteristicks of Men, Manners, Opinions, Times*, in which he associated the "flourishing and decay" of societies with governmental systems. But it was Winckelmann whose 1764 project was to make a systematic ordering of ancient art (based primarily on sculpture) as determined by systems of government and topography. Winckelmann's writings also came to influence greatly the aesthetic evolution as defined by Hegel at the start of the nineteenth century. Along with Kant's definition of a universal aesthetic value and response, this Hegelian progression from Symbolic to Romantic art became the foundational base of the traditional history of art as we know it today.

The first art historical writing, the founding of the academic discipline and its institutionalization, coincided with the period of Europe's explicit imperial interests in the East and Africa. As Eagleton has pointed out, the development of the concept of the aesthetic has its own complex background in relation to local identity and ideology in what was later to become Germany (1990). But theories of the aesthetic also came to be defined as universally applicable and depended to a great extent on the comparison between classical Greek and non-European traditions. Earlier West European forms of writing on art, in which the focus had been solely on the personalities of particular individuals and their lives, were superseded during this period by aesthetic theories defining works of art and architecture as reflections of race, of topography, and of systems of government. And while the idealization of antiquity had certainly been fundamental to the Renaissance, the utilization of the classical ideal as a sign of superiority, defining the European West from the remainder of the world only came to be fully articulated during the eighteenth and nineteenth centuries. This process occurred not only through the means of the institutionalization of the classical ideal in academic writing but also through travel literature and visual imagery, and (later on) through museum displays and exhibitions. At the same time, these enterprises set out to differentiate between European cultural and aesthetic production, and the alien mysterious or exotic world beyond.

The Transcategorical Primitive

The History of the World is the discipline of the uncontrolled natural will, bringing it into obedience to a Universal principle and conferring subjective freedom.
—*Georg Wilhelm Friedrich Hegel (1956:104)*

By the end of the nineteenth century, aesthetics and artistic styles became an established means of categorizing the identities of peoples and cultures in comprehensive and encyclopedic world systems. As organizing tools, they enabled a stratification according to developmental differences manifest in cultural monuments, and cultures were defined as part of a single linear evolution with a universal origin and a telos in the modern West. This unification of cultures into a monogenetic progress was seen as a liberal view in the latter part of the nineteenth century. Its argument for the unification of all humanity was made in opposition to the contemporaneous belief in polygenesis, a viewpoint that was favored by racialist thinkers, as we shall see below.

The interest early art history displayed in the origins and categorization of the arts and architecture of the world developed in the context of the concurrent interest in the origins and evolution of man in general. Universal cultural comparisons were thought necessary in order to distinguish levels of development attained by different societies, and these were seen as part of the general progress of man in the world. In eighteenth-century racial theory, human beings were classed as part of the animal kingdom, according to a hierarchical scale of beings: first apes, then Africans and so on, all seen as different species in the dominant scientific view. Abolitionist liberals argued for a single species, a monogenetic evolution of mankind, as a case against enslaving fellow human beings. By the nineteenth century a contesting faction argued for a polygenetic evolution with different races being different species, thus making their subjugation and/or extermination more ethically acceptable (Young 1995).

During this time it became common for racial theorists to back up their arguments by reference to historical monuments, and cultural artifacts were analyzed as symptomatic of racial groups. Numerous books appeared on this subject with titles such as George Gliddon and Josiah Notts's *Types of Mankind; or, Ethnological Researches Based upon the Ancient Monuments, Paintings, Sculptures and Crania of Races, and Upon their Natural, Geographical, Philological, and Biblical History*, published in London in 1854. Another such scholar is Robert Knox, who was instrumental in the development of racialism in the mid-nineteenth century. He claimed that the idea of supporting ethnological propositions by ancient monuments was his (Knox 1862). Robert Young points out that racial theory was never simply scientific or biological in the minds of its developers. The racial was always cultural as much as biological. As scientific scholarly notions or concepts, culture and race were developed together so that the one became the uncontestable evidence of the other (1995).

Culture was seen as an organic process, a natural growth of human development, and by the eighteenth century refined cultures came to be called civilization (Williams 1983:87–93). This term was essentially a comparative one. It was used to refer not only to the refined outcome of a long historical process but also to the process itself (Williams 1983:58; Young 1995:32). This teleological reformulation of history as a series of stages or periods leading from savagery to civilization became the standard European interpretation of the history of the world. Civilization was thus a process of refinement that involved everyone, and according to these terms, the European colonization of the world was justified as beneficial in the advancement of this process. While in the eighteenth century an economic four-stage model of hunting, pasturage, agriculture, and commerce plotted degrees of development of various peoples, by the nineteenth century this was changed to the three-stage model of savagery, barbarism, and civilization, which were defined as specifically racial categories. Theoreticians such as John Stuart Mill, Lewis Henry Morgan, and Matthew Arnold described these categories as racial-historical stages of man with the European, of course, as the superior civilized race. Some racial theorists went so far as to describe the first people as black and saw skin color variations as gradual stages of lightening of the skin due to the process of civilization (Prichard 1813; Young 1995:35). Savagery and barbarism were thus located geographically elsewhere, and the civilizing mission to this elsewhere was devised at the same time as these theories of culture.

In this conception of social development, the study of the New World and the increased interest in the exploration of the Old World provided the raw data for this stratification of cultures. The colonial extension of Europe's territorial control, therefore, can be said to have directly enabled the development of this scientific knowledge of non-European cultures. Yet, the increased awareness of other areas of the world also presented a threat to the idea of the monolithic history of human progress and the concept of Greek precedence in the origins of civilization. This matter then came to be resolved by maintaining that some areas of the world remained static while others progressed. This resolution enabled a separation of a non-Western chronology from a proper historical time, the latter being qualified as the thread that weaves itself into a unilinear world narrative toward European civilization. According to this conception, New World "Indians," for example, were primitives, so their characteristics and customs were studied and attempts at their explication made by recourse to the writings of ancient authors. And the reverse was also applicable: ethnographic accounts of "latter-day primitives" written by travelers or missionaries were reapplied to the study of such things as Near Eastern antiquity. An example of such scholarship is the work of Antoine-Yves Goguet, who studied travelers' descriptions of native Americans as a means of understanding the peoples of the ancient Near East in biblical times (Goguet 1758). Such an approach was not considered anachronistic because stages of the development of mankind were all equivalent when they did occur, the only difference being that they might occur in different historical periods, depending on such factors as climate, terrain and so forth, and in some places this development was arrested into a static moment. Temporality, chronology, history, and cultural manifestations and categorizations within these were of paramount importance in creating the modern European identity as the apex of civilization. These structuring horizons reigned in a variety of phenomena into a single progressive evolution, and the universe *qua* totality of the Great Chain of Being became one of the foremost symbolic fictions of colonialism.

Both the monogenetic and the polygenetic theories common at the time depended on a hierarchical scale, though monogenesis was the more liberal view in that it saw all people as belonging to the same species. Polygenesis was a more racist position that equated a difference in race with a difference in species. The monogenetic liberal view is best exemplified by *Outlines of a Philosophy of the History of Man* by Johann Gottfried von Herder (A.D. 1784–91), the first global formulation of historicism.

Herder defined it as "a philosophy and a science of what concerns us most nearly, the history of mankind at large" (Herder 1966:vii). He emphasized diversity and the value of the different cultural contributions of knowledge and technology of all societies. All cultures, according to Herder, participated in the development of civilization to modern Europe, and all mankind is one brotherly race (264). In his system, each culture or nation was formed by climate and topography, and its developments could not have happened elsewhere. His cultural diversity was thus very locus centered, but his emphasis on topography led him to criticize the views of writers such as Winckelmann who saw fit to use the classical ideal as a standard of cultural development, especially in the arts and architecture. Herder felt that to judge Egyptian works of art by Greek standards, for example, was ridiculous. Egyptian works of art could only have been produced in Egypt and Greek works of art only in Greece because all cultural developments are strictly local. It is not that he saw Egyptian art or society as having an equal level of success or value as Greek; his developmental system was definitely hierarchical, but Herder's categorization of these times and places meant that to judge the products of one locus by those of another was pointless. Many of Herder's liberal opinions were thus based on the belief in the importance of topography. His opposition to slavery, for example, was based on his opposition to the movement of races from native lands. And his dislike of colonialism was due to the fear that it would lead to the destruction of the colonizing race (Young 1995:38). The unnatural enlargement of a nation, he felt, would lead to a wild mixture of races resulting in degeneracy. Empire was thus for him the exact opposite of an autonomous unit of nation. Paradoxically, his notion of the progress of civilization, based on cultural contributions of different areas of the world at different moments in time, meant that he believed that a grafting of various cultures into one progression was necessary. Thus, he seems to have been both an adherent of isolationism and diffusionism at the same time (41). Herder's relatively liberal views were taken up to form the basis of many conservative racialist doctrines in the nineteenth century, and these too were anticolonial at times. Polygenesis was the theory espoused by those who saw different races as being different species, but by the end of the nineteenth century, racist theoreticians of the far right had also appropriated monogenesis as a means of demonstrating the gradual progression of culture and race to white European civilization (123).

In this scheme of world history, an integral aspect was that Near

Eastern civilizations manifest a gradual decline, and their decrepitude is an important part of this narrative history. Travelers saw the ruined state of cities such as Babylon or Nineveh as proof of the divine intervention of the Christian God. Constantin-François Volney is one such commentator, and the same was declared by Hegel in his *Philosophy of History:*

> The general thought—the category which first presents itself in this restless mutation of individuals and peoples, existing for a time and then vanishing—is that of *change* at large. The sight of ruins of some ancient sovereignty directly leads us to contemplate this thought of change in its negative aspect. What traveller among the ruins of Carthage, of Palmyra, Persepolis, or Rome, has not been stimulated to reflections on the transiency of kingdoms and men.[6]

If the East was of interest as the beginning of the flourishing of culture in this narrative, it was equally so as an example of decay. Elsewhere, Ottoman misgovernment was described simply as evidence of the gradual decrepitude of the east, which had contributed its part to the progress of human civilization in antiquity and fell into decline after that significant moment.

In this system of thinking on historical development, language played a central role and was closely linked to art and government. At the end of the eighteenth century the descriptions of internal mechanisms of operations and rules of languages were succeeded by evolutionary models, arranged in ascending progress; thus, language too was subsumed by this evolutionary historicism (Kristeva 1989:193–216). Definitions of nations and cultures such as Herder's always emphasized language as being as integral a manifestation of a nation as the soil itself or its technological products. The origins of language was an important part of the origins of civilization. Scholars such as Quatremere de Quincy associated language and architecture, explicitly describing both as forms of expression of human development. The ability to speak and the ability to construct a surrounding environment were equally defined by him as characteristics of man (Lavin 1992). In this view, also expressed in the writings of Jean-Jacques Rousseau, language was closely related to politics and forms of government.[7] This focus on the correlation of race and language—the belief that the spirit or essence of peoples is to be found in their language—led to the concept of philology as a scientific discipline (Foucault 1970:280–300). The sociolinguistic evolution, like cultural progress, was also described as something that was not necessarily chronological. Instead, it could be plotted from primitive to enlightened on the basis of the degree to which the objectivity of language is developed. This objectivity meant the distance or proximity between the word and the thing to which it referred or the level of resemblance between them manifest in each language.

The difference between natural and artificial language is important here. According to this theory, in primitive cultures a natural language exists that is more or less onomatopoeic, or alternatively, communication is made through bodily gestures. As A. W. Schlegel describes it, "Protolanguage will consist in natural signs, that is signs found in an essential relation with what is designated" (Schlegel [1801] 1963:239; Todorov 1982:228). More-developed societies make use of a language of conventionally defined or regulated associations between the word and the thing to which it refers. It is a more rationally and socially evolved form of speech or communication; thus, it is a language of logic or reason. Language and the way it functions, especially in writing and its development, came to be considered a valuable objective measure of development. By the start of the nineteenth century, the categorization of writing on the basis of levels of abstraction was supplemented by a newly established philology. During the period of 1780 through the 1820s the discovery of families of languages made their divisions a new realm of inquiry. Philology became important in tracing origins of, and links between, certain language groupings, such as Indo-European or Semitic. This inquiry was added to notions of ethnicity and race that were based on physiological or anatomical difference, although the latter continued to be stressed by some in the nineteenth century.

Michel Foucault pointed out that the study of the structure or comparative grammar of languages was linked to the study of anatomy, that the constitution of historicity through linguistics followed the same model as that of the sciences of living beings, and that philologists such as Schlegel stated this parallel mode of operation explicitly (Foucault 1970:280). Whereas in the eighteenth century the main interest was in the sign's proximity of resemblance to the real, or its arbitrariness as a sign, in the nineteenth century the study of the development of world language subgroups was added to this. Grammatical structure came to be as important as the representative form of writing, in scripts (Foucault 1970:290). This amounted to a proper historicity of language and its development, but at the same time it was yet another technique of exegesis, or an internal interpretive mode, which Foucault describes as a characteristic discursive turn in the ordering of knowledge in the nineteenth century.

Language was seen as a useful means of establishing a historical development of civilization because it was, like anatomy, a basic characteristic of people. Moreover, language, and especially writing, was seen as a sort of key to mental evolutionary processes. But this sociolinguistic evolution came to be equally associated with the arts and architecture, even though the former was considered the realm of the aesthetic whereas the latter was the realm of the functional. According to the architectural historian James Fergusson:

A still more important use of architecture, when followed as a history, is found in its ethnographic value. Every different race of men had their own peculiar forms in using the production of this art, and their own mode of expressing their feelings or aspirations by its means. When properly studied, it consequently affords a means as important as language for discriminating between the different races of mankind,—often more so, and one always more trustworthy and more easily understood. (1874:2)

Fergusson goes on to explain that his study is "an architectural ethnography" that "fixes identities of race from art" (52–58).

Thus, language, the built environment, and aesthetic production all reflected human development in this ethnological system. All were considered to reflect the rationality or irrationality of the cultures producing them. Key in all of this was the idea that the classical ideal could be expressed only in ancient Greece. Pre-Greek cultures were by definition incapable of being aesthetically evolved because of the theory of interrelation of the arts, language, and forms of government, which by the end of the nineteenth century was posited as an established scientific fact. The world was therefore a book. The world as the book of nature was not just a metaphor for the nineteenth-century scientific view. Scientific progress could be grasped as revealed in nature or in culture. Seen this way, the modern scientific view was not so ontologically different from that of pre-Enlightenment Europe, even if epistemologically the shift toward a different worldview was extensive. In pre-Enlightenment thinking, such a reading of nature's signs was achieved by finding correspondence between such things as plant shapes and their possible uses (Foucault 1970; Todorov 1993). By the nineteenth century, language, the arts, and architecture all came to be seen as scientific manifestations, as signs of the divine structuring of society. Cultural production thus took the place of divine symbols with all the implications of their sacred character as messages from God. And this was not simply an analogy between language and the visual arts or architecture. The linkage was fundamental because all three were seen to reflect the essential nature or spirit of peoples as determined by divine intent.

The Natural History of Art

History in general is therefore the development of Spirit in Time, as Nature is the development of the Idea in Space.
—*Georg Wilhelm Friedrich Hegel (1956:72)*

Throughout the second half of the twentieth century, art historians increasingly came to question the methods and models of art history. The validity of a concept of a canon of masterpieces was challenged, and the teleological nature of the history of art as the history of style developing in a single linear evolution toward the modern West was heavily criticized from several positions.[8] Further questions have been raised more recently regarding the processes of art historical writing and its relationship to issues of gender, race, or class. An area that still needs to be confronted in all these reassessments of the disciplinary structure of art history is how art historians evaluate and categorize the arts and aesthetics of other peoples and societies, how they create a taxonomy of world art. It may seem unnecessary to bring up this question now, after the onslaught of disciplinary criticism that flooded the art historical literature of the 1980s and 1990s, but this is one issue that has not been addressed. Just as the advanced practice of art history today has come to openly discuss the hierarchy of the canon or the marginalization of certain groups of people, art history's history as a means of categorizing people and monuments, and its related colonial history must be taken into account in any assessment of the analytic processes upon which the discipline depends. Nor should this context be considered relevant only for current academic writing but also to pedagogical practices in the university, the exhibition of alien art in museums, and the treatment of such works in the realm of the market. The latter, for example, often depends on the humanist notion of art belonging to all the world as a justification of its (often illicit) sale to a primarily West European and North American market.

    The remnants of a nineteenth-century racialist polarization of the civilized mind/savage mind can still be traced in the disciplinary division of Western/non-Western art today. However, the inclusion of the arts and aesthetic practices of non-European traditions was never a simple bipolar opposite across the board. Since some form of non-European art was always an integral part of this narrative, the idea that non-Western art was added at a later moment to a pure European canon is misleading. The liberal multicultural separate-but-equal stance has still to confront how an academic tradition that was so deeply embedded in racialist theories of culture and civilization came to formulate the canonical concept of a universal history of art.

Disciplines like social anthropology have unambiguously defined their origins as being established for the study of primitive cultures in colonized countries (Asad 1973; Fabian 1983; Clifford and Marcus 1986; Comaroff and Comaroff 1992), while art history generally maintains a rarely questioned ethic of objectivity in its evaluation and classification of world art although such a system was never far removed from the practices of social and cultural anthropology. Therefore, assessments of visual arts often continue to reinforce the perceived inequalities in capacity between a European and non-European mind established in the last century. This differentiation is most obvious in the arts and architecture of cultures that have been defined as primitive by anthropologists in opposition to Western modernity. Art historians specializing in the arts of Africa or the pre-Columbian Americas, for example, are now certainly aware of how the aesthetic production of this part of the world has always been viewed as inferior, childish, and nonsensical (Oguibe 1993; Blier 1987, 1995; Schele 1986). These are areas that were always outside art history, outside a conception of civilization and its progression.

Non-Western cultures that were not labeled primitive by anthropology (those designated barbaric rather than savage in the tripartite progress of civilization) were allowed into the field of art history as producers of art, even if that artistic production was defined as a lower evolutionary rung. A similar mediation of objects and aesthetics naturally occurs in presenting the arts of these areas to the West, yet no critical light has been cast on this mediation in the way it has in areas traditionally defined as primitive or savage and relegated to anthropology. The visual arts of Asia (including the Middle East) and North Africa have played a different role in this cultural hierarchization. They have always been admitted as art and formed an integral part of the history of art from its inception as a separate area of world knowledge. Their racial, historical, and cultural alterity has been used every step of the way in the development of the Western art historical narrative and for upholding the grid of a taxonomy of world aesthetics.

The anthropology of art, which became an established area of knowledge by the 1960s and 1970s, was revolutionary in its call for relativism in aesthetics because it allowed the aesthetic productions of non-European traditions to be valued as art. Raymond Firth and Anthony Forge, for example, both argued that the criteria for determining and evaluating artistic quality exists independently of culture (that such criteria are based on transcendental aesthetic judgments) (Firth 1951; Forge 1967). As a method, the anthropology of art rejected the application of the European genres of painting, sculpture, and so on to non-European art by showing the difficulty in such cross-cultural applications, but it retained the notion of an aesthetic judgment as universal. The anthropology of art, still practiced today in various forms, is in effect based on a category of objects that can be separated as art because it is comprised of objects that are not purely utilitarian. But such a category is obviously derived from a modern European conception of high art and more specifically is very much influenced by the Kantian concept of the aesthetic and aesthetic judgment (Kant 1790).[9]

Very often the anthropology of art assumes that the art category, at least, is universal, even if those arts have differing local manifestations that must be considered in cultural contexts and the position of the anthropologist is taken into account in their interpretation.[10] In art history, on the other hand, assessments of alien arts and architecture are still often presented as pure aesthetic judgments, formal analyses of works of art, isolated from the position of the analyzing art historian and his/her institution. If art, unlike other enterprises, is universal, and it is above contamination by the worldly sphere, then an art historical knowledge is possible that can be applied across temporal and geographical boundaries, especially if that knowledge is careful to avoid applying Western categories cross-culturally. An ethnographic approach by necessity continues to be utilized in any discussion of non-Western art, but rather than applying its methods across space as a means of assessing geographical difference, as in a standard ethnography, it is in art history equally applied across time in descriptions of the alien past. But whereas anthropology—its methodological cousin—has a very strong system of self-critique and is in a constant state of self-consciously investigating its own interpretative practices (Asad 1973; Fabian 1983; 1990; Clifford and Marcus 1986; Stocking 1987;

Comaroff and Comaroff 1992; Taussig 1993; Thomas 1994), such self-reflexive thinking has yet to be applied to art historical interpretations of non-European cultural production. It is remarkable that even much of to-day's theoretically inclined scholarship, which has readily taken up the concerns of postmodernism or poststructuralism, is not willing to admit the relevance of the place of the art historian in his/her own work. Textuality, subjectivity, discourse, and the problematic of context are presented as issues that apply only to the past culture under study as if they could have no relation to our own positions as historians and how we reconstruct that past.

In the anthropology of art there has been a categorical shift from artifact to art object in dealing with alien cultures.[11] This recategorization was a result of a broader focus and critique of representation and discourse in anthropology, the humanities, and social sciences in general. However, renaming objects as art and arguing for their equal place in cultural institutions is not a solution by itself. In many ways it actually works as a hegemonic device. By simply relegating objects as art, it is felt that the right thing has been done, and therefore, a fair assessment has been made equally across ethnic divides. In this way estimations of quality and descriptions of the characteristics of ethnic or national styles are considered objective because the objects have been placed into the category of artwork, worthy of esteem, and by naming them art works, scholarship has already been objective and unbiased in the formation of judgments and opinions. This approach is best exemplified by the genre of the museum exhibition catalog. But there are still important issues that need to be addressed. While concern regarding the transhistorical applicability of the tools of art historical analysis within the European tradition have been voiced clearly and articulately, it has always been taken as common sense that the same difficulties of a transhistorical analysis must apply across geographical boundaries to the study of alien arts. The very different nature of such an enterprise, and the complex factors that determine the interpretation of foreign art, of past or present, needs to be acknowledged for areas that have been admitted to have art. Such arts are subjected to what is thought to be pure disinterested aesthetic judgment rather than ethnological observation. This aesthetic judgment is considered objective precisely because it has already allocated these works to the level of art. But clearly the evaluation and categorization of these works involve a specific set of factors—factors that are related to ethnography and cultural difference.

During the 1970s and 1980s anthropology became increasingly concerned with the poetics and politics of representation and anthropology's relation to colonialism. A series of anthropologists, among them Talal Asad, Johannes Fabian, James Clifford, George Marcus, and Michael Taussig, all argue that analytic categories are embedded in the observer's own cultural and social conditions. This fundamental argument was taken up by art historians who specialize in areas of art history that had previously been defined as primitive. Again, one area that seems to have fallen through the cracks of the disciplinary divide is non-Western art from areas that have always made up part of the canon of world art. Certainly a sociology of art has been utilized for the study of non-Western art from complex societies, especially in the past fifteen years. In this approach the artwork is historically contextualized and observed as part of a larger cultural domain by what is considered a neutral set of analytical tools. But art history, like ethnography, is a form of cultural knowledge. It is a study of cultural difference in monuments, masterpieces, and artifacts. In anthropology it is no longer possible to speak of objective ethnographic observation. The relation of the history of the discipline, and of the scholar to the object of study, has become an integral part of the study of cultures. In art history, this incorporation of disciplinary history and existing relationships of power need to be carefully analyzed for this middle area, that was neither outside the Western historical narrative, nor considered capable of producing the same level of high art as the Western tradition. As a consequence of its position in history, there has been a distinctive ambivalence toward this middle area. It yields neither real art nor ethnographic data. Methodologically, traditional art history and social historians of art speak of difference with regard to the arts of China, India, or Islam, yet they are classified as art, not objects of ethnological study like those of societies that had been classified as primitive. Therefore, a contemplation of these objects as art categorized by fair and disinterested aesthetic observation is still firmly in place.

Art history and anthropology are both disciplines in whose discursive arenas evaluation and definitions of culture are made. In art history an autonomous aesthetic domain needs to be maintained in order to have an object of study, but as has been demonstrated with regard to the so-called primitive cultures, this separation of art/artifact or utensil is never neutral. There is some questioning now of why products of the non-Western world are left out and a call for their inclusion as art (see, for example,

Price 1989). And within the Western tradition itself there has been a further questioning of the distinctions between high art/popular culture in contemporary Western art worlds. Critics of such Eurocentric aesthetic writing generally believe that a bipolar distinction has always been made between primitive small-scale societies and complex Western ones (for example, Marcus and Myers 1995). Thus, a questioning of Western aesthetic practices and their applicability with regard to the former has occurred. But in the realm of the latter, the autonomy of the aesthetic is questioned only with regard to media, gender, or class distinctions within European Western art itself.

More recently, an ethnographic critique has been applied in the case of Western art worlds, renegotiating the relationship between art and anthropology within Western art in contemporary life.[12] This critical approach calls for the integration of the two traditionally separate disciplines of art history and anthropology. Thus, a new critical anthropology of art has been formulated that concerns itself with the realm of culture as we live it today.[13] This is a remarkable state of affairs in aesthetic discourse, where the problematic of cultural translation is an issue at the forefront of Western accounts of contemporary Western art and society but has yet to be taken into account in the analysis of the art or cultural production of the area of the world that led to the development of postcolonial criticism in the first place. In the scramble for what Gayatri Chakravorty Spivak calls the "commodification of the marginalized in the academy" (1985), we as scholars have been eager to worry about ethnographic concerns when it comes to the demimonde of New York City but have failed to see the need to question our interpretations of Asian and North African arts and aesthetics. The continuous cultural hierarchization that takes place within this nonprimitive category has yet to be confronted. And the relegation of the cultural products of numerous non-European traditions to the same autonomous sphere of world art, the standards and analytic tools of which are of European manufacture, ought to be taken into consideration.

Art history has depended upon opposition and difference in its practices (Moxey 1994; Preziosi 1998). The influence of anthropology has brought about an interest in the cultural particularity of artistic production, but comparison is still a necessary part of relativism, for statements of cultural difference, and we must become more conscious of the implications of ethnographic critiques for our own field. As Spivak argued was the case for European literature, art history's empirical mode continues to be practiced in many places without consideration of imperialism's cultural representations and its relation to pedagogy. In Spivak's view such neglect allows a continuation of the ideologies of imperialism within the academy today. The analysis of colonial discourse reveals that history, far from being disinterested, is in itself "a process of epistemic violence" (Spivak 1985:130).

In conclusion, it is important to restate that the narrative of the progress of civilization, in which cultural difference plays a significant role, is not, nor ever was, a simple opposition of primitive non-Western and developed Western civilization. Alterity is positioned within the formation of the narrative itself and not merely as a radically exterior other. It is also important to remember that art history and aesthetic philosophy were fundamental in the creation of a scientific notion of culture in the nineteenth century. Just as anthropology's project of studying non-Western peoples provided a stable alter category of primitive as radically differing from Western modernity, aesthetic discourse presented a series of spacial and temporal worlds in which the category Oriental was parallel to the category of primitive, or, conversely, modern. It may seem an unnecessary exercise to dwell upon these points at this time, but the same narrative structure remains at the basis of a global history of art, even though its origins have been forgotten.

The establishment of a universal grid of aesthetics, particularly in eighteenth- and nineteenth-century German philosophical writing, formed the basis for the discipline of art history. The earliest art historical writings established a canon of works of high art, masterpieces or works of genius with which every educated European, and later, American had to become familiar. At first these art historical texts were written for an elite group of Europeans who participated in the well-known but vaguely defined journey called the Grand Tour as part of their education. The main focal points of this trip were Italy and Greece, but North Africa and the Near East also came to be included, and here ancient monuments were established as destinations of the tour and defined as part of the topography (Liverani 1994; Chard 1995). In more recent years the global art history survey textbook has replaced the Grand Tour as an educational introduction to the world beyond. Artistic culture is still presented in many institutions of higher learning, especially in North America, according to the nineteenth-century Grand Tour model. World culture is described in the North American university system as one long evolutionary process with several malformed steps along the way to the ideal Western humanism. But the early art survey texts were not an isolated academic undertaking. They might be seen as a part of the general desire to create a modern European identity (Schwartzer 1995). Nor were these texts originally used for university teaching; instead, the intended audience was the educated public, travelers, scholars, and also government officials.

The role of government officials should not be underestimated in the standardized categorization of world art and aesthetics. In the related field of ethnography, administrators of overseas imperial possessions, missionaries, and travelers were considered equally valid sources of information regarding the alien culture of that country as scientifically trained scholars. In describing the art and architecture of colonized lands, political officials, and explicit colonial agendas often played an important role. A a prime example of such a scholar in nineteenth-century India is James Fergusson, whose writings make very clear that the reason for his study is "the question as to whether the natives of India are to be treated as equal to Europeans in all respects" (Fergusson 1974:vi). Fergusson also worked extensively on the reconstruction of the Assyrian architecture uncovered in Iraq. Archaeologists working in the Near East (such as Austen Henry Layard and Emile Botta) were, more often than not, employed in the Colonial Service. Henry Rawlinson, decipherer of cuneiform script, was a representative of the British East India Company in Baghdad. Rawlinson, who originally held the title Political Agent for the British Colonial Administration, in fact refused to take up another government position offered to him because it was not in the Colonial Service (Larsen 1996:48, 359). He was instrumental in defining colonial policy and in 1859 became British ambassador to Teheran. He had strong views regarding the Great Game and the competition for power over Asia in general. Layard acted as a member of British parliament and in 1861 became vice minister of Foreign Affairs (Larsen 1996:359). All museums during this time relied on military personnel, colonial administrators, and missionaries for ethnographic and cultural information, which was always presented as unquestionably scientific and accurate (see figure 1). It was the expansion of colonial activity in the Near East that created the museum collections of antiquities still intact today, as museums came increasingly to rely for material on colonial officials. This acquisitions policy defined the character of the collections that were not quite seen as ethnographic, like those simultaneously acquired artifacts from Africa or Australia, but nevertheless predicated upon difference.[14] Thus, it is by no means an exaggeration to

Figure 1. Henry Layard in the Archive Chamber, Kouyunjik, described as "sketched on the spot by C. Malan," 1852. From A. H. Layard, *Nineveh and Babylon* (London: John Murray, 1853), p. 345.

say that colonial expansion set the stage for the new discipline of Near Eastern archaeology and defined, to a large extent, the interpretations of Near Eastern cultures.

The notion of the history of art as the history of styles was, of course, fully developed by Hegel in the early nineteenth century. Hegel's famous tripartite division of the evolution of art into Symbolic, Classical, and Romantic phases had far reaching effects in the academic discipline, and only in recent years has this stylistic evolution come to be questioned at all. Some have justifiably pointed out that such a stylistic history disregards many important factors in the development of the visual arts, that to think in terms of teleologies is simplistic. But what needs to be added to that critique is that this framework of stylistic history and its description of national styles is a racially and politically charged field of knowledge. The use of aesthetics and style for defining national cultures and racial identities is the very basis of the discipline of art history. By analyzing aesthetics, an entire national and racial identity is made accessible. Nor should we, as Mario Liverani points out, in our complacent multiculturalism become blind to the continued desire to control other countries, though the new political strategies of neocapitalism have replaced colonialism (Liverani 1995). Culture and history are still strategically operative in the so-called postcolonial world, and the aesthetic is crucial for the definition of culture and for plotting historical stages. Failure to confront issues of alterity, ethnography, and cultural translation can turn art history into a mechanism by which ethnocentric hegemony will continue to be maintained through notions of a hierarchy of culture and civilization formulated by the racialist scholarship and racist politics of the days of European imperialism. And the East will always remain, as Hegel said, the realm of the symbol.

2

The Extraterrestrial Orient:
Despotic Time and the Time of the Despots

Perhaps we have not sufficiently demonstrated that
colonialism is not simply content to impose its rule
upon the present and the future of a dominated
country. Colonialism is not satisfied merely with holding
a people in its grip and emptying the native's brain of all
form and content. By a kind of perverted logic, it turns
to the past of the oppressed people, and distorts,
disfigures, and destroys it. This work of devaluing pre-
colonial history takes on a dialectical significance today.
—Frantz Fanon (1963:210)

Our familiarity, not merely with the languages of the
peoples of the East but with their customs, their
feelings, their traditions, their history and religion, our
capacity to understand what may be called the genius of
the East, is the sole basis upon which we are likely to be
able to maintain in the future the position we have won,
and no step that can be taken to strengthen that
position can be considered undeserving of the attention
of His majesty's Government or of a debate in the
House of Lords.
—Lord Curzon, address to House of Lords,
September 27, 1909 (quoted in Said 1978:214)

BY 1909 the importance of the production of knowledge for the British
colonial enterprise in the East is neither implicit in political rhetoric nor
subtly expressed. The necessity for the development of the discipline of
Oriental studies was not thought of as that of an esoteric scholarly endeavor. In Lord Curzon's words it was "an imperial obligation . . . part of
the necessary furniture of Empire" (quoted in Said 1978:214) The need
for this knowledge was stressed as an integral part of the process of colo-

nization and one that would facilitate the continuation of European authority over the East. The development of the discipline of Mesopotamian archaeology and its discursive practices during this time cannot be isolated from this colonialist enterprise. Nor can it be divorced from the general Western historical narrative of the progress of civilization, which was necessary for the aims of a civilizing imperial mission. In this chapter I will contend that this narrative of civilization was heavily dependant upon a discourse of otherness that posited a Mesopotamia as the past of mankind, and furthermore, I will maintain that the *presencing* of Mesopotamia through this imperialist discourse constitutes the ground whence today many Mesopotamian archaeologists continue to unearth what counts as historical fact and to decide upon its accepted mode of comprehension. First, in order to locate Mesopotamia's position in the Euro-American historical tradition, I will consider the historical dimensions of space and time as structuring horizons for the framework of Mesopotamia. Second, I will argue that this framework, which, in Heidegger's words, "serves as a criterion for separating the regions of Being" (1962:61) cannot be divorced from the cultural abstraction most commonly used to identify Mesopotamia: despotism.

Postcolonial critiques of the totalizing forms of Western historicism have pointed to how the process of imperialism was not limited to the overt economic and political activities of Western governments in colonized lands. An entire system of representation and classification through the arts and sciences was necessary for the success of the imperial enterprise in the East and in Africa (Said 1978, 1993; Fabian 1983; Clifford and Marcus 1986; Dirks 1992; Pratt 1992; Bhabha 1994; McClintock 1995; Young 1995; Preziosi 1998). Mesopotamian archaeological practices must be considered within this system not only because this field concerns a region that was of geopolitical interest to the West but because of its crucial place within the metanarrative of human culture. A number of archaeologists have already pointed to archaeological practice as a mode of presencing, open to human agency, and thus not fixed in its own realm of empirical data (Hodder 1986, 1992; Hodder et al. 1995; Shanks and Tilley 1987). Such a mode of presencing depends to a great extent on the production of texts, but this aspect of archaeology has received comparatively little attention and virtually none by Mesopotamian scholars. Archaeology, like other human sciences such as anthropology and history, allowed a European mapping of the subjugated terrain of the other. While ethnography portrayed the colonized native as a savage requiring Western education and whose culture needed modernization, archaeology and its practices provided a way of charting the past of colonized lands.

Mesopotamian archaeology is a discipline concerned with defining a particular past, and a particular culture within this past, and as in other archaeological or historical enterprises, two of the basic constituents structuring the discursive practices of this discipline are space and time. These ontologically obvious measures are not neutral in archaeological practices. In fact, if we apply Heideggerian terms, it is within this structure of space and time that Mesopotamia was revealed as a Being-in-the-world. As an ontic phenomenon, therefore, Mesopotamia is prefigured by the temporal structure of European metahistorical narrative. In other words, as I aim to show here, Mesopotamia, as archaeologists generally think of it today, is a discursive formation.

The relationship of power to praxis in archaeological research has received some attention in recent years. Issues such as the promotion of one historical interpretation over another or the focus on one sector of society at the expense of all others have been confronted and discussed at great length by a number of scholars. In this essay it is not my intention to liberate a true Mesopotamian past from the power of Western representation. Rather, by analyzing Mesopotamia as a phenomenon within archaeological and art historical discourse, I hope to show how a particular Mesopotamian identity was required for the narrative of the progress of civilization as an organic universal event. My intention then is to question the ontological, or rather, ontic, concept of Mesopotamia as it has been determined by recent Western discourse and to consider the ideological components of this phenomenon. In other words, I would like to open up the field of politicizing inquiry in archaeology here to consider Mesopotamia not as a factual historical and geographical entity waiting to be studied, excavated, and interpreted according to one set of conventions or another but as a product of the poetics of a Western historical narrative. I hope to show that through the structuration of time and space, and through a tropical or figurative discourse Mesopotamia came to play its crucial role in the story of the progress of civilization.

In the narrative account of a world past, Mesopotamian identity came into being as an earlier embodiment of civilized (in other words, Western) mankind. "The cradle of civilization" is the metaphoric epithet that every schoolbook associates with Mesopotamia, in both East and West, and it is in this cradle of civilization that civilization-culture had its infancy. My aim then is to show that this cultural cradle, as we commonly know it from archaeological textual representation, is a product of European efforts to come to terms with a problematical historical domain.

Today many Mesopotamian scholars continue to work according to paradigms of research established in the last century, according to the imperatives of imperialism, yet they maintain that the discipline is scientific, objective, and free from worldly affiliations. For Mesopotamian scholarship, considerations of the relationship between politics and archaeology has meant two things only: interpreting the material and textual remains from ancient Iraq primarily as manifestations of political propaganda of Babylonian and Assyrian kings and, more recently, pointing to the Iraqi Baathist regime's use of the pre-Islamic past for propagandistic purposes. We as Mesopotamian scholars do not question the nature of our discipline, its parameters, and its interpretive strategies. As a high cultural activity and a humanist discipline, we do not question its institutional character or presence. Mesopotamian scholarship assumes that the colonial context of its creation is irrelevant, except as a distant, indirectly related historical event. This attitude is not limited to archaeologists of Western origins. I do not use the word *we* because I am a Middle Eastern scholar educated in the West. Eastern archaeologists work within the same parameters and according to the same interpretive models as do Western archaeologists due to the fact that archaeology is a European discipline that only became instituted in Middle Eastern countries while they were under European rule. Therefore, Mesopotamian archaeologists, regardless of nationality, have been slow to reflect on the circumstances under which the constitution of the field of Mesopotamian archaeology occurred and how its textual practices have formed ancient Mesopotamia as an area of modern knowledge. This is particularly surprising in the case of indigenous archaeologists who have so wholeheartedly embraced the methods and interpretive strategies of this discipline without question.

On the level of the overtly political and ideological, ancient history and archaeology have certainly been areas of contestation, as in, for example, Palestine-Israel and Cyprus. However, it is not only such geographic areas and histories that can be contested. In this chapter I would like to define and contest another terrain: the conceptual territory that functions in the production of Western culture as narration.

Space and Despotic Time

Archaeology, like all studies pursued with a scientific method, is based on comparison. It is constantly comparing unknown with known, uncertain with certain, unclassified with classified.
—*Bernard Berenson (1948:230)*

During the second half of the nineteenth century the myth of Mesopotamia as the origins of Western civilization became institutionalized into the humanist tradition. This tradition can be defined as a metatemporal teleological discourse that is based upon the concept of culture as an organic natural whole, one that encompassed the entirety of the world. The organicist model portrayed history as an integrative natural phenomenon and even relied to a great extent on tree metaphors in its narrative (roots, branches, flowering, and so on). Thus, human culture was presented metaphorically (and very often visually in diagrams) as a tree with its roots or lowest shoots being Mesopotamia and Egypt (see figure 2). Alternatively, and even more commonly, the progress of civilization was described in the vocabulary of the growth of a human organism with infantile and mature phases. Time, in this cultural narrative, was visualized according to this organic structure and its potential evolution. The past was seen as a necessary part of the present Western identity, and its place in the serial development to the present was of paramount importance.

Michel de Certeau (1988) has defined the act of historical writing as a perpetual separation and suturing of the past and present. In the case of Mesopotamia the cut and suture are not limited to the separation and adhesion of past and present time as abstract phenomenological concepts. This reconstructive historical act has severed Mesopotamia from any geographical terrain in order to weave it into the Western historical narrative. In the standardized orthodox textbook accounts of Middle Eastern history, Sumerian, Babylonian, and Assyrian cultures can have absolutely no connection to the culture of Iraq after the seventh century A.D. Instead, this past is grafted onto the tree of the progress of civilization, a progress that by definition must exclude the East, as its very intelligibility is established by comparison with an other. This other can change, according to requirement, from the foreign, the mad, the past, and so forth all groups that can be classified and studied through the social sciences. The otherness of the Oriental past, however, plays a double role here. It is at once

Figure 2. *Tree of Architecture* by Banister Fletcher. From *A History of Architecture* (New York: Charles Scribner's Sons, 1905, first published 1896).

the earliest phase of a universal history of mankind in which man makes the giant step from savagery to civilization and an example of the unchanging nature of Oriental cultures. The dual aspects of this role may seem irreconcilable at first glance. However, it is this very paradox that reveals the place of the Oriental past as a problematical historical domain, both "ours" and other, belonging at once to the diachronic progress of civilization and the synchronic time of the Orient.

In historical scripture, then, the Mesopotamian past is the place of world culture's first infantile steps: first writing, laws, architecture, and all the other firsts that are quoted in every student handbook and in all the popular accounts of Mesopotamia. These firsts of culture are then described as being passed, as a torch of civilization to the Graeco-Roman world. If Mesopotamia is the cradle of civilization, and civilization is to be understood as an organic universal whole, then this Mesopotamia represents human culture's infancy. Already by the 1830s, even before the start of scientific excavations in the Near East, Hegel's lectures on the philosophy of history defined this area as the site of the infancy of human civilization (Hegel 1956:105). European historical writing had provided an interpretive framework in which the development of history was likened to the growth of the human organism and in which the cradle of that organism was the East. When Mesopotamian material remains actually came to be unearthed in the decades following Hegel's lectures, this evolutionary model was firmly in place. Mesopotamian archaeological finds then were interpreted according to a preestablished model. Conversely, architectural structures, visual and textual representations as well as every other aspect of culture were used to confirm a model of progress that had been established before these same cultural remains had been unearthed.

The temporal organization of this evolution of human civilization puts Mesopotamia into the distant primeval past of mankind, a time that is both "ours" (in other words, the West's) and that of a barbaric, not yet quite civilized, civilization. The temporal placement of Mesopotamia then, also determines the spatial organization required for this system to function. In terms of geographical land, Mesopotamia is not to be associated with Iraq, as it can inhabit only a temporal and not a terrestrial space. Thus, in this case the will to power, which is often turned to the production of history, has established as historical fact the development of culture as one Olympic relay with its starting point in a place that needs to remain in the realm of the West although its savagery can never be totally overcome.

However, the Western historical narrative is not a coherent discourse that merely uses the East as the origins of civilization for its own political ends, in the sense of appropriation of land, history, or the declaration of cultural and moral superiority; nor does the ancient Orient simply appear within this narrative as a representation of otherness. The exercise of power may often work on the level of the consciously political. But at the same time, academic discourse, as an apparatus of power, with its metaphoricity and rhetoric, is a matrix in which unconscious desire also manifests itself symptomatically. The representation of the ancient Near East within the Western historical narrative, then, is not limited to overt racial comparison and hierarchization through linear time; it is also a form of control and fixing of that uncanny, terrifying, and unaccountable time: at once ours and that of the Other.[1]

In the simplest terms, if the earliest signs of civilization were un-earthed in an Ottoman province inhabited primarily by Arabs and Kurds, how was this to be reconciled with the European notion of the progress of civilization as one organic whole? Civilization had to have been passed from ancient Mesopotamia and Egypt to Greece. Therefore, the contem-porary inhabitants of this area had to be dissociated from this past, and this unruly ancient time was brought within the linear development of civilization. However, as a sort of primeval European past, it was also con-strued at the same time as an era of despotism and decadence, and para-doxically, Orientalist notions of nineteenth-century Eastern culture, systems of government and economy were projected backward in time and applied also to Babylonia and Assyria. From within this matrix the unruly despotic past continues to resurface in descriptive language and in-terpretive methods.

The structuring of historical time is not only a teleological device. It is my contention here that this temporal framework is necessary for the operations of taxonomy, which, as Edward Said and numerous others have shown, was so crucial for the colonialist project. It has often been stated that in the evolutionary process of civilization the telos is equiva-lent to the West. Countless texts from the Western historical tradition de-scribe how civilization was passed from the Near East through Greece and Rome to the modern West, and this construction is hardly a point of con-tention any longer. However, it is my belief that this unilinear time also acts as an organizing device for a taxonomy of political systems that are then aligned racially to particular past cultures that are in turn seen as the developmental steps of the human cultural organism.

According to Montesquieu, the so-called founder of political science, there are three species of government: the republic, the monarchy, and despotism. The republic was the ideal government of classical antiquity and monarchy that of the West. Despotism, according to Montesquieu, is the government of most Asian countries, and as Louis Althusser has pointed out, the first feature of despotism in Montesquieu's definition is the fact that it is a political regime that has no structure, no laws, and lacks any social space. Despotism is the government of extreme lands with voracious climates, and (as Althusser states) the location of the despotic regimes already suggests their excess. In Montesquieu's system, despotism is the last in the progress of governments. It is a decadence and a deterioration, even a derangement of politics itself, and he saw this despotism as existing in the Orient in his own time. However, this despotism, by its very timeless nature, was always the government of the inert, static Orient and its unprogressive culture. Despotism, then, is both the first and the last in Montesquieu's developmental system of politics. Montesquieu represents despotism as "the abdication of politics itself," hence its paradoxical character as a political regime that does not exist, as such, but is the constant temptation and peril of other regimes (Althusser 1972:82). According to Althusser's description of Montesquieu's characterization, despotism is "space without places, time without duration" (Althusser 1972:78).

Despotism's timeless quality, then, explains how latter-day Middle Eastern despots can be converged with a primeval past world (for example, in Lewis 1996). Mesopotamia, therefore, exists within despotic time as the mythical time of despotism or civilization's unruly malformed past. I have discussed this abstraction elsewhere (Bahrani 1995) and will address it further below; however, here I would first like to focus on how the process of naming the historical region in question was so indispensable for its placement within the Western cultural narrative. Because, as we have learned from the ancient Mesopotamians, a thing does not exist until it is named.

Name and Being

When, on high, the heaven had not (yet) been named
(and) below the earth had not been called by name.
—*First couplet of the Babylonian Epic of Creation*

The earliest European interest in the remains of the ancient cities of Baby-lon and Assyria stemmed from the desire for the validation of the Bible as a historically accurate document. As early as the twelfth century A.D., Western travelers such as Benjamin of Tudela and Petahiah of Ratisbon attempted to identify remains of cities mentioned in the Hebrew Bible around the area of the city of Mosul in northern Iraq. However, it was not until the seventeenth and eighteenth centuries that a number of Eu-ropean travelers began to record their attempts at the identification of an-cient sites, sometimes with illustrations of those sites accompanying the written descriptions. The first organized archaeological expeditions or missions in Mesopotamia began in the mid-nineteenth century. This is also the time that a number of terms came to be applied to this geograph-ical locale: Mesopotamia, the Near East, and the Middle East. While the latter two names were interchangeable originally and encompassed a larger geographical terrain, Mesopotamia became instituted as the name of the pre-Islamic civilization of the region that under Ottoman rule was known as Iraq. This name, *Iraq,* had already long been in use by the local inhabitants of the region by the time of the writings of the geographer Yakut al Rumi (born A.D. 1179/A.H. 575) and the early tenth-century A.D. (fourth-century A.H.) descriptions of the region by Ibn Hawqal.[2] A map drawn by al Idrisi in A.D. 1154 clearly designates the area as al-Iraq (see fig-ure 3).[3] However, most scholars of Near Eastern antiquity believe that the word *Iraq* is a post-Ottoman term. In a book published in 1995, for exam-ple, Henry Saggs states that archaeologists should not use the word *Iraq* because "it has political and nationalist overtones which make it inappro-priate. An older and more relevant name for the region is Mesopotamia, a term of Greek origin, meaning between the rivers" (1995:7). Saggs and many other Mesopotamian specialists seem unaware of the history of the term *Iraq* and that the word *Mesopotamia* is in fact a nineteenth-century British designation revived from late Hellenistic and Roman usage (classi-cal Greek texts actually use the term *Babylonia*). While the term *Iraq* in-deed designates a modern nation state today—a nation state that has certainly used archaeology for its own political imperatives—Near Eastern scholarship's presentation of Mesopotamia as a more relevant, apolitical term can be said to serve yet another kind of political agenda.

The terms *Middle East* and *Near East* came into use in Europe and North America in order to identify more clearly the vast geographical ter-rain that had previously been referred to as simply the Orient, an area that encompassed basically the entirety of Asia and northern Africa. In order

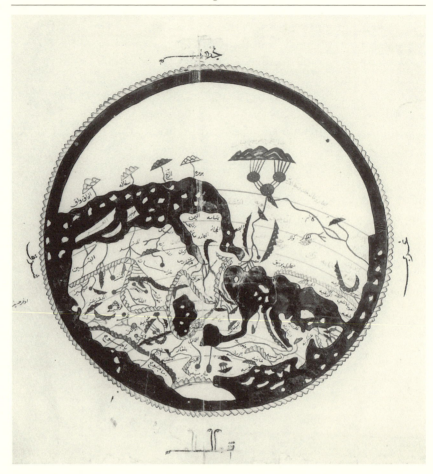

Figure 3. Map of the world by al Idrisi, A.D. 1553 (A.H. 960) after A.D. 1154 original (MS. Pococke 375). Permission of the Bodleian Library, University of Oxford.

to distinguish what was nearer to Europe, in a time when European interest in this vast area was intensified, a closer definition of what Europe was
dealing with became necessary. The term *Near East,* which was first applied at the end of the nineteenth century, soon fell out of general usage.
Nevertheless, it has survived until today primarily as a designation for the
same geographical locus in the pre-Islamic period, the place named the
Middle East. This is especially true in academic literature produced in
the United States. The name *Middle East* was coined in 1902 by American

naval historian Alfred Thayer Mahan, for whom the center of this region, for military strategic purposes, was the Persian Gulf (Mahan 1902; Lewis 1994). In this way a distinction came to be made between the region before and after the advent of Islam that implied the death of one civilization and its replacement and eradication by another. Within this disciplinary organization the term that came to be the acceptable name for Iraq in the pre-Islamic period is *Mesopotamia*. This revival of a name applied to the region in the European classical tradition came to underscore the Babylonian and Assyrian position within the Western historical narrative of civilization as the remoter malformed, or partially formed, roots of European culture, which has its telos in the flowering of Western culture, and ultimately, the autonomous modern Western man. Thus, the term *Mesopotamia* refers to a temporal rather than a geographical entity, which is, in the words of A. Leo Oppenheim, a "Dead Civilization" (1977). This civilization had to be entirely dissociated, by name, from the local inhabitants and contemporary culture in order to facilitate the portrayal of the history of human civilization as a single evolutionary process with its natural and ideal outcome in the modern West.

Bernard Lewis states that only "two of the peoples active in the ancient Middle East had survived with a continuing identity and memory and with a large impact on the world. The Greeks and Jews were still Greeks and Jews and still knew Greek and Hebrew; in these ancient yet living languages, they had preserved the immortal works of religion and literature, which passed into the common inheritance of mankind" (1994:10). Therefore, according to this still commonly held view, the torch of civilization was passed from Mesopotamia to Europe via the two Eastern ethnicities that are acceptable to the West: Greeks and Jews. Paradoxically, in the two main sources of the Western cultural narrative—classical texts and the Bible—the Assyrians and Babylonians, and their successors, the Persians, are the hostile other, presenting a constant threat to the political freedom of democracy and the worship of the true God. The earliest archaeological expeditions to Mesopotamia, then, were unambiguous in defining the purposes of their mission. Since human civilization was thought to originate in Mesopotamia, and this civilization was transferred from the East to the West, the two justifications for the archaeological expeditions were repeatedly stated as being the search for the roots of Western culture and to locate the places referred to in the Old Testament.

This desire to disassociate the past of the region from its present and to present it instead as a primitive stage in the evolution of mankind facilitated the concept of Mesopotamia as the rightful domain of the West, both in a historical and a geopolitical sense. A separation and division of (Sumerian, Babylonian, and Assyrian) cultures and an exclusion of the later history of the region was successfully articulated through the act of naming. Furthermore, the dimensions of time and space in this metanarrative of civilization established Mesopotamia as an ephemeral temporal entity, one that I argue positioned Mesopotamia at the crossing of a latitude and longitude that have no cartographic space and can be appropriately defined as extraterrestrial. Mesopotamia was outside the limits of geographical boundaries, existing in time but not in space or rather, within despotic time because of its suspect place and duration. In this way Mesopotamia is "space without places, time without duration," thus fitting into Althusser's definition of despotic time. Mesopotamia, as the extraterrestrial Orient, then, is a nonplace, just as colonized land is always terra incognita or *terra nulla* in colonial descriptions of geographical conquests, Mesopotamia was also such a nonplace, available for colonization as the site of the beginnings of a Western identity and on the more practical level, for the very real European imperial interest in the area.

The structuring of historical time, according to Mikhail Bakhtin, allows the surmounting of the unaccountable and the frightening (1986:34), both of which, as Homi Bhabha points out, are aspects of the uncanny (1994:143). Thus, the structuring of historical time also enables the otherness of the semisavage Oriental past to be controlled and fixed through its authority. What is outside the spatial geographical boundary and cultural identity is thus brought within the cohesive limits of Western tradition, its uncanniness almost turned to sameness through this incorporation. However, the otherness and unruliness of this ancient despotic Orient continue to resurface within the discourse of Mesopotamian archaeology in its descriptive language and paradigms of interpretation.

The acquisition of monuments and works of art that were shipped to London, Paris, and Berlin in the nineteenth century was thus not seen solely, or even primarily, as the appropriation of historical artifacts of Iraq but the remains of a mythical pre-European past. Mesopotamian cultural remains unearthed in the first days of archaeological exploration, then, served to illustrate how the modern West had evolved from this stage of evolution and that biblical accounts were true, thus that the Judeo-Christian God was the true God.[4] Yet these were certainly not the only needs that dictated the archaeological endeavor in Mesopotamia. And more importantly, the European concepts that formed Mesopotamia are not limited to the earliest days of archaeological work in the region. It is even more important to realize that the construction of a Mesopotamia within the discourse of nineteenth-century colonialism is not a thing of the past. The structure of this colonialist discipline continues today, virtually unchanged, and remains all but unquestioned.

A new and worrisome development in Near Eastern scholarship is the recent fashion for titles that refer to nationalism, colonialism, and empire (see, for example, papers in Gunter 1992; Larsen 1996). These works are presented as investigations of the colonial origins of the discipline, yet they continue to stress that there is no relationship between the development of the discipline and the political imperatives of empire despite the fact that nineteenth-century statesmen and politicians repeatedly described anthropology and archaeology as indispensable for empire building. Likewise, numerous publications have appeared in the past few years with titles that promise an investigation of politics and the practice of archaeology, but in reading them one finds that the association of nationalism, politics, and archaeology is a phenomenon limited in scholars' minds to Middle Eastern and East European counties. There is little discussion of the West's use of the past, nor is there much interest in how the position of a Western archaeologist approaching an alien culture may or may not relate to the object of study. Again, it is perhaps necessary to stress that I am not against the arguments presented by these scholars regarding the political uses of the past in Middle Eastern countries or in Eastern Europe. This is certainly the case more often than not. What I find remarkable is that these same scholars fail to see similar processes at work in their own tradition, even when they address issues of empire directly.

On March 30–31, 1990, a conference titled The Construction of the Ancient Near East was held at the Arthur M. Sackler Gallery of the Smithsonian Institution in Washington, D.C. (Gunter 1992). To date, this is the most recent and comprehensive engagement of ancient Mesopotamian scholarship with the issues of imperialism and Orientalism, with the construction of the field of Mesopotamian archaeology during the height of Western imperialism. Yet, surprisingly the contributors confined themselves to the workings of the field of ancient Near Eastern studies—whether publications, excavations, or funding—to pre–World War II Europe and North America, and maintained that the field today is untainted by any political power interests. Matthew Stolper seems to be the exception when he says, "The European literary and intellectual history that shaped the study of the ancient Near East is not to be separated from political history" (1992:20). More significantly, however, although the contributors refer to the construction of the discipline during the period of Western imperialism, the major consensus seems to be that Near Eastern archaeology is the "stepchild of imperialism," thus having only an indirect relation to it, and was never used as a tool of imperial power.[5] A reading of the papers presented at this conference indicates that the silence in Mesopotamian studies regarding the colonial context of the field is not an oversight. The issue has indeed arisen, but it has also been dismissed.

Exactly one year after the conference at the Smithsonian, at the annual meeting of the American Oriental Society in 1991, the organization voted against signing a letter in condemnation of the allied bombing of Iraqi archaeological sites because the consensus was that the society must remain politically neutral. In July of 1997, at the meeting of the Rencontre Assyriologique Internationale in Venice, the organization repeated its refusal to become involved by rejecting the signing of a proposed letter to UNESCO (United Nations Educational, Scientific and Cultural Organization) calling for the protection of Iraqi cultural heritage. Thus, the myth of ancient Near Eastern archaeology and its practices in general being above the realm of politics continues today. While conferences such as the one organized at the Smithsonian and articles written by a handful of scholars attempt to engage with issues of Orientalism and colonialism, these endeavors, especially in the area of Mesopotamian archaeology, have been limited to positivist historical documentation of the origins of the discipline in the late nineteenth and early twentieth centuries. There has been no engagement with issues such as representation, cultural translation, or prevalent paradigms of discourse, which have been major areas of focus in related academic disciplines. Thus, although there has been some concern with the recording of the events that occurred in the earliest days of Mesopotamian archaeology, there has been a decided lack of questioning of the (internalized) structure of the field and its practices. The rhetoric of objectivity and realism is today still operative in Mesopotamian archaeology. However, what is equally disturbing is that now this objectivity is at times presented in the guise of politically correct postcolonial approaches that are alternatives to the hegemonic mainstream of the discourse.

The superficial incorporation of the vocabulary of dissent from the margins into the hegemonic discourse of the center without any reassessment or awareness of the epistemological boundaries of the discipline only serves to neutralize and deflect, thereby allowing the central system of practice to remain dominant and effective. In Gramsci's sense of the word hegemony is not ideology and manipulation. Hegemony constitutes the limits of common sense for people and even forms a sense of reality.[6] Thus, the vague references to Orientalism and imperialism in the contemporary discourse of Mesopotamian archaeology have only served further to validate the status quo and preserve the conventional epistemological limits of the field. It seems that a principle of silent exclusion is in operation, barring any real oppositional views through the adoption of their vocabulary into the central dominant discourse.[7] Therefore, this mimicry and subsequent neutralization of counterhegemonic terms within the parameters of hegemony are decoys of sorts that lure the possible danger to the integrity of the discipline by deflecting any oppositional realities.[8]

Mesopotamia, then, in its guise as a manifestation of civilization's past remains a phenomenon taken as historical fact. If we view Mesopotamia as a *phainomenon* in the original Greek sense of that which shows itself, which is manifest, then we should take into account that *phainomenon*, on the other hand, is also semblance: an appearance of something that makes itself known but also conceals something of itself in that very appearance. In other words, it means a distinctive way something can be encountered (Heidegger 1962:24–35). Mesopotamia is the manifestation of the remote past of world civilization. The "itself," which may be concealed in this appearance, is yet unnamed, even if we are to assume that some reality beneath upholds this *phainomenon*. However, whether the utterance of the name is the *hermeneuein* through which a proper identity is accessed, as traditional Western ontology maintains, or whether the name, as the Mesopotamians believed, creates the being, archaeology must consider its own taxonomies and the processes of identification and categorization that they require.

Time of the Despots

> *Entstellung, translated as "distortion" or "transposition," is what Freud shows to be the general precondition for the functioning of the dream, and it is what I designated above, following Saussure, as the sliding of the signified under the signifier, which is always active in discourse (its action, let us note, is unconscious).*
>
> —*Jacques Lacan (1977:160).*

Once identified and placed within a Western matrix of knowledge, Mesopotamia as the cradle of civilization began to be reduced to characteristics that were identifiable by, and recognizable to, (scientific) research. A number of powerful abstractions, not unlike those upon which ethnographers depended in order to get to the heart of a culture more rapidly, graphed a diagram for Mesopotamian archaeological practices. Components of this framework consisted of essential identities of the East that discerning scholars could access through objective inquiry into every realm of culture. However, if we analyze this "value-neutral" research on the level of the mimetic description of the data, we can see that the creative distortion inherent in all mimesis, as Aristotle describes it, forms a dominant mode of discourse. Furthermore, this discursive mode is heavily dependent on the prefiguration of the master tropes of metaphor, metonymy, and synecdoche for its prosaic mimetic image of antiquity.[9]

In metaphor, which is literally transfer, a figure of speech is used in which a name or descriptive word is transferred to an object or action through analogy or simile.

Metonymy (name change) works through displacement. The part of a thing may be substituted for the whole, cause for effect or agent for act, whereas synecdoche (regarded by some as a form of metonymy) uses a part to symbolize a quality presumed to inhere in the whole. Synecdoche and metonymy can be seen as types of metaphors; however, they each differ in the effect they have on the figurative level. Hayden White describes metaphor as representational, metonymy as reductionist, and synecdoche as integrative (1973:34). This latter trope permits the reconstruction of the totality from one part in a way that allows access to culture as if it were a hologram in which each part contains the whole.

The main recurring abstraction in the textual practices of Mesopotamian archaeology is that of despotic rule. Working within the rhetorical boundaries and signifying processes of essentializing metonymy and synecdoche, scholarship has further identified a despotic Mesopotamia as a historical fact, and it is this abstraction of despotism that has allowed Mesopotamia to assume its position as a nonplace. The representation of Mesopotamia as a despotic entity is found in all manner of archaeological interpretation regarding this culture, from agricultural production to religion, and recurs repeatedly in descriptions of the arts and architecture. Decay, violence, inertia, and excess, all characteristics of despotic lands in Montesquieu's classification, are abstractions through which Mesopotamian culture is represented. Here, I will point to how despotism resurfaces in the form of metaphor, metonymy, and synecdoche in the descriptions of aesthetic traditions and artistic genres of Mesopotamian culture. An early example is seen in the writings of James Fergusson, the architect and architectural historian who worked with Austen Henry Layard in reconstructing the Assyrian palaces: "Khorsabad formed a period of decay in Assyrian art . . . but this is even more striking when we again pass over eight centuries of time and reach Persepolis, which is as much inferior to Khorsabad as that is to Nimrud. In Persepolis, the artists do not seem to have been equal to attempting portrayal of an action, and scarcely even of a group. There are nothing but long processions of formal bas reliefs of kingly state."[10] In this passage decay and repetitive inertia are characteristics of an architecture that is metaphorically defined for us, in Montesquieu's terms, as despotic. Such a viewpoint, published in London in 1850, during the period of British colonial expansion in the East, should come as no surprise. However, tropical abstractions of decay, repetition, inertia, and despotism appear quite often in descriptions of Mesopotamian material culture today. In the past two decades there has been a series of articles and books on Assyrian palatial art that have focused on its function as state ideology. At first the propagandistic messages of wall reliefs were studied by Irene Winter (1981) in an insightful article that considered the placement of images within the architectural space. Then this idea was taken up by others and extended to everything from single objects to entire architectural structures.

Following this method, an entire building, Sennacherib's Palace without Rival, can be described as an oppressive propagandistic structure:

The decoration of Sennacherib's "Palace without Rival" was thus a response to and an expression of a series of linked oppositions. Its audience consisted of insiders and outsiders: Assyrians and foreigners, residents of and visitors to the palace. The media are text and image, each exploited with a clear awareness of its strengths and limitations, each displaying marked innovations when compared with examples by Sennacherib's predecessors. The subjects are Sennacherib's military and civic accomplishments, contrasted and balanced in both texts and images. And the message—expressed in the reliefs and in the texts displayed on the bull-colossi— was that Sennacherib's aims were twofold: the maintenance of the boundaries of empire and the creation of a center. In the decorative program of Sennacherib's palace, these dual aims were inextricably entwined, as nonsubmissive peoples from the periphery of the empire served as labor for the construction of the palace at its center, while the palace in its awesome magnificence in turn served to reduce potential troublemakers to submission. (Russell 1991:267)

According to this interpretation, then, the palace itself, including the building, its bull colossi, texts, and wall reliefs, is a despotic entity for reducing potential rebels to submission. The architectural structure of the palace is described metaphorically as having the awesome magnificence of all Oriental despots and the power to reduce troublemakers to submission, both in Assyria proper and in distant lands. By means of synecdoche here, consciously political propaganda is the part of Mesopotamian cultural practices taken to stand for the whole, integrating the entirety. Despotism is embodied in cultural monuments, as in the body of the tyrant himself. The ideology of despots has clearly become a handy ethnographic abstraction through which archaeologists can get to the heart of Mesopotamian culture and describe its aesthetic practices more easily and quickly than if they were to accept the possibility of a certain amount of variation of purpose or means in its cultural production.

Once again I must stress that I do agree with these scholars to an extent. Political rhetoric and propaganda were certainly important components of Assyrian and Babylonian cultural production. In fact, I argue that no representation, regardless of its country of manufacture, can be entirely separated from politics and ideology. But in the case of Mesopotamia all manifestations of culture have been reduced through essentializing metaphors, by means of synecdoche and metonymy, into one identity. And there is certainly a confusion of the terms *ideology* and *propaganda* in such scholarship.[11] While sculpture and architecture created under royal patronage was no doubt infused with some form of propaganda, many other factors went into its creation besides the consciously political. Reading all Mesopotamian cultural remains as nothing more nor less than the propagandistic utterances of the king reduces this Mesopotamian identity to the epiphenomenon of articulate ideology and thus serves the rhetorical strategy of Oriental despotism. In this way current scholarship repeats and diffuses the prototypes of imperialism. Through the power of writing, abstractions that are colonial in principle are left intact.[12]

This kind of essentializing metonymic and synecdochic representation does not take place solely in text. Since the mid-nineteenth century, objects collected from Mesopotamian archaeological sites by travelers, missionaries, adventurers, and archaeologists have been displayed in Western museums as a metonymic visual presence of that culture. The categorization of these objects, and their display in Berlin, Paris, and London, in museums that were built or enlarged specifically for that purpose was unquestionably part and parcel of the imperial project in the East in the nineteenth century. At the British Museum the original installation of the Assyrian finds was advertised to the general public as both an antiquarian object of study and a national prize or trophy (Bohrer 1994). Today similar methods of display continue to be utilized occasionally for Near Eastern antiquities. A group of Mesopotamian royal monuments, including the famous *Stele of Naramsin,* formed the main focus of an exhibition titled "The Royal City of Susa" at New York's Metropolitan Museum of Art in 1992. These monuments had been mutilated and carried off to Iran by the Elamites in the twelfth century B.C. According to the established tradition in scholarship, the didactic material and the catalog entries expressed horror at this act of theft and destruction. Oriental violence and cruelty were seen as a valid explanation for these actions, but I will return to this particular abstraction in Chapter 6.

What is more interesting for my purposes here is that neither the didactic material in the exhibit nor the wall maps made mention of the words *Iraq* or *Iran.* The reasoning behind this is, no doubt, that only the ancient names should be represented in a "high cultural" institution. However, I shall venture to say here that this is not common practice with exhibits representing ancient Western cultures within the same institution nor others like it in the United States. The museum and its representation of alien cultures is clearly not a value-neutral domain since this is the arena in which information and representations of other cultures are disseminated to the general public. The omission of the names *Iran* and *Iraq* from these maps and descriptions has only added to the general conception of this area as nonplace and further strengthened the disassociation of the past and present of a particular geographic region (one which, whether relevantly or irrelevantly, happened to be at the moment either at war or without diplomatic relations to the United States) while paradoxically presenting these cultures as typically Oriental.

My insistence on the political ramifications of this exhibition through its omission of names from the map may seem unwarranted, or at best misguided; however, references to it in the popular press and leading newspapers in the United States indicate that its message was successfully deployed and understood. The following is an excerpt from an article in the *Houston Chronicle* after a U.S. air attack on Iraq: "Before initiating his pre-inaugural raids on Iraq [Clinton] should have visited the exhibition at New York's Metropolitan Museum of Art called 'The Royal City of Susa.'

Had he attended the exhibit, he would have seen that, like Saddam Hussein, the kings and queens of ancient Mesopotamia lived in mortal fear of losing face before their enemies" (Makiya 1993).

The writer clearly associates an oppressive antique despotism with the dictatorship of Saddam Hussein although confusing Iranian for Mesopotamian artifacts in his comparison. This is hardly surprising, considering the exclusion of the names from the exhibition maps and descriptive texts. The omission of the names, and the confluence of Iran and Iraq as one despotic entity, is traceable to an established Western concept of the East that is still intact from the days of Montesquieu—namely, that everything east of the Mediterranean is one vast oppressive country. Because of the omission of the names and the nature of the display, the writer came away from this exhibition with a general vague notion of violence and oppression, which he was able to apply generically and racially to Middle Eastern dictatorship—the contemporary Oriental despotism.

The Extraterrestrial Orient

How many miles to Babylon?
Three score and ten!
Can I get there by candle light?
Yes, and back again!
—*Victorian nursery rhyme*

Space and time are the transcendental horizons within which the identity of Mesopotamia came into being as an extraterrestrial despotic entity. Through this structuration Mesopotamia became a world in between, neither East nor West, neither civilized nor completely savage. The borderline identity that it acquired allowed its incorporation into the realm of world history while at the same time enabling its otherness to remain intact as the sign for the very limit of civilization. Mesopotamia as the origins of human culture, therefore, not only acts as a zero point for the computation of time. Because it is the origin of historical time for the narrative of the progress of human culture, it serves as a limit, in being a beginning for the chronology of civilized mankind. But just as it is a chronological zero point, it is also the limit of humanity, differentiating more than human history and prehistory. It is a border between (in the dialectical antithesis of savagery and civilization) earthly and unearthly, while at the same time it is the originary nonplace upon which the beginnings of history could be written, the terra incognita of the historical voyage of discovery and conquest.

This identity, formed through the limits of space and time, was made further effective by means of the designation of the name *Mesopotamia*. Indeed, the utterance of the name was indispensable if Mesopotamia was to exist as a historical entity, separate and in every way dissociable from the historical development of the geographic area from which Mesopotamian remains were unearthed. The name became a definition of this culture as the infancy of world civilization. The land between the rivers was also the land between civilized and savage man, temporally delineating the borders of the domain of the West. Mesopotamia's coming into being then, its configuration as a *phainomenon*, is a manifestation that allowed its transformation into the necessary terrain, to be encoded in the coordinates of a metaphysical imperial cartography.

The creation of a historical narrative in which space and time became transcendental horizons, for the Being-Mesopotamia was part of the larger discursive project through which Europe attempted its mastery of the colonized. The narrative of the progress of civilization was an invention of European imperialism, a way of constructing history in its own image and claiming precedence for Western culture. But this narrative of world civilization is a representation and one that necessarily requires what is described by Adorno and Horkheimer as "the organized control of mimesis" (1944:180). The economy of rhetorical structures in this mimetic organization certainly depended on prefigurative tropological languages; however, it also involved a metaphysical cartography that provided a conceptual terrain necessary for the narration. And the charting of an extraterrestrial Mesopotamia was essential for the success of this representational enterprise. Edward Said points out that "in the history of colonial invasion maps are always first drawn by the victors, since maps are instruments of conquest. Geography is therefore the art of war" (1996:28). Historical cartography is also drawn according to the requirements of the victorious, and archaeology is instrumental in the mapping of that terrain.

Likewise, representation in archaeological writing is not a duplication of reality; it is a mimetic activity that cannot be neatly separated from questions of politics and ideology. The ancient Greeks were well aware that mimesis always involves distortion, but through a gradual rhetorical change we have come to think of mimesis as an exact realistic copy.[13] In the *Poetics*, Aristotle defines representation as differing in three ways: in object, manner, and means of representation. The first is the thing or action that is represented, the second is the way in which it can be represented, and the last is the medium of representation. While the choices involved in the first and last aspect of representation are addressed in Mesopotamian archaeological theory, the second remains mostly disregarded, as if considering the manner in which something is represented is simply a postmodern affectation, unrelated to scholarly interrogation. The image of Mesopotamia, upon which we still depend, was necessary for a march of progress from East to West, a concept of world cultural development that is explicitly Eurocentric and imperialist. Perhaps the time has come that we, Middle Eastern scholars and scholars of the ancient Middle East both, dissociate ourselves from this imperial triumphal procession and look toward a redefinition of the land in between.

3

Ethnography and Mimesis: Representing Aesthetic Culture

Descriptions of the uncivilized sign (that of others) are
uncivilized descriptions of the symbol (our own).
—Tzvetan Todorov (1982:223)

ANTHROPOLOGICAL STUDIES TELL US that for societies in which high art does not exist, art arises in two specific domains: the first is in the realm of rituals, especially political rituals where power is legitimized by association with supernatural forces in representations, and the second is in the area of commercial exchange, where artifacts may be technically sophisticated, but such sophistication consists of the technological transformation of materials for commerce (Gell 1992; Coote and Shelton 1992). In art historical terms, as defined by Ernst Gombrich (1960), both of these domains require processes of "making" as opposed to "matching." They create objects or images that do not imitate a preexisting reality but conjure up an entirely new thing, and in both cases the creation of the artifact is impelled by social forces. In the first case political rituals distort reality for the sake of control, often relying on an association with the divine. In the second case artifice and skill create luxury items for material gain or social exchange rather than for the sake of beauty or pure aesthetic value. Matching, on the other hand, is a mimetic activity. It involves the objective copy of an original or the faithful yet creative representation of the real. In the logical scheme of the representational evolution, Gombrich points out, making comes before matching (Gombrich 1960:116–45). It is the process employed in a less advanced stage of human development. Children's art, for example, is an art of making (we were all makers in the beginning, according to Jean Piaget).[1] The childhood of mankind, primitive cultures (the societies in which fine or high art does not exist according to traditional anthropology) also make things rather than matching reality, and finally, foreigners also seem to have this same predilection for making as opposed to matching. According to Gombrich and numerous others before him, matching, or proper mimesis, as a representational process began with the maturation of human society, which took place in classical Greece. It forms the basis for fine arts.

It may seem an unnecessary exercise to dwell upon these outdated polarities, yet they have not been entirely dismissed in current art historical accounts, despite the fact that notions of art, and of levels of resemblance in images, are now admitted to be culturally constructed and to be variable rather than stable categories. The assumption of a universally applicable model that approaches images in terms of natural and arbitrary representation of a preexisting entity remains fairly well intact. Mimetic and symbolic art—matching and making—are assigned to different parts of the world, to particular societies, to classes within societies, and even linked to specific political systems and religions. However, as concepts— perceptual and conceptual—making and matching are clearly dialectically related to one another in a similar way to the linguistic opposition of sign and symbol. It is because of this dialectical link that I wish to return to the issue here.

In recent years representation as an aesthetic concept, a textual process, and a political category has come under increasing scrutiny and criticism. In the field of art history there has been a great deal of theoretical concern with the nature of representation and how it functions as visual imagery in particular cultures or historical moments as well as a rigorous questioning of the tradition of perceptualism in which art history has worked for so many years. In the first two chapters of this book, I have stressed the great extent to which the global map of art and archaeology is itself a representation.[2] Here I would like to go back to the working opposition of Western/non-Western in order to bring into the open the basic binary formulations upon which this opposition depends. The way that global art history organizes itself as a discourse, or a form of knowledge, I argue, hinges on such oppositions.

Postmodernism's questionings of the truth claims of historical narratives, and its critiques of the possibility of autonomous authorial identity have particularly important implications for the study of non-Western art. Yet, while questions of textuality, writing, and discourse have had some impact in the Euro-American tradition, there has been little critical reflection on, or sustained analysis of, the writing of a non-Western history of art by scholars working in the Western academy. In this chapter I will discuss two matters that seem of importance with regard to the current practice of a global art history. The first is the necessity to recognize the position of the art historian in relation to the object of study, a relation that I argue places the scholar as a translator of culture. My argument is that the relationship between observer and observed, the subject and object of study, can no longer be ignored as if these were issues relevant only to the nonaesthetic realm. If art history studies the aesthetics or visual products of cultures, then the problematics of culture and cultural translation cannot be put aside. The second issue, which is not unrelated to my mind, is the dependance on mimesis as a point of reference in many art historical accounts. This issue has been treated in great detail by Norman Bryson in his 1983 book, *Vision and Painting*, and in his later work as well. Here I will return to Bryson's arguments in order to rethink the polarity of perceptual/conceptual image making at the level of an organizational structure that is thought to allow access to historical and ethnic identity through a "psychology of perception." In other words, my contention is that it is not enough to say that mimetic/symbolic or perceptual/conceptual are categories inadequate for understanding non-Western traditions because they are alien or anachronistic, as many have already argued. No matter how well meaning it is, that approach assumes non-Western art is the undervalued aesthetic of a homogenized other. It is more important that we consider the functional position already allotted to non-Western art in its relation to European aesthetics. Without questioning the prevailing practices of transcultural art historical practice, any theoretical reconsideration of non-Western aesthetics will remain limited by the same "structures of reference" that allowed colonialism to map the place of the other.

The Art Historian as Ethnographer

> *Both history and ethnography are concerned with societies other than the one in which we live. Whether this otherness is due to remoteness in time (however slight), or to remoteness in space, or even to cultural heterogeneity, is of secondary importance compared to the basic similarity of perspective . . . in both cases we are dealing with systems of representations which differ for each member of the group and which, on the whole, differ from representations of the investigator.*
>
> —*Claude Lévi-Strauss (1963:16–17)*

One of the main occupations of art history is the tabulation of cultures and cultural production, both across the globe and transhistorically, comparing cultural practices and aesthetics as a matter of course. Methodologically, art history still takes cultural difference as a definable entity to be found in the visible and finite objects of non-Western traditions whereas in related academic disciplines culture and cultural difference have emerged as two of the most problematic and complex theoretical issues of recent years. For the most part, art history has focused on the exclusionary nature of the canon, and a concerted effort has been made to expand this canon to include cultural artifacts from non-European traditions. This is cultural criticism's equivalent to the first wave of feminism, when art historians first began to ask why works of art by women were excluded from the canon. As far as the study of non-European traditions is concerned, at best it allows for a relativist conception of art and art historical interpretation so that all voices (as the multicultural maxim goes) can be heard. The notion of cultural difference as a relative listing of a diversity of cultures is rejected by recent anthropology, postcolonial criticism and cultural studies. Instead, cultural difference is understood as a process that occurs at the borders or frontiers of disciplines and concepts. In other words, from the postcolonial position, cultural politics is not in any way a demand for recognition as part of a universal humanity. The point is rather that the condition of cultural knowledge itself depends upon a splitting of subjectivity.[3]

Colonial discourse constructed panoptic accounts of reality to serve its own ends, presenting such accounts as objective and external to the position of the observer. The desire of colonial discourse can thus be described as a desire for complete mastery of its object of knowledge, an ordering of things according to the imperial gaze. Such a separation of subject and object, however, is impossible because knowledge, and the processes of signifying that form of knowledge, do not occur outside the boundaries of the self. Quite simply, cultural difference is not a graspable knowledge of other people and places. Knowledge regarding diverse cultures and aesthetic practices is not an objective system of categorization of recognizable entities. Because representations of others are also ways of making ourselves, of defining our own identities, such knowledge cannot be contained and uncontaminated. If we accept this anthropological stance, then art historical concepts of culture need to be rethought in order to come to terms with the structure of difference itself, which enables the construction of cultural knowledge. The possibility of an objective mapping of the aesthetics of other people and places would thus be called into question.

There are four related points I would like to make here and will discuss further below. The first is that art history can be roughly equated with ethnology because these disciplines are methodologically related in their modes of observation and classification. The second (and, in my mind, crucial) point is that ethnology cannot be defined as just the study of culture but of cultural difference. This distinction brings up the third point: far from being obvious concepts, both culture and difference are theoretically problematic domains. They are not the transparent areas of knowledge that art historical discourse imagines. The fourth issue emerging from the previous three is that of the relationship between art historical and ethnographic authority. If I am correct in seeing a parallel between art history and ethnology, then transcultural art historical writing can be equated with ethnography.

Ethnicity and culture are concepts that have always been heavily relied upon in art history, especially in its basic pedagogical form of the global art survey, even if, as in methodological terms, they are often left undefined. While the definition of a priori terms and concepts have become a focus in much art historical writing, very little attention has been paid to definitions of culture or the processes of cultural translation. At the same time, critical theoretical approaches that investigate the workings of power—political, patriarchal and economic—are still generally applied to the historical period or society under research rather than to the processes of writing and interpretation of which the investigating scholar is part. While one can say that there has been a serious paradigm shift in the practice of art history, the fundamental relationship of art historian to the culture or the past that she/he studies has not been much of an issue, and consequently the idea of a historical reality as an unmediated presentation of data by the historian is maintained intact. Many poststructuralist concerns are happily considered in relation to the context of study but then set aside as if the relationship of the scholar to the context did not exist. The idea that texts represent and configure truth—that they do not stand alone but are part of an entire system of representation, of a problematic context—and the idea of the text as mediation is seemingly acceptable for all but the texts that we construct. Art historians do not often see the relevance of these theoretical arguments for their own work as production of knowledge. However, a number of scholars have moved away from the singularities of class and gender as the only conceptual

categories of an identity politics and have called for an awareness of subjectivity and its place in the art historical narrative, and in the interpretation of works of art. Taking up Hayden White's arguments with regard to
the writing of history, Michael Ann Holly further points out that the rhetorical language of the text, its tropes and metaphors, have a great deal to
do with the meanings or values that are generated regarding the art object. Holly's argument is that such language is a result of a narrative splitting of sorts in which authorial subjectivity is bound to weave itself into
the descriptive language of the text (1990).

My main concern here is with the implications of these crucial arguments when we consider that subjectivity is bound up with issues of cultural and racial alterity. Long before art history became concerned with
these issues, Hayden White and Michel de Certeau had both likened
historical writing to a "sort of uncanny passage" into text in which discourse attempts to apprehend the strange or the threatening through a
"metonymic dispersion of its elements" (de Certeau 1988; White 1978:
5–7). Art historical descriptions, it can be argued, are a similar uncanny
passage through which the cultural other is categorized and organized according to an orderly system of knowledge. Aesthetic discourse, like historical writing, is played along the margins of separation that outline and
define a social and spiritual identity of the civilized against a background
that is both its temporal origin (in terms of a past in which it was originally chaotically merged and from which it became separated) and its
other, primitive, or barbaric self. The very limit between self and other
then becomes "at once the instrument and the object of study" (Foucault
1972:5–8). Art history needs to question the mode of representation of
otherness—how the display of difference circulates in its discourse—as
part of the general concern with the practices of art history.

Numerous studies have by now argued against a globalized conception of art and its transcendental evaluations, and the Enlightenment concept of an aesthetic realm has been gradually replaced by a multicultural
appreciation of varied art practices. However, becoming aware of a diversity of artistic-cultural productions requires a new conception of art history that aims at a retrieval of the original function of the artwork within
its culture as, for example, proposed by Hans Belting (1987). This approach is certainly preferable to the universally applied (European) formal
analysis that predominated the first half of the twentieth century in art
history. Nevertheless, this focus on context has allowed the perpetuation
of a myth that the analysis of place of production, or circumstances of

production and use, is more objective than the analysis of form, that it can give access to a true cultural identity. The idea, stemming from social history and Modern anthropology, is that to situate the native point of view in its appropriate context is to arrive at an accurate social record or historical account. In art history this method is taken as means of knowing the true value of a work of art gained through a knowledge of its original use, practice, and intention.

Instead, what I have begun to argue elsewhere and what I am stressing here, is that the study of non-Western art within the discipline of art history is an *enunciation of cultural difference*, and so it can be defined as a discourse of the other (Bahrani 1995). In other words, what I am calling for is the serious consideration of Homi Bhabha's definition of culture as an enunciative site (Bhabha 1994) and a theoretical reflection upon the implications that this definition has for the practices of a globalizing discipline of culture like the history of art. The questions that arise out of such a methodological shift are questions that concern themselves with the epistemological limits of cultural description and the dynamics of writing and textuality that determine non-Western art as non-Western, and permit a reconstruction of "native cultural context."

In art history, when an alien culture is at issue, the ability to access or recognize aesthetic value, or to differentiate art/artifact, falls back methodologically onto the safety net of "context" (and its web of indigenous ideas of aesthetics) as neutral evaluative procedures. As a result the construction of social context becomes in itself a powerful interpretational base, but we must come to terms with the fact that context is also produced through certain choices by scholarship. In his essay "Art in Context," Norman Bryson has enumerated a number of assumptions operating behind the concept of context in art history (Bryson 1992). The most important among these is the opposition and implied pure separation between the work of art and the context. Bryson argues that the evidence that makes up context is no less to be explained than the work of art or visual text. We have furthermore learned from anthropology, cultural studies, poststructural literary theory, and philosophy that contexts are never just *there*. They are constructed by (among other things) scholarship and therefore can be said to depend on analytic categories that are not less compromised than the evaluative categories of a European formal analysis. For the distant past, the same concerns regarding the problematic of accessing original meaning have also been raised by postprocessual archaeological theory in relation to the reconstruction of ancient contexts

(Hodder 1982, 1992; Shanks and Tilley 1987; Shanks 1999). In the study of non-Western arts, searching for native or original cultural context does not lead to objectivity. It is not the collection of factual data by dispassionate observers. Indigenous notions of aesthetics in alien cultures are established by means of anthropologically determined categories that appear to be contained and "found" but are nevertheless determined by interpretation. While this form of contextualizing art practices is certainly preferable and more fruitful than a universally applied perceptualism or phenomenology of vision, it clearly brings its own set of theoretical problems with it. These problems are not just formal misunderstandings of works of art, or misreadings of original intent or context, they are misreadings (or misrecognitions) that, as processes of articulating cultural difference, carry a number of ideological implications. By returning non-Western art to its original context, we do not simply have a means of understanding or appreciating it on its own terms. If relations between self and other are relations that involve power, and if subjectivity is inseparable from ideology, then a relativist contextualization is not in itself a solution.

While it is most important to historicize as fully as possible our understanding of works of art within specific cultural and sociopolitical contexts, it is equally important to become aware of the processes by which we re-create such historical contexts. In other words, if representation and power are related, then this link must also apply to our own representational practices in the formation of texts.[4] Attempting to access "original intent," indigenous notions of art, or the aesthetic is therefore, a process fraught with an entire set of interpretive problems that need to be addressed. Keith Moxey has argued convincingly that the focus on the intention of the work of art assigns it a "terminal role in the life of a culture, a location representing a synthesis of ideas current in the culture" (1986:271). Moxey's statement makes clear that the search for original intent can become a means of translating culture-as-sign, of reducing cultural identity into one terminal location. This phenomenon is what Bhabha describes as a "desire to see, to fix cultural difference in a containable, *visible* object" (1994:50).

Thus the prevailing method of searching for indigenous notions of aesthetics, and indigenous aesthetic value, does not take into account that aesthetic value as a desirable universal concept remains problematic, even if that value is considered to vary according to time and place. As Moxey points out, a work of art may have aesthetic value in one culture that is not recognized by another. Therefore, an aesthetic object can be reduced into a nonaesthetic object, and a nonaesthetic object can become aesthetic by means of its placement into a museum context, for example (Moxey 1991). However, there are times when the cultural artifact is not only changed in aesthetic status through decontextualization. Such an artifact can certainly be turned into a nonaesthetic object or converted to an aesthetic object depending on change of context. It can be exoticised, but it can also be reduced to a degenerate aesthetic object and redefined as abject. When this happens, the cultural artifact is not simply being misunderstood according to a different set of notions of aesthetics or ideas of beauty, nor is it just that its original function and meaning are lost as a result of the loss of context. The object itself becomes a sign of the limits of civilization, an opposition to the concept of the aesthetic itself. The art object becomes what Bhabha describes, in the context of colonial discourse, as a "metonymy of presence" (1994:89). This is a metonymic replacement (similar to the function of the stereotype) in which partial presence allows a circulation of definable and recognizable identities in the system of knowledge of colonial discourse. The terminal location of the object—discovered by means of context or intent—becomes the site of fixing a recognizable cultural difference. Like the racial metonymy of presence in stereotype, it can be exotic (beautiful or alluring), but it can also be degenerate.

According to Bhabha, cultural difference is constituted through the social conditions of the enunciation of that difference. Thus, without a reconsideration or reassessment—a change in the conception of the site of the enunciation—the same structures of reference are maintained. Therefore, Bhabha suggests that rather than focusing on a Manichaean divide, we might better attempt an investigation of "the processes of subjectification" made possible by discourse (1994:67). The contention here is that the hegemonic position remains intact if we assume that there can be an unproblematic, relative appreciation of multiplicities of cultures. As a theoretical domain, culture can no longer be defined in a clear-cut manner. Since the very concept of culture is linked to difference, the problem of cultural knowledge, of understanding cultural difference, cannot be limited to the search for indigenous terms and practices. If culture and difference are inseparable—if culture is produced through the processes of signification rather than found and observed—then an egalitarian cultural relativism in global art history is not a viable solution for discriminatory practices.

Instead, we might reflect on this shift of focus from culture as an epistemological object of knowledge to culture as an enunciative site. This shift has a number of implications for art historical practice. The first and most obvious issue is that we can no longer have an unproblematic access to or a means of knowing non-Western cultures and appreciating them "on their own terms" in a multicultural celebration of diversity. This is what I have been arguing thus far. The second implication of this focal shift is that if culture is an enunciative site, then the position of the art historian clearly becomes one of the translator of culture and can therefore be defined as an ethnographic position. The relationship between aesthetic description and ethnography requires urgent attention as a result of this methodological shift. The third point that needs to be stressed is that a shift from culture as epistemological object to enunciative category opens possibilities for investigating cultural meaning in new ways. Far from being a nihilistic paralyzing move that presents an impossibility in the realm of research, as some might fear, this shift can be a liberating discursive strategy in that it can allow views that are contestatory to hegemonic representations that are often still fixed in their colonial form. At the same time, it can also enable working outside the closure of the binary polarities of Occident/Orient, white/black, and so on, which counterhegemonic politics can often fall into. Culture thus becomes contingent and hybrid.

Bhabha's argument, explicated by means of his theoretical terms of *mimicry* and *hybridity*, is that it is exactly this conception of culture as hybrid that allows a subversive strategy of subaltern agency "that negotiates its own authority through a process of iterative 'unpicking' and incommensurable, insurgent relinking" (1994:185). Far from being some pure indigenous voice, the subject as agent is in itself a product of ideology and is contingent and intersubjective. In referring to the *contingent* aspect of culture, he stresses that the word contingent contains the meaning of contiguity and metonymy but also the temporality of the indeterminate. Thus, contingent is the indeterminate as well as being a link. The result of all this argumentation is that alterity remains an issue, even when we think that we are doing our best to access and appreciate original context and indigenous ideas of art. We cannot simply step outside our own sociohistorical context.

Alterity, as Michael Taussig writes, is an alter world that mimics the world of substance (our own ethnocentric world) and is modeled on it, always maintaining a relationship with the world it parallels (1993:122). He argues that the representational act is in fact inseparable from colonial history; mimesis and alterity worked together in what Taussig describes as "the colonial mirror of production" (1993:66). Therefore, it is not simply that cultural hierarchization requires differences and discriminations for its discursive practices; these differences—including what is articulated as the aesthetic—were in themselves inherently bound into the creation of the political identity of the West.

Taussig and numerous postmodern anthropologists have stressed the importance of keeping in mind that alterity is not simply a pure essence that the ethnographer discovers. It is a complex of relations created exactly *in relationship* to the position of the ethnographer. The scholar's subjectivity comes to play a role in the retrieval of this context, which we imagine to be an untainted area of study, even when it is contemporaneous, in the same space and time. In other words, there is always a narrative splitting of the subject; the observer is part of the observation, and so ethnography is a hybrid activity. One may also add that it is an activity that has many spatial practices. As a methodological term, it is not limited to recording fieldwork among "tribal peoples." The anthropologist Johannes Fabian describes ethnography as genre. It is a genre concerned with forms of intercultural relation (1990). It is a taxonomic mode of writing the difference of culture. Modernist ethnological anthropology set out to survey a full range of human diversity and its progress through levels of culture and civilization. These encounters were described in ethnographic texts. Canonical art history similarly focused on cultural monuments and the progressive development of culture as art and architecture. In anthropological terms, cultures are by definition ethnographic collections (Clifford 1988:230). It is only by imposing a hierarchy of civilized and primitive cultures that the project of art history is separated from ethnography. If we accept the perspective that global art history is a form of cross-cultural description, then we must also consider ethnographic concerns and their implications for art historical descriptions.

In anthropology the position of the ethnographer has emerged as a complex problem discussed at great length in the past twenty years. Foregrounding the identity of the scholar, calling attention to the place of the ethnographer in the text in order to point to the conditions under which the text is written has been a major turning point in anthropological theory as a whole and has had both epistemological and political ramifications (Marcus and Cushman 1982; Clifford 1983). These discussion have specifically cautioned that even if ethnographers set out to be as objective and as truthful as possible, ethnography can only ever be a partial truth, and its message cannot be separated from the rhetoric of the text.

In *The Practice of Theory*, Moxey calls for a politically engaged form of art historical interpretation that would acknowledge the narratives that we construct and become aware of how they are products of our own value systems (1994:14–15). For the study of non-Western art fields, Moxey's advice becomes politically crucial. Disregarding the position of the historian in this case can be described as an explicit political stance because it presents the description of other cultures as a form of knowledge unaffected by any worldly experience. We would thus have to accept the implication that it is the only area of intercultural relations in which ideology is irrelevant. Moxey argues that art historical discourse is dialogic and intersubjective. The relationship of author to the object of study is what forms interpretation to a great extent. Art history is therefore a dialogue. It is not a unidirectional description of art objects from an isolated position. The possibility of an apprehension of cultural artifacts is never a direct form of knowledge since cultures are represented by virtue of these dialogic translations. Moxey uses the term *dialogic* not as a simple dyadic exchange, of an autonomous observer and observed, but in Bakhtin's thoroughly socialized sense. Such a view obstructs the possibility of claims to retrieving an essential, inherent, or pure knowledge of a cultural artifact and its context, and thwarts the implicitly political hierarchy of cultures as we know it.

But does art history remain a monological genre in another sense? Since Western scholarship has laid down the terms in which the arts, aesthetic practices, and cultural history of others may be represented, is it by definition inescapably Western? If art historical descriptions of the world beyond Europe can be made only from a Eurocentric position, then it will remain not only a monological genre but might even be described as a lingering colonial discourse that (as in the example of nineteenth-century ethnography) denies the possibility that the object of observation, the foreign culture, might be populated by speaking subjects. And the teaching methods and scholarship of art and archaeology will continue to be what Sartre described, in his introduction to Frantz Fanon's *The Wretched of the Earth*, as an echo of Western humanism across the globe (Sartre 1963:7).

Sign/Symbol

Once we get used to the idea of "representation" as a two way affair rooted in psychological dispositions we may be able to refine a tool which has proved quite indispensable to the historian of art and which is nevertheless rather unsatisfactory: the notion of the "conceptual image." By this we mean the mode of representation which is more or less common to children's drawings and to various forms of primitive and primitivist art.

—Ernst Gombrich (1963:180).

Todorov describes a territorial, temporal, and biological taboo with regard to the symbol in language: "It is as if a vigilant censor had authorized us to speak of the symbolic only if we were to use borrowed words such as 'insanity,' 'childhood,' 'savages,' 'prehistory' " (Todorov 1982:223). In Gombrich's model of making and matching, and in the Hegelian system that inspired it, a similar disavowal of the symbol and its reattribution to the realm of the other occurs. Conceptual art is seen as an art of conventional signs and therefore symbolic while perceptual art is theoretically similar to both the natural sign in imitating nature accurately and to the linguistic phonetic sign in being a rational, and even at times a scientific, method of rendering the world. Today such a subdivision would perhaps seem amusing to most art historians. Nevertheless, until fairly recently it was standard to think in terms of a Western illusionistic representation that is mimetic or realistic and conceptual art as a broad inclusive category roughly equivalent to most image making outside the European tradition. For approximately two centuries such a model of representation dominated any critical discussion of art. Perceptual and conceptual were referential categories that were thought to be universally applicable because they had been derived from a universal human cognitive system. Both modes of representation were seen as schemata or patterns by which humans portray their surrounding world, and these modes were distinctive of particular traditions in the West and elsewhere. Of course, there were always exceptions, but a pervasive feeling has existed that a subdivision of perceptual and conceptual arts along geographical frontiers was generally possible.[5] In this way perceptualism, the successful form of mimesis, came to be seen as the civilized mode of artistic production and in so defining civilization also contained the equally necessary function of delineating what is external to civilization and civilized behavior: children, primitives, and pagans in general.

Gombrich set forth these principles of art historical development in his 1960 book, *Art and Illusion*. For Gombrich, making is distinctive of the ancient Orient, of Africa, and the greater part of Asia during most of its history, and matching is the aesthetic production of the West, developed under democratic government. In the chapter titled "Reflections on the Greek Revolution" he argued rather eloquently that what he termed *matching* or perceptualism is a result of democracy, equating the freedom of movement portrayed in the stone sculpture of antiquity with political freedom. Making and matching, then, could be plotted clearly in terms of space, time, and political system. Matching is confined to particular areas of the world, and according to historical time, it is limited to a definitive period of Western history.

Gombrich's model was perhaps "the climax of the perceptualist tradition," as Norman Bryson put it in his rigorous investigation of this subject in *Vision and Painting*. And even if perceptualism is a rather recent way of approaching works of art, it has, as Bryson has said, become almost natural for us to think of a work of art as a record of perception (Bryson 1991:62–63). In answer to the question "what is painting?," Gombrich had declared that "painting is the record of a perception." Bryson pointed out the fundamental flaw with this statement and proposed that rather than thinking of it in terms of a record of perception of reality, painting should be approached as "an art of signs." He further explained that "painting in the West manipulates signs in such a way as to conceal its status as sign" (Bryson 1983:xii–xiii). This then is what we read as a mimetic representation and what has traditionally (especially by Gombrich) been seen as the ideal goal in "a doctrine of progress towards the essential copy" (Bryson 1983:15–16). In Bryson's words, "At the level of theory, the concept which suppresses the emergence of the sign as object of art historical knowledge is mimesis" (1983:38).

In his work on the primacy of perceptualism, Bryson has made a number of observations that are vital for any rethinking of approaches to non-Western arts. He has pointed out that the difference between natural and arbitrary resemblance, between signifier and signified, is not a given because it is culturally produced and constantly changing. Lifelikeness and its opposite depend on the perception of the audience because what is real is historically relative and variable. The scale between natural and conventional signs must therefore constantly shift. When considering Near Eastern art, and perhaps various other non-European traditions, Bryson's argument needs to be heeded and even radically amplified.

Lifelike or schematic, arbitrary or natural, conceptual or perceptual—all obviously refer to a mimetic relationship between art and nature or between representation and an external world. All these terms are concerned with either an affirmation or denial of a given, unproblematic realm of the real. Even arguments at the opposite end of the semiological thesis—that all representation is arbitrary and that there is no such thing as natural resemblance—leave an unquestioned real intact. By this term, I mean the ontic real as it is conceived of at various times and places, and not simply the social context of the cultural artifact. The differences between artifice and reality, *physis/tekhne*, nature/culture are not universals. They are historically and culturally determined concepts of comprehending the world. There can be no universalizing scales of lifelikeness or arbitrariness in art just as there can be no such scale for measuring levels of arbitrariness in languages. What I am referring to here, of course, is the domain of metaphysics that Jacques Derrida describes as "the white mythology which reassembles and reflects the culture of the West: the white man takes his own mythology, Indo-European mythology, his own logos, that is the *mythos* of his idiom, for the universal form of that he must still wish to call Reason" (1982:213). Derrida characterizes Western metaphysics in terms of its equation to reason and the subject of reason as a specific historical, cultural, and racial subject. The principles of reason upon which (what we consider) the real rests are called into question. But even aside from this deconstructive argument, it is possible to demonstrate that reason, rationality, and the real are culturally specific. When it comes to the realm of art or image making, Derrida's critique of metaphysical oppositions is invaluable for understanding the ontotheological foundations for a historically situated Western concept of the aesthetic and representation as mimesis. But for the study of non-Western arts it is important also to heed his statement regarding the question with which art has been approached. If we continue to ask the same question, to repeat this question "without transforming it, without destroying it in its form, its question-form, its onto-interrogative structure," then we leave the notion of art as understood. Art remains predetermined or comprehended in the question form, and "this can be verified: teleology and hierarchy are prescribed in the envelope of the question" (Derrida 1987:22). With Derrida's warning in mind, I would like to return to the question of the difference between perceptual and conceptual representation.

Mimesis is the process by which a representation functions as a record of the perception of reality, corresponding to that reality and matching it—whether successfully or unsuccessfully. Perceptual and conceptual art can thus be defined as terms for evaluating levels of correspondence between the mimetic image and what it represents or the proximity of resemblance between sign and referent. This is the standard separation of *physis/tekhne*, nature/art, with its implication that art, the concept or the material thing, has a unity and an originary meaning separate from nature. In other words, far from belonging to another realm, as a concept, conceptual art is merely an aspect of perceptual art, both being polarities of mimesis. This binarism is more or less parallel to the categories of natural and conventional signs in semiology.

In Charles Sanders Peirce's classification some signs are motivated and have an intrinsic relationship to the thing they mean to signify. This is the category of index. In the index the relation of sign and referent is one of contiguity: smoke means fire, footprints indicate the person or animal (Peirce 1940:98–119). In Peirce's system the symbol is the opposite of the index in that its relationship to the signified real is arbitrary and based purely on convention. There is no direct, natural link to the reality behind the sign; an example of the symbol would be scales representing justice. The third category in Peirce's model is that of the icon. This category includes the image, in which the relationship is based on direct external resemblance, and the diagram, in which the relationship between signifiers is parallel to the relationship between signifieds. Peirce's classification, which is considered to be relatively independent of the linguistic model, is still based on the levels of proximity between each type of sign and the thing in reality that it may represent. What I will demonstrate in the next four chapters is that, at least for one ancient society, such a divide between representation and the real cannot be maintained. It is not just what counts as realistic representation that needs relativizing according to culture and time, but the difference between reality and artifice as well. Furthermore, if it is the goal of mimetic realism for the viewer to accept the image as reflecting the real, it is not only that reality which is constantly changing and differing across culture. Not all cultures see images as reflecting a preexisting real (whether perceptually or conceptually) that is a relationship of mimesis. I will show by means of the Assyrian record that conceptual representation (if such a term is not entirely wrong) cannot be thought of as the opposite of an essential copy or realistic image. There are traditions in which what art history has labeled conceptual art was in the view of the culture that produced it quite literally an essential representation, or an indexically linked image—a relationship that according to the standard subdivision would fall under natural signs as opposed to arbitrary or conventional signification. An image can be conceived of as an essential copy without resemblance at the level of *eidos*, or what in Peirce's terminology would be the icon. In fact, the subdivisions of natural/conventional, perceptual/conceptual, and so on are not only inapplicable to Near Eastern antiquity because they are anachronistic. They actually become contradictory and have a tendency to collapse as sustainable categories. However, such contradiction is not unusual for a theory of the symbol in Western aesthetic discourse itself.

The categorical distinction between perceptual and conceptual images as defined by art history is a distinction of ideologically freighted oppositions similar to numerous ethnological dualisms that we know from anthropology, such as complex/simple, modern/primitive, rational/ritualist. Like these oppositions, making and matching, or perceptual and conceptual, representation purport to reveal the empirical realities of cultures. And like the philological definition of sign and symbol, or natural and conventional signification, the two realms of making and matching have come to be defined as culturally distinctive referential modes. Although Western philosophy had argued that visual and verbal signification were entirely separate realms that do not coincide, during the nineteenth century their systems of classifications were explicitly linked in both aesthetic discourse and philology, even if this correspondence is sometimes inverted or seemingly contradictory. Aesthetics and rhetoric came to be conflated in the thinking of this period because both areas were ruled by the principle of imitation (Todorov 1982:111, 128).

Traditionally, Western thought has relied on an opposition of word and image as fundamentally different modes of signification: images are mimetic; words are dependant on convention. They do not resemble or imitate the thing represented but refer to it in a more arbitrary manner. A word can never be taken for the thing itself. According to this tradition, hieroglyphs, pictographic, and ideographic scripts are inferior to phonetic alphabets because they retain an image in the signifier rather than depending on pure conventional marks that are a more conventional means of rendering spoken language. At the same time, in the art historical tradition works of art (before the modern period) are natural signs; they are faithful copies of the things in the world which they represent. Art is thought to represent an already existing autonomous essential world.[6] These natural representations are contrasted to the conventional images of pagan and primitive people. The latter are generally thought to have a more arbitrary relation to the thing represented, being nonmimetic, more abstract. Mimesis is the natural image, it signifies through imitation in that it resembles the thing it represents while conceptual art (its posited opposite) relies on convention for its signifying processes. It is here that the reversal occurs in the natural/conventional sign division by which word and image have been categorized as forms of signification. W. J. T. Mitchell has already pointed to how this categorization defines Western images as natural signs and how they are contrasted to images that are seen as conventional signs and described as less real or unnatural (1986). Such images are less accurate or objective because they are not based on external resemblance. They represent a conventional idea of the thing in reality rather than depicting it as it is. In terms of the written sign, however, it is the conventional marks of what is seen as purely phonetic script rather than the natural signs of pictography that are superior because they are uncompromised by imagery.

In Western thought, proper and figurative meanings of words are seen as dichotomies that do not coincide with one another. Proper language is thought of as being made up of pure unmotivated signs and thus in the realm of reason and logic. It is unaffected by such things as metaphor and analogy. Symbolic thought exists where there is no reason or logic and is the realm of the other: children, primitives, and the insane. In art, or concepts of image making, a parallel distinction occurs in that the Western representation of reality is traditionally thought to be a faithful and more accurate, thus logical and technologically advanced, representation (for example, perspective-based representation). Non-Western art is symbolic. An opposition has thus been formulated whereby Western signs (word or image) are objective and logical, and non-Western signification is the realm of the symbol. Word and image in the West are representations of reason, and reason, in turn, is conceived in terms of mimesis while symbols are the representations of others—foreigners or the childhood of the West. The description of the uncivilized sign (the symbol) as that of the other (in Todorov's words) thus also occurred in descriptions of art and aesthetic practices since non-Western art forms are described as an inversion of mimesis proper.

Conceptual art can exist only as the opposite of perceptualism. Thus, it is a useless exercise to call for a greater appreciation of conceptual art. It is more important to acknowledge that as a theoretical term, it describes only what is opposite to Western representation. As a concept, it has no means of approaching non-Western art from its own varied ontological or ontotheological conceptions of art or image making, which, at least in some cultures, may not include mimesis. Conceptual art has nothing to do with the aesthetics of anything other than the European tradition.

In art historical deconstruction the concept of the aesthetic and the activity of aesthetic judgment have been discussed in some detail in recent years. The focus has been on two aspects of the aesthetic: the autonomy of the aesthetic judgment as an internalized subjective activity rather than a socially and historically determined act, and the value of autonomous art as free from monetary value. Both these ideas have been carefully taken apart and shown to be unviable because the aesthetic as a concept exists only as an ideology in Western philosophy (see, for example, Rodowick 1994). The main impetus behind these discussions in art history has been Derrida's deconstruction of Kant's aesthetic theory, especially his essay "Parergon" (Derrida 1987). However, the emergence of the aesthetic in the eighteenth century was also linked to theories of representation in general. This ideological relationship between semiology and aesthetics has been given a great deal of attention by deconstructive philosophy, although not similarly investigated by art historians.

In his *Aesthetics*, Hegel stresses the arbitrariness of the sign as differing from the symbol's essential or conceptual correspondence to the thing expressed (Hegel 1975). Numerous earlier and later writers in the Western tradition have made the same distinction. For Hegel, the sign is better than the symbol because it is independent and objective. It is able to maintain its autonomy while at the same time pointing to the referent. Hegel believes in the necessity of a distinction between sign and symbol, yet he also seems to warn of the possible tendency to conflate the two and in fact uses the terms *symbol* and *symbolic* in a number of seemingly incongruous or contradictory ways (de Man 1996:91–104). A recurring interpretive problem in any reading of Hegel is thus the sense in which the term *symbol* is used. In his well-known subdivision of the history of art into three parts, *Symbolic, Classical,* and *Romantic,* he uses *symbolic* to refer to a historical period. Many commentators on Hegel's work have seen the symbol as a diachronic or vertical term describing a past that is preclassical. Yet Hegel clearly meant it also synchronically. To him, the symbolic was never totally overcome. Classical art (in other words, Greek antiquity) is postsymbolic, but because all art belongs to the order of the symbol, "it follows that a classical style can in essence no longer be symbolic in the more precise sense of the term, although some symbolic ingredients remain intermittently present in it" (Hegel 1975, II:20).

As a historical period, symbolic is opposed to classical mimesis; it is the time of making as opposed to the time of matching, as Gombrich might say. As an ethnographic term in Hegel's writing, the symbol enables an anthropological charting, and its use in this case seems more closely linked to a philological or rhetorical distinction between sign and symbol: the traditional differentiation in which the sign is a detached, objective rendering of the real and the symbol is an attached and motivated sign. It is therefore the sign in this case that is natural and not the symbol because the sign represents, faithfully, objectively, a truth or concept. The symbol (as exemplified in hieroglyphic script) instead has a contiguous relationship and is therefore compromised by being motivated by the thing it indicates. In other cases (as in the Egyptian pyramid) the symbol is a total form in itself and therefore not a representational sign at all. There are many passages in Hegel's writing in which sign and symbol seem to be exchanged, leaving us with the impression that he was often unclear about the distinction although he set out to argue this distinction in a rigorous and logical manner. The symbol cannot be divorced from the sign, neither diachronically in the historical aspect of art history nor synchronically in its ethnological register. In both axes it is a necessity of differentiation in canonical art history, yet Hegel himself warned us of the conflation of what we have often seen as binary opposites when he said "The symbol is prima facie a sign" (1975:304).

In Hegel's system art proceeds from the Absolute Idea. It is the sensuous presentation of the Absolute itself. Art's task is to present the Idea to immediate perception in a sensuous shape. Spirit has to go through a course of steps to reach true concept, and the Spirit as art gives itself a consciousness of itself in this course. In other words, it gives itself artistic shape. This development of the Spirit is universal and comprehensive. Spirit unfolds into a sequence of forms of artistic configurations (70–73). Hegel stresses that we must look at Spirit's opposite, matter, in order to understand Spirit. In his aesthetics, symbolic art manifests matter (1956:17; 1975:303–426). It is the stage when matter overwhelms Spirit. He further points out that the symbol is the beginning, the threshold of art, thus it belongs to the East, which is the place of beginnings. According to this developmental view, the symbol seeks what the classical finds and the romantic transcends.

As Jacques Derrida and Paul de Man have both demonstrated, the place of semiology is central in the logic of Hegel. Derrida points out that in the system of metaphysics the sign can be treated only as a transition and that indeed "metaphysics is even indistinguishable from such a treatment of the Sign" (Derrida 1982:71). The implications of this critique for the art historical subdivision of Western/non-Western art are clear. For Hegel, the place of the aesthetic is the moment of transition between Objective and Absolute Spirit; thus, the aesthetic sign is a transition in more than one sense. It is a transition from Objective to Absolute Spirit. It is also a transition from content to expression, referent to representation. The symbol borders the sign so that it is in effect a transition unto itself from nonsign to sign. It is the limit of signification; as such, it actually belongs to the sign as *parergon*: that which is defined as external to the work of art proper, or the *ergon*, in Kantian aesthetics, such as ornament or frame. Therefore, the sign/symbol opposition is necessary for the aesthetic, but not simply as an example of radically different modes of representation. The symbol is the border, the frame of the sign. Derrida also suggests that all of these characteristics of the sign as transition, a bridge, and as something that unites, are reducible to a question of truth. How truthful is the presence of being in the sign? How adequate is its form to its content? At a certain level, then, the division between sign/symbol becomes a distinction between a truthful and an untruthful representation.

In Paul de Man's investigation of this semiological aspect of Hegelian philosophy, he writes that the "assertion that art belongs unreservedly to the order of the symbolic is made in the context of a distinction between symbol and sign that in the realm of art does not seem to apply" (de Man 1996:95). But it is precisely in order that the proper sign may exist that the symbol is distinguished by Hegel, even though on some level he is always aware of the difficulties inherent in his system. Both de Man and Derrida have shown that the internal system of aesthetics requires the outside of the aesthetic in order to sustain itself as a category. De Man argues that Kant's *Third Critique* and Hegel's *Aesthetics* both end up "undoing the aesthetic as a valid category" (de Man 1996:70–104). The system of the aesthetic cannot ground itself, he concludes, on its own internal principles. It is not self-sufficient.

Conceptual art, or alien art, can be likened to the *parergon* within the space of the canon of art history. It forms the frame of perceptualism. Aesthetic detachment requires this attachment in a parallel condition to the necessity of the *ergon/parergon* pointed out by Derrida and the requirement of the symbol for the sign as shown by de Man. In art history, cultures such as those of the ancient Near East and Egypt are defined by their placement as both spatial and chronological borders of the universal aesthetic evolution. Africa, Islam, and East Asia take over that position of the limits of civilization in primarily spatial terms because their development is outside the real time of world history. In this way Kant's description of *parerga* fits the art historical canon well: "It is only where taste is still weak and untrained (ie. at the very limits) that, like aliens they are admitted as a favour, and only on terms that they do not violate the beautiful" (Kant [1790] 1952:67). Derrida's deconstruction of the *parergon* demonstrates that the entire possibility of the *ergon* rests on the possible encroachment of the alien *parergon*. But this alien already inhabits the *ergon* and cannot be expelled without destroying its host (Derrida 1987).

Derrida asks how what is outside the text can be understood or even conceived of, the point being that like sign and symbol, *ergon* and *parergon*, the one is inconceivable without the other or, to use his words: "Thus one could reconsider all the pairs of opposites on which philosophy is constructed and on which our discourse lives, not in order to see opposition erase itself but to see what indicates that each of the terms appear as the *différance* of the other, as the other different and deferred in the economy of the same" (Derrida 1982:17).

Sign and symbol, matching and making, are clearly such terms that emerge as the *différance* of the other "in the economy of the same." When Derrida asks us to reconsider the formulation of the question what is the meaning of art, it is not just the division of art/artifact or, the work of art/utensil that is at issue but *physis /tekhne*. Derrida shows that mimesis, which is opposed to *physis,* is really only its *différance* (1982:3–27). What we imagine as two entirely opposite realms are actually interdependent. Binary oppositions, we should recall, work by the suppression of one term in favor of the other. The two terms are not opposed in an autonomous separation. They differ in relation to one another and are therefore "in the economy of the same." It is thus that in terms of alterity, the enunciation of difference works through an attribution of bipolar oppositions to self and to other. Paraphrasing Michael Ann Holly (1990), we can say that in cross-cultural aesthetic descriptions we may be talking about other people's works of art, but we are also talking about ourselves.

The uses of art in societies where fine art does not exist are described by the anthropology of art as being in the domain of ritual and the domain of commercial exchange, where materials are transformed for commerce. These ethnological descriptions of cultures that lack a notion of high art, mentioned at the beginning of the chapter, are clearly also descriptions of two examples of the uses of art in the European tradition. In defining them as the art, practices of primitive societies or alien cultures such scholarship also describes its own European culture. Tzvetan Todorov's theorem that "descriptions of the uncivilized sign are uncivilized descriptions of our own symbol" seems justified when the sign and symbol are those of aesthetic theory and art history.

4

Being in the Word:
Of Grammatology and Mantic

The one who will shine in the science of writing will
shine like the sun.
—a scribe

O Šamaš, by your light you scan the totality of lands as
if they were cuneiform signs.
—Assyrian hymn

These three ways of writing correspond almost exactly
to three different stages according to which one can
consider men gathered into a nation. The depicting of
objects is appropriate to savage people; sign of words
and propositions, to a barbaric people; and the alphabet
to civilized people.
—Jean-Jacques Rousseau, *Essai sur l'origine des langues*

Alphabetic script is in itself and for itself the most
intelligent.
—Georg Wilhelm Hegel, *Enzyklopädie*

THESE QUOTATIONS ARE from the exergue of the first chapter of Jacques Derrida's *Of Grammatology* (1974:3). They were chosen because the author wants to show that writing is always ethnocentric, that it is not separable from culturally specific concepts of reason or science. Mesopotamian writing, being considered the earliest by the majority of historians of language and philologists, makes the inclusion of an Assyrian prayer an appropriate choice for juxtaposition with post-Enlightenment conceptions of writing.[1] By beginning with these quotes, Derrida wants to say that there are many ways of viewing the sign in history but that they are all ethnocentric. Each system is the system of reason and logic to its users and although developed in local contexts, is assumed to be valid universally. In Western thought from Plato onward, phonetic writing is equated with objective truth and its accurate representation. Writing in this tradition has always been considered as an external matter to speech and as a record of speech. It does not proceed from nature but is rather a supplement to it. In philosophical thinking it thus has the same exteriority to nature as a utensil. Such a priori distinctions, then, indicate that the structure of writing has a significance beyond its own limited field. It is from writing that metaphysics emerges. Derrida invokes an Assyrian statement to remind us that other forms of writing are also equated with reason and science as the anonymous scribe's words make clear. Although he is not interested in recounting a history or a genealogy of writing and its progress in world civilization, according to the classical teleological model of histories of writing, he nevertheless seems well aware of the cuneiform writing system and how it functions. Derrida in fact adapts the renowned Assyriologist Ignatius Gelb's term *Grammatology* from the latter's *A Study of Writing: The Foundations of Grammatology* for his own study (Derrida 1974:323). He also states, provocatively, that grammatology (in his sense) could have opened up historically at the moment of the decipherment of ancient non-European scripts, but did not. In other words, Derrida's thinking on the relation of language and metaphysics was influenced by his study of nonphonetic scripts such as cuneiform and Chinese.

Ignatius Gelb's book, first published in 1952, was what is known as a classical historical study of the development of language. It was remarkable in its time for the addition of its final chapters that were critical confrontations of the (by then standardized) notion of the monogenetic origin of language and the related concept that writing was the factor that spurred the birth of civilization. Gelb explained the term *grammatology* as the descriptive treatment of writing; thus, what he seems to have had in mind is a sort of metawriting that would allow a questioning of received knowledge regarding script. In this, Gelb, like Derrida, approached the classical historical model of unilinear progress with skepticism. Although Gelb's book went through two editions in the 1950s and 1960s, it has been out of fashion among Assyriologists for the last thirty years, being replaced by a preference for a narrower scope in philological scholarship. Derrida's *Of Grammatology* (and his work in general), on the other hand, has been one of the most influential texts in the Western humanities during this same time, and Derrida himself is heralded as perhaps the most influential philosopher of the postmodern era.

Postmodern criticism and arts, the ethos of postmodernity, and the project of deconstruction are characterized as exemplifying a crisis in representation. The issue of representation, especially how the object of study is represented in texts, is at the center of postmodern thinking. Such thinking breaks with the belief in the unmediated real by questioning the possibility of a pure mimetic representation. Texts, it is argued, transform the object of study into a simulacrum or anamorphosis of the thing because texts must always be an indirect, mediated, perspective. Thus, the process of coding and decoding, the relationship between the signifier and the signified, is an issue that has been at the fore of critical thought for some time now. In the visual realm the distinctions between the referent and representation, essence and appearance, original and copy are at the heart of postmodern discussions and postmodern aesthetics. The study of representational practices through an analysis of semiotics and rhetoric, as well as the concept of mimesis, have become standard theoretical inroads for investigation in art history, literary criticism, cultural studies, and anthropology. All concern sign systems and their relation to the real: image, representation, convention, words, and so on; they have also been defined as modes of presencing. This latter concept has also been taken up by archaeological theory to apply to the retrieval, organization, and presentation of data from the past as a mode of presencing of that past (Shanks and Tilley 1987; Hodder 1992). These approaches are not, as many who are in opposition to theory and theoretical analysis in archaeology have stated, a method that abandons all references to the factual real. Rather, the point of a semiotic or deconstructive approach is to complicate it as a concept by rethinking the relationship between sign and referent, signified and signifier, nature and convention, as well as word and image.

The comparative method of visual-verbal representation has been utilized in the study of ancient Near East since the earliest days of the discipline. Near Eastern art historians and archaeologists have always been very much interested in the text, or verbal communication, as well as the visual. Historical narratives are often compared to representations on Assyrian reliefs, and myths and literary texts are used to explain iconography wherever possible. These approaches are of great value for an understanding of Near Eastern cultural remains, and what I am outlining here is not a suggestion for an abandonment and a replacement but for what I hope will be an expansion of these investigations. As in other fields, the visual and the verbal are traditionally neatly separated as disciplinary specialties, and the two subfields are kept from merging. They are seen as two modes of communication, which are at times parallel but most often are not and which as parallel codes mostly convey the same message, repeated according to another sign system. Recently some scholars of the ancient Near East have begun to span this disciplinary divide in order to consider the two areas together (most notably, Anthony Green, Julian Reade, Franz Wiggerman, and Irene Winter). Their work has focused on the ancient texts and the information that they provide on images and aesthetic practices. In addition to the groundbreaking endeavors of these scholars, I propose two theories: In Assyro-Babylonian material culture it is possible to recognize a similarity of representational structures in both the fields of the visible and the readable, which is not always an underlying linguistic (or narrative) structure, nor even a pictorial one; for ancient Iraq and perhaps other ancient Near Eastern cultures, especially Egypt, the interaction of visual image and text is constitutive of representation itself. This is what I will refer to as the word-image dialectic.[2] Therefore, when I refer to an underlying representational structure, I do not mean that language dictates the pictorial, nor do I mean that the pictorial determines script. Rather, my argument here is that it is the indissociable relationship between the two that is distinctive of Assyro-Babylonian beliefs.

A clarification of this relationship between sign and referent, signifier and signified in the thought of the ancient Near East, an investigation of how visual and verbal signification functioned in Assyro-Babylonian ontology, can be useful as a contribution to the discussion of the problematics of representation in general, currently being investigated from a variety of perspectives, as well as for further study of signification and practices of representation in the ancient Near East. What I mean to address here is not a reading of texts as sources of information for images (narrative or otherwise) but rather the structure of a word-image dialectic that I will demonstrate shifts between the visual and the verbal realm in every sense and forms the basis for an Assyro-Babylonian conception of representation. In order to demonstrate this claim, I will describe the cuneiform system of writing in the traditional historical-developmental manner, but with the additional insights that a poststructuralist or semiological investigation of writing can give.[3]

The Script and the Quest for Origins

The origin of spoken language, or the historical processes of the formation of language, which as we have seen was important for the charting of
a global history of mankind, is still a problem of interest in linguistics, anthropology, psychoanalysis, and theology, and it is not one upon which
any agreement has been reached. The earliest writing systems, on the
other hand, seem to be fairly securely identified as the scripts developed in
the ancient Near East. From the fourth millennium B.C. until the first
century A.D. the cuneiform script and system of writing were used in Iraq
and the surrounding Near Eastern countries (see figures 4a and 4b). This
is the first writing system known and may have influenced the later Egyptian, Indian, and, some think, perhaps even the Chinese system of writing
(Liverani 1998:102). The cuneiform script was used to record a large variety of languages, primarily Sumerian and Akkadian but also Hittite, Hur-
rian, Urartian, Elamite, Eblaic, and others. Throughout its 3,000-year-long
use, it underwent several changes, always adding on new uses but never
abandoning the earlier ones. Writing was thus invented for the first time
in southern Iraq sometime during the last part of the fourth millennium B.C. but quickly spread throughout the Near East. In many historical and anthropological accounts it is this invention of writing that has
been described as the impetus for the origin of civilization. And writing as
a characteristic of ancient Near Eastern culture has been a major factor in
the inclusion of the Near East in the standard progress of civilization.

The term *cuneiform*, used to refer to this Near Eastern writing, is of
course a modern term applied to the script because of its wedge-shaped
signs. *Cuneiform* thus refers to a script, not to a language. The language
for which it was developed was most likely Sumerian, the earliest-known
language used in Iraq, and cuneiform continued to be used for Sumerian,
at least throughout the third millennium B.C., although not exclusively.
Sumerian is classified as an agglutinative language, meaning that it translates the grammatical correspondences by juxtaposing prefixes, suffixes,
and affixes to all the essential "full" words, be they nouns or verbs, but it
seems to be linguistically unrelated to any other language grouping (Bottéro 1992:68). Earlier in this century some scholars argued that the script
was in fact first invented for another language, now lost to us, and only
later adopted for Sumerian. I. J. Gelb, for example, in *A Study of Writing*,
refers to the "X-Element" as the ethnic group in question (1952:63). The

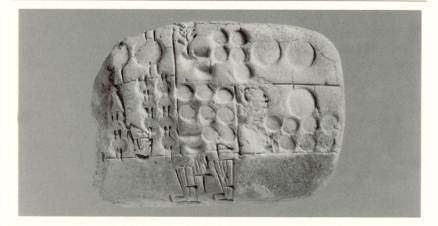

Figure 4a. Uruk III tablet (recto), ca. 3100 B.C. Courtesy of the Metropolitan Museum of Art (Purchase, Raymond and Beverly Sackler Gift, 1988).

Figure 4b. Uruk III tablet (verso), ca. 3100 B.C. Courtesy of the Metropolitan Museum of Art (Purchase, Raymond and Beverly Sackler Gift, 1988).

influence of this view, which predates Gelb, is still found in some standard texts on the ancient Near East although no argument is explicitly made for it. E. A. Speiser pointed out in 1930 that a number of names of cities and terms for certain professions, such as carpenter, are most likely non-Sumerian and can be said to reflect a "sub-stratem" language spoken by a race of people that preceded the Sumerians as inhabitants of southern Iraq. However, there is very little reason to believe in the existence of the "X-Element," and the general desire to attribute the first writing to a mystery race is perhaps better explained in the context of the intellectual history that formed the background of most scholars working in the field at the time of the discovery of the earliest texts, and of Sumerian. The related question of the land of origin of the Sumerians seems to also derive from the nineteenth-century desire for a racial classification of historical development. By the late nineteenth century, especially in Britain and France, a racial linguistic categorization corresponding to levels of civilization was fairly well established as scientifically sound in the academic disciplines (see Chapter 1). During this time, arguments for a Turanian people who were racially classified as proto-Aryan, having been the instigators of early civilizations as far apart as Egypt, Etruria, and Mesopotamia, were made, based on no other evidence than the assumption that only Aryans were capable of creating a civilization.[4] Assyriologists such as Henry Rawlinson and William Kennet Loftus felt that the Mesopotamians originated in Ethiopia, but after a Sumerian element had been discovered in Iraq, archaeologists such as Hermann V. Hilprecht began to differentiate between an indigenous people and the "invading Semites." The theory of the non-Sumerian occupation put forth by Speiser was taken up by scholars such as Benno Landsberger but refuted by the art historian Henri Frankfort. Frankfort attempted to identify a Sumerian style in the period preceding the Early Dynastic era, referred to by archaeologists as the Jamdat Nasr period (3100–2900 B.C.). Frankfort studied physical features on statuary of both periods in order to recognize a racial similarity through physiognomy. He applied the same methodology to the earlier Uruk period (3800–3100 B.C.). Later, some scholars took up Frankfort's view, but others argued against it. The art historian Anton Moortgat, for example, concluded that the identification of Sumerians based on cranial measurements of skeletons was problematic because cranial types uncovered in excavations did not always seem to match up with those found in Sumerian sculpture. Therefore, it seems that both sides of the argument in the 1930s and 1940s were based on dubious racial classifications and fueled by the political climate of that era.[5]

According to the predominant model of the nineteenth century, all racial-cultural groupings in world history could be explained and made to fit into a tripartite classification of savage, barbaric, and civilized cultures (see Chapter 1). As a means of coming to terms with the archaeological discovery of sophisticated cultural remains in regions of the world that in the nineteenth century were peopled by specimens of the barbaric stage of ethnic development, Turanians were clearly a practical solution. As a proto-Aryan race that was responsible for the origins of civilization, Turanians could solve the problem of civilized artifact in barbaric or primitive places. Though all Near Eastern scholars would today find such an allegation of a proto-Aryan presence preposterous, vestiges of this older scholarship have survived, in a diluted form, yet the origins of such arguments have by now been totally forgotten. These vestiges are not debated because of the unfortunate general lack of interest in the historiography of the field, which like any other discipline has its fair share of skeletons. Thus, it is often stated in general handbooks or student texts that the Sumerians came to the Tigris-Euphrates valley "from the north" although there is no archaeological or linguistic evidence for such an assertion, and it is never really clear where north is meant to be. Bottéro points out that since a homophonic function, based on the Sumerian language, was utilized in the Mesopotamian script by as early as 3000 B.C., a Sumerian invention is most likely, but the place of origin of these Sumerians was still questioned by him. At this point the evidence for cuneiform script being invented for the writing of Sumerian, whose speakers lived in the area of southern Iraq, is yet the strongest (Bottéro 1992:80). But the matter is certainly complicated by the fact that Mesopotamia is likely to have been always multilingual, not unlike Iraq today.

As for the impetus behind the development of the cuneiform script, a theory most widely publicized through the work of Denise Schmandt-Besserat proposes that clay tokens used as counting devices throughout Western Asia from the ninth millennium B.C. onward were the forerunners of written records, In which case (one might conclude that) the origin of writing could be sought elsewhere. This hypothesis is highly conjectural especially because the so-called tokens are often artifacts of dubious nature that are difficult to distinguish and, furthermore, rarely have a recorded archaeological context (Zimanksy 1993). Added to this is their alleged distribution over the entirety of South Asia and the Near East for a period of over five millennia (Michalowski 1992).[6] More recently, Piotr Michalowski, Jerrold Cooper, and Jean-Jacques Glassner have all argued, contrary to this developmental model, that the earliest script we know of was invented as a system in one moment, that it was an "invented technology" (Michalowski 1992:58; Cooper in press; Glassner 2000).

Regardless of the ethnic identity of its inventors, cuneiform writing came to influence much of Assyro-Babylonian thought in the later history of this culture. The decipherment of this cuneiform script, begun by the

German scholar George Friedrich Grotefend and the English politician
Henry Rawlinson in the middle of the nineteenth century, is a story that
has been recounted so often that I will not repeat it here (see Bottéro
1992:55–66). Suffice it to say that it was first the Old Persian cuneiform
script used in Achaemenid royal inscriptions that was deciphered, and after that Babylonian and Assyrian, both of which are dialects of Akkadian,
and lastly Sumerian, which is linguistically unrelated to the others. Although the script was first devised for Sumerian and continued to be used
for Sumerian, by about 2500 B.C. the script began also to be utilized to
record the Akkadian language, which is classified as Semitic because of its
affiliation with Aramaic, Hebrew, and Arabic. Cuneiform script was also
adopted for the languages of the neighboring countries in Iran, Anatolia,
and Syria, and by the second millennium, Akkadian language written in
cuneiform script became the lingua franca of royal and diplomatic correspondence as far west as Egypt. This predominance of cuneiform writing
has led scholars to speak of it as the script of the first half of the history of
the world, referring to the three millennia of written history in which the
majority of documents are in this script (Hallo 1971).

The Script and the World

The earliest shape that this script took, however, was not cuneiform but
pictographic. The earliest stage of writing seems to be that used in the
texts uncovered in 1928–29 at the city of Uruk (modern Warka) in southern Iraq (see figure 5). Here, more than one thousand clay tablets were
found, using a simple pictography for what seems to be the recording of
economic transactions. These tablets were retrieved from the archaeological level IV, and the name *Uruk IV* has subsequently been applied to the
earliest script. The signs used in this Uruk IV writing are word signs, expressing numerals and objects. This stage has therefore been described as
logography, or word writing, "a script of things" (Gelb 1952:65; Bottéro
1992:73). An abbreviated picture of the object represented that object; for
example, an ox head or sheep head for an ox or sheep; a fish for a fish, in-
tersecting and opposite semicircular shapes for the sun (on the horizon); a
pubic triangle for a female; a penis for a male; and so on. But this method
soon evolved into a system that worked through association so that a picture of the sun could also refer to the qualities associated with sun, such
as day, bright and so forth, a foot could refer to that bodily part but also

Figure 5. Uruk IV tablet, ca. 3200 B.C. Courtesy of Hans Nissen.

to the act of walking, a mouth next to bread could signify "to eat," and the pubic triangle placed next to the sign for mountain could indicate a slave girl. This last example made sense in a country where the mountains were associated with foreign land, from whence slaves could be acquired. In this way verbs of action and abstract ideas could also be represented through the script of things.

This system was still limited, however, because it could not express parts of speech or grammar. The intended meaning had to be read in the context of signs, and difficulties were also great for recording personal names. Personal names in Sumerian and Akkadian, as in the Middle East today, were very often statements or entire sentences in themselves, such as Enlil-ti (Enlil has given life) and were as common as names like Abdallah (servant of God) are in Arabic. The difficulty of recording such names was eventually solved by the development of phoneticization. Ignatius Gelb believed that it was the problem of the personal names rather than the necessity of indicating grammatical elements that originally spurred this development (Gelb 1952:66). In the phonetic system, words and concepts that could not be easily indicated by pictures came to be recorded through homonyms and combinations of homonyms. This could be accomplished by either total or partial phonetic transfer. In the case of the latter, two or more separate words could be joined for their phonetic values to form a resulting single word. In the case of the former, a simple and direct homonymic transfer could be achieved by using the picture of one thing, the name of which could indicate another. An example is the verb to live or the concept of life, ti in Sumerian, which could be written with the sign for arrow, also ti phonetically. The word for onion, sum, could be used for the verb to give, sum. An example of partial transfer is the combination of ti (arrow) and gi (reed) to form the word tigi, a type of drum (Bottéro 1992:81). These signs thus became syllabic, no longer denoting their original meaning of arrow or reed, but used for their phonetic value to refer to something else.

Over time the cuneiform system of writing developed into a cursive, linear form in which it is no longer possible to see an indication of the pictorial origin of the script, but the development of the script into abstract cuneiform signs is not a transformation based solely on unmotivated phonetic values or semantics. Formal qualities, the shapes of words, were also taken into account in this system. In some cases things that were conceived of as having some sort of affinity or similarity were denoted in the script by similarly shaped signs:

šiptu   ašipu

These two words refer to an incantation (šiptu) and exorcist (ašipu).

Unlike Egyptians, Babylonians and Assyrians did not maintain a pictographic script for public monuments. In ancient Egypt a cursive writing also developed out of pictographic hieroglyphs and came to be used in daily life. However, pictography continued to be utilized as a script in public contexts, for temples and funerary monuments. In ancient Iraq, while not remaining pictographic in form, the script always retained its pictographic origin within its logic as a system. Throughout its long history the script preserved a mixture of logograms and syllabic spellings, logograms being used mostly for nouns and verbs, syllabic signs for personal names, pronouns, and grammatical formations. And traditionally this has been seen as the one great limitation of cuneiform writing: that it was never to develop into a pure and detached phonetic system, like the alphabet.

Anyone who has even a slight knowledge of ancient Iraq knows that for that culture writing is associated with magic, and elsewhere I argue that it is this very power that makes images function (see Chapter 6). But this magical quality of writing is not only of significance for witchcraft incantations and substitution rituals. A similar power can be seen at the level of what I will purposely call Babylonian grammatology, referring back to both Gelb's and Derrida's definitions of this word. Written signifiers, in the Assyro-Babylonian system, were thought to be in a continuous influential relationship with the signified in that each was capable of controlling the other in different contexts. In referring to this as a magical power of writing there is some danger that readers who are not familiar with Assyro-Babylonian culture will imagine an esoteric belief, limited to the initiated priests. While it may be true that only a limited portion of the population was able to read and write, the association of concepts of signification and the workings of the cuneiform script need not mean that people were literate, just as we know that Babylonian divination and oneiromancy were deductive systems related to the workings of cuneiform writing but that knowledge of unsolicited omen reading and dream interpretation, and/or belief in them, was certainly not limited to those who could read and write. One might further add to this the fact that royal public monuments displayed in city centers or temple courts always bore inscriptions that the majority of the population may not have been able to read.[7] They were written, however, because the very fact that writing appeared made an impression on the nonliterate viewers. Be that as it may, there is more than ample evidence to indicate, as Bottéro has already argued in some detail, that Assyro-Babylonian ontology was firmly grounded in notions of representation that are related to the structure of the writing system.

In a series of articles that discuss writing and its relation to other forms of knowledge in Mesopotamia, Bottéro put forth his theory that the structure of the cuneiform script, and the fact of its invention in Mesopotamia, formed what he designated as "the scientific spirit" of this culture.[8] Deductive divination and oneiromancy, religious and medical knowledge, all have a similar underlying structure, which he demonstrates as related to the system of writing. Divination functioned as a system of "deciphering pictograms" in nature, in the entrails of sacrificial animals, in the physiognomy of people or animals. Similarly, oneiromancy functioned by "reading" the images in the dream (see figures 6a and 6b), and medicine worked by reading the symptomatic signs in the body of the patient.

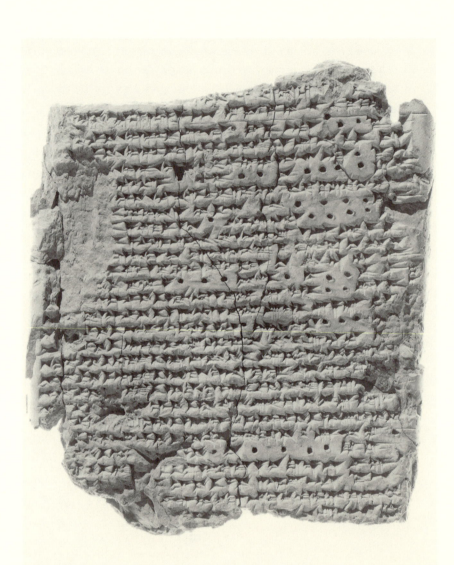

Figure 6a. Assyrian Dream Book tablet (recto), seventh century B.C. Courtesy of the Yale Babylonian Collection.

Figure 6b. Assyrian Dream Book tablet (verso), seventh century B.C. Courtesy of
the Yale Babylonian Collection.

All of these scientific activities were recorded in treatises and texts that organize and classify similar signs or symptoms into groupings. The treatises or manuals provide information by listing possible occurrences in a bipartite system of *protasis* and *apodosis*, a principal proposition introduced by a conditional clause. An example of this system is the following interpretation from the Assyrian Dream Book: "If (in his dream) one gives him water: his days will be long" (Oppenheim 1956:280). The *protasis*, if one gives him water, directly produces the *apodosis* of long life. The latter is derived from the former and linked to it. This system of *protasis* and *apodosis* used in omen texts is also used in medical texts and in law codes, and is perhaps best known from the codex Hammurabi, where the articles of the code are listed in the following manner: "If a man has destroyed the eye of another man: they shall destroy his eye."[9]

Bottéro explains divination as a sort of pictography. The appearance of a pictogram in nature conveyed a message to those who had the ability to read it. These pictograms could appear in anything from common, everyday occurrences, such as the formation of a puddle of water in front of one's door, the inadvertently overheard words of passersby, or the movements of stars and planets. Other types of divination were also practiced. A well-known method is the analysis of the entrails and liver of the sacrificial animal. In this type of divination, signs were also present in the entrails that could be read by the priest. All methods of divination functioned through the same belief that the gods had written into creation: "Si les vieux Mésopotamiens imaginaient en vérité que les dieux écrivaient en intervenant dans la 'création,' tout l'univers visible, pour autant qu'il dépendait de la causalité divine, constituait donc, au moins virtuellement, comme une immense page d'écriture" (Bottéro 1974:161).

The fragment of an Ashurbanipal hymn to the god Šamaš, quoted by Derrida and repeated at the beginning of this chapter, refers to this deity's aspect as the revealer of oracles, "O Šamaš, by your light you scan the totality of lands as if they were cuneiform signs." One of the epithets for this god is *pašir šame u erṣeti*, "the exegetical reader of heaven and earth."[10] Omens and oracles, then, could be read in nature through a hermeneutic system like textual exegesis.

For those who are unfamiliar with ancient societies, this concept of signs in nature may be seen as a general habit of primitive peoples. However, in antiquity, Babylonia was unique in the fact that this view was one that encompassed everything. Their whole world was seen as ominous. Babylonian divination and astrology were thus renowned throughout the ancient world. In ancient Egypt, for example, diviners were famous for their talents in oneiromancy only. Dream interpreters from Egypt were counted among the war booty of the Assyrian king Esarhaddon and were consulted for this oneiromantic purpose in Ashurbanipal's reign (Oppenheim 1956:238). But dream omens are the only omens that were recorded in Egypt. In contrast, thousands of omens concerning all aspects of the world were recorded and cataloged in Mesopotamia, covering all manner of phenomena, conscious or unconscious, and quite often extending to what in our minds would seem like impossible occurrences.

The assertion I am making here, that ontology is grounded in notions of representation, should come as no surprise to anyone who is a scholar of the ancient Near East, nor to anyone who is aware of the postmodern investigation of philosophical categories. Metaphysics, Derrida tells us, is the separation of *physis* and *tekhne* and is not separable from the establishment of a phonetic system of writing where words are no longer conceived as being related to what they represent. In other words, what we consider metaphysics proper was established with the invention of a system of writing that is as different as possible from cuneiform in its representational logic because the total phoneticization of the alphabetic script separated the realms of word and image, and name and thing. The signifier became an external, conventionally attributed means of denoting the signified rather than being in a closely linked relationship with it as is the case with the cuneiform system. Bottéro's important argument for the relationship between cuneiform script and Assyro-Babylonian ontology has many more ramifications than those that he has discussed. This, I think, becomes clearer if we view the relationship between the signifier and the signified as moving in more than one direction. Bottéro saw, and brilliantly argued, that the well-known principle of names of things controlling those things, recorded in Mesopotamian religious texts, was only a facet in this system, that homophony and similarity in shapes of signs forming words were all seen not as random epiphenomena but as part of the logic and destiny of the signified indicated through them. This sliding of the signified under the signifier was thus of great concern to the Mesopotamians. What I propose may be added to this description of the system of the script and its influence on thought is that the relationship of signified and signifier was not unidirectional in the thinking of the Mesopotamians. It is perhaps better conceived, metaphorically, in terms of a circle or a chain of signification. Certain characteristics of this system of writing can be explained through such a shift in focus, and this sort of logic can be demonstrated in other areas of ancient Mesopotamian culture as well.

Since in the earliest writing, pictograms were used to indicate things, one generally thinks of a direct, unmediated representation through image of the thing in question, the kind of image that in the semiotic terminology of Charles Sanders Peirce would be termed an icon (Peirce 1991; 1931–58). But already at the earliest stage of the writing system a large number of the pictograms were not only abbreviated linear drawings of things (the pictorial quality of which had to be learned anyway, no doubt), but the system often used a *pars pro toto* sign. Thus, parts of things came to stand for the whole things in the pictographic script.[11] I would like to suggest that, if read as a figurative mode, this stage in the development of writing can be described as being, at least in part, a metonymic or, to be more exact, a synecdochic stage. In the second stage, as we have seen, these pictograms, whether whole pictures or synecdochic parts, were used to indicate other things by association so that a pubic triangle that metonymically indicates woman or girl, placed next to the standardized line drawing of mountains that refer to foreign lands, could be read as slave. Or more simply, a foot could refer to walking, the sun to brightness, and so on. Rhetorically, then, this stage can be described as metonymic because an associated object comes to stand in for the thing, and metaphoric because some signs are based upon the use of one thing for another derived from cultural conventions like that of the mountains as the land of the slave of foreign origin. The third stage of development was reached when these same signs were used for phonetic value. These signs then could also be used as a rebus through phonetic transfer; thus, we have the example of ti (arrow) being used to indicate life, also pronounced ti in the Sumerian language. This stage can therefore be described as homonymic.

All of these tropes or rhetorical modes (metonymy, synecdoche, metaphor, and homophony) were used as keys of sorts in divination and dream interpretation, as I will demonstrate. In a dream, for example, a message is transmitted by a replacement of certain words or acts by others. It is a mechanism of substitution that often depends on the rhetorical logic of tropes and homophony, and requires the interpretation made by a *pašīru* in order to make sense. The *pašīru* is basically one who can practice exegesis in order to read the words of the gods. Through a hermeneutic reading he or she is able to grasp the meaning of the signs in the dream. Just as in the script, tropes and homophony provide the polyvalence of the signs that lead to the understanding of the dream. Thus, we have the following examples from the Assyrian Dream Book:

1. If a man in his dream eats a raven (*arbu*): income (*irbu*) will come in.
2. If in his dream someone has given him a seal with his name on it: he will have offspring.
3. If one gives him a bolt: his secret will not leak out.

In these examples the relationship between *protasis* and *apodosis* is based on homophony between the word for raven (*arbu*) and the word for income (*irbu*) metonymy and synecdoche in that the seal is a metonymic representative of the person in question and his name is a synecdochic extension that is equated to the extension of offspring, and a metaphorical association of the bolt with the confinement of a secret.

The possibility of encountering the same concept, thing, or referent through different substances or signifiers was thus not overlooked by the Mesopotamians. This possibility became an area of scientific investigation and a means of attempting some understanding of the workings of the universe. In Mesopotamia, therefore, one could encounter the same things or phenomena through mimetic iconicity, metonymic or synecdochic abbreviation, metaphoric or allegorical association, or homophonic relation. These forms of signification can conceivably be divided further into groups based on resemblance, including the areas of iconicity and homophony; and participation or association, including metonymy, synecdoche, and metaphor. The first group can be seen as signification through substitution whereas the second group defers or displaces the signified. None of the above modes of signification seem to have been privileged as granting a more direct access to the referent, what in Western ontology Kant defines as the Thing in itself (*Ding-an-sich*), or to a Heideggerian realm of Being.[12]

In Western tradition we have learned from Kant to distinguish between the phenomenal and the noumenal as two separate modes of knowing, the phenomenon being the object of perception, the noumenon that of thought. Kant also differentiates between the transcendental object and the *Ding-an-sich*. The latter is independent from our perception. It is what the Thing is in itself, regardless of our relationship to it. The transcendental object, which is quite similar to the Thing in itself is slightly different because it is what underlies our perception of the thing. It is the underlying ground of the thing's appearance. In other words, it is the Thing, but as thought by us. In postmodern critiques of the philosophical categories of the Enlightenment it has been argued that the *Ding-an-sich* is a mirage, that the distinction between the transcendental object and the *Ding-an-sich* cannot be maintained (Žižek 1993:35). According to Jacques Lacan, whose psychoanalytic writings are fundamental in this argument, the Thing in itself can only be retroactively produced through signification, through the symbolic. Thus, the gaze creates different shapes of the Thing (Lacan 1986:67–105). The latter critique can perhaps help us to better understand the Mesopotamian conception that the meaning of things and things themselves could be encountered through a variety of signs or symbols, certainly in writing but also in the world at large.

Thus, to go back to the beginning, the original pictogram designates one object or referent, either by what may have been regarded as a direct iconicity, or in part, metonymically. This pictogram, however, could never be privileged as the most faithful direct access to a signified because the signified could constantly evoke another in turn, through resemblance or contiguity as well as through a homophonic parallel. This point is of importance because standard studies of writing have always described a teleology of symbol to sign in which early cuneiform writing and Egyptian hieroglyphs are examples of the symbolic stage. Such writing is defined as symbolic because the signifier is interpreted as evoking the signified directly in a contiguous manner and is thus seen as motivated. This motivated symbolic writing is thus opposed to unmotivated, purely abstract signification, like that of the alphabet (Todorov 1982). But a system such as cuneiform has unlimited possibilities for signification. Each sign used, whether for pictographic or phonetic value, always had the potential for evoking other referents that constantly remained contained within it. Thus we have the example of ti, which can be read as arrow, or rib (life), or to live as well as for its phonetic value of the sound ti.

In Western tradition, going back to Plato's *Cratylus*, words are autonomous, they have a signifying power in themselves but also when combined with other words create other meanings, and the combinations can go on to signify something else, through sentences. For Mesopotamia, it is not just the unidirectional additions of words that provide further meanings. Signification is a continuous chain:

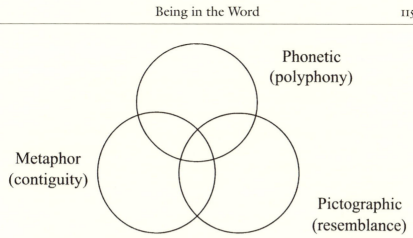

Phonetic
(polyphony)

Metaphor
(contiguity)

Pictographic
(resemblance)

This chain should be autoreferential and self-contained, and we know that scribal lists attempted a standardization of possible meanings to be read from the usage of such signs. But the principle of resemblance and contiguity through polyphony, metaphor, and other conventional associations led to a polysemy, beyond the standardized prosaic readings to the well-known Mesopotamian study of hermeneutics, and the consequent notion that omens are to be found in the world. The conceptual chain of signification was continuous. Therefore, the standardized lists of meaning were by definition perpetually incomplete. In illustrating the possibility of hermeneutic readings, Bottéro uses the example of the god Marduk, upon whom the gods had bestowed fifty names, all of which characterize the powers of the god. All the multiple attributes identified by the different names of Marduk were included in the names themselves. For instance, one of his names, Asari, had the conventional syllabic division, *a-sar-ri*. But when redistributed as *a-sar-ri,* the main components of which are a (water), sar (grain, greenery, and agriculture), and ri, which is equated to ra or ru (bestowing gifts), the name makes Marduk one who gives fertility (Bottéro 1992:94). All known aspects of Marduk were contained in his names, but the total knowledge was impossible because through homophony and contiguity many other meanings could emerge.

Names of things and people, even names of gods, were their destiny. This is why the Mesopotamians believed that fate was written by the gods on the Tablet of Destinies. Divination worked by reading things literally but not as simple iconic pictograms. Rather, any aspect of the entire semantic constellation of metonymns and metaphors could provide an omen or a message from the gods. Nor should the importance of homophony be forgotten in this system. If nouns are not arbitrary epiphenomena, neither are phonetic parallels or similarities. Thus, in dream interpretation we have cases like the one which states that if the dreamer dreams that one gives him lion tallow, he will have no rival. The logic of this conclusion is based on the similarity of ur.mah (lion) with *mahiru* (rival), even if the syllables are reversed. Similarly, if he dreams that someone gives him *mihru* (wood), he will have no rival. Or if he dreams he eats a raven, income will come in because of the homophonic association between raven (*arbu*) and income (*irbu*). Divination, as Bottéro states, was the gods' code, which was the code of cuneiform writing inscribed into the world. Following a model set up by Claude Lévi-Strauss, Bottéro argues, quite convincingly, that divination is a scientific, deductive method. But it can be argued in addition that Mesopotamian divination also reflects a "science of presence and absence" or a metaphysics of sorts in which the material world is never separable from signification the way it is for the modern world. And this, for want of a better term, is a form of philosophy. The Assyro-Babylonian concept of writing as a chain of signification is thus more easily understood in light of poststructuralist developments in the field of signification and Derridian deconstruction than in the traditional methodology of linguistics, established at the start of the nineteenth century. I am not suggesting that we apply poststructuralist linguistic theory to cuneiform. Rather, I suggest that poststructuralism and deconstruction's deliberate breaking away from traditional binary divisions of signifier and signified allows us to reconsider our own analyses of a system of writing in which such binarism is both alien and anachronistic.

The continuous referential chain that I describe as being the most characteristic aspect of Assyro-Babylonian notions of signification illustrates what Derrida terms *différance*. This is one of Derrida's main theoretical motifs, which he describes as being both difference as well as deferment, both senses being present in the French verb *différer*. The distinction between elements in writing enables one to refer to the other *and* be distinguished from it (Derrida 1982:1–29). Thus, if we take cuneiform writing to illustrate this point, the referent is indicated by a cuneiform sign, such as ti (the referent arrow), which differs from another referent. But in order to differ it is constantly deferring other meanings that work through metaphor, metonymy, and so on. Thus, what remains in ti (arrow) as a sign is the differential structure that forms it as that signifier. It is *différance* that produces the differential structure of our hold on "presence," never producing "presence" as such but only that differential structure (Spivak 1974:xliii). These Derridian concepts can be taken further toward an understanding of Mesopotamian ideas of signification. Another aspect of Derrida's grammatology is that he does not just address content or syntax but also shapes of words (Derrida 1974:97ff), and in his later work he develops the concept of words as both having revelation and concealment lodged within. As a basis for this, Derrida uses Sigmund Freud's syntax of dreams in which the pictographic language of the dream utilizes what Freud defines as *condensation* and *displacement* (Freud 1959). These terms were later rhetorically translated by Jacques Lacan as metaphor and metonymy (Lacan 1977:146–78). The dreamer in this way both reveals and conceals things in the language of the dream that are to be interpreted by the psychoanalyst. This notion, described by Derrida and Lacan, that the verbal text is as much concealment as revelation is not unlike the Assyro-Babylonian conception of words referring to things, thus revealing them, but always containing the concealed contiguous and iconic relationships of metaphor, metonymy, or homophony. However, a fundamental difference from the psychoanalytic unconscious language described by Freud is that such displacements in Freud's notion of a re-pressed language imply a displaced truth or reality whereas in Derrida's conception, as in the Assyro-Babylonian belief, such revelation and con-cealment are always present. For Mesopotamians, it seems that no one element can ever express the entirety of a limited and definable referent directly. The "whole" refers to further realities because of the trace of other referents within. Derrida suggests that if the sign is a structure of difference as defined above, what opens up the possibility of thought is not merely the question of being but that ever-present difference. Since the being of the sign is always partially not there, the structure of the sign retains the trace of that other part, which is always absent (Derrida 1974:50). This trace is exactly what the Mesopotamians seem to have been concerned with in their system of writing and ontology.

Mesopotamian pictograms, in the traditional Western approach of Hegel or Ferdinand de Saussure would be considered symbols, as op-posed to the arbitrary signs of the alphabet, which is an "external sys-tem." Writing, which is purely phonetic, is seen in this traditional view as less compromised, as objective, as Derrida puts it: "Saussure confronts the system of the spoken language with the system of phonetic (and even alphabetic) writing as though with the telos of writing. This teleology leads to the interpretation of all eruptions of the nonphonetic within writ-ing as transitory crisis and accident of passage, and it is right to consider this teleology to be a Western ethnocentrism" (Derrida 1974:40). This teleological trajectory to phonetic writing has caused several laments, even in our own scholarship. Both Gelb and Bottéro, among others, feel as though the cuneiform system of writing in Mesopotamia never reached its logical conclusion:

> The [cuneiform] script never did attain the logical conclusion of its evolution, which we have already described as perfect syllabism. It never rid itself of its antique pictograms (which one can better call *ideograms*, as we have seen, from the moment that the stylization of the characters does not permit seeing in them the "drawings" of anything at all) to the benefit of phonograms only. Almost every one of these 400 or so cuneiform signs in common use has one or more double values: ideographic (i.e. it indicates a thing, a word or concept, if you will) and phonetic. Thus the sign of the mountain can designate *the land* (*mâtu* in Akkadian), *the mountain* (*šadû*) and also the idea of conquest, of reaching (*kašadu*); and it can be read phonetically—*kur, mad, lad, šad*—and have other values which are more unusual. (Bottéro 1992:85–86)

The script, according to Bottéro, was always to keep "profound traces of its primitive and imperfect stage" (86). However, one need not see this as an unfortunate limitation to its development. Perhaps instead, it shows the Mesopotamian concern with, and awareness of, the fundamental problematics of signification. In Assyro-Babylonian thought, images and words were never completely separated. The script functioned through a combination of both, but even this concept of *both*, of a *word* without *image*, is alien. Each of these notions, as we think of them, was always already affected by the other, and what we think of as the real was also affected in this way. Ontology, like the script, never "rid itself of its antique pictograms," and this has been seen as the unfortunate limitation to the development of a true science of things in the world separate from illusion. But perhaps it is our own illusion, that we can come face to face with an unmediated real, that limits our apprehension of the world.

The lament regarding cuneiform never abandoning its pictorial aspect and reaching a pure phonetic textual representation is no doubt due to the long tradition in Western philosophy that sees visual images as more motivated, primitive, or childlike as a mode of signification. Words are better because they are conventionally coded representations of the real as language. Such a division is anachronistic to ancient Iraq where the determining logic of the writing system was as much the visual shape of things as the phonetic sound of things as spoken words. Thus, the name creates a being, and by the same logic of the dialectic system the external shape of the being could also affect its destiny in the world in a *real* way. Conventionally, then, according to the developmental theory of linguistics, cuneiform writing (and Egyptian writing) failed because it was never able to free itself from the realm of the symbol in order to become a pure mode of signification, in order to enter the realm of the sign. In the post-Enlightenment science of the world, sign and symbol were repeatedly used to separate civilized from primitive, science from magic.

What I have attempted to demonstrate here is not that ancient Mesopotamians were unaware of writing and pictures as different modes of communication. Rather, they observed that the distinction between the two is always unstable. As media, therefore, they function in a dialectic relationship. If (as I have been arguing here) cuneiform writing can be defined as literally an *image-text*, then the conceptual binary opposition with which we work can become an obstacle, limiting a rich field of investigation that could potentially contribute not only to the further knowledge of Assyro-Babylonian culture but also to issues of verbal and visual representation that are at the center of Western philosophical and critical thinking today. When we speak of language or script as a coded system of signs that are conventionally determined, the conventional reading of a sign is therefore not the only place in which meaning is generated in a culturally specific way. In other words, if we depend on de Saussure's signified/signifier or Charles Sanders Peirce's triangle of object, sign, and interpretant, we cannot limit ourselves to the latter categories of each grouping when considering cross-cultural interpretations of the sign. *Object, signifier* and *sign,* as well as their divisions, must be taken into consideration when attempting to access the representational practices of cultures such as that of ancient Iraq. For Mesopotamians, writing was constituted as a mode of signification, but it was never a transcription purely for vocal exchange; thus, it could not be a phonetic writing. Although the phonetic was an important and integral part of the system, it was never a phoneticism that could be removed from the original concepts represented. Alphabetic script depends on the conceptual breakup of the sign/referent. Cuneiform's failure to achieve this pure phoneticism can be explained as due to a conception of *la langue* in which vocal speech, graphic signs, and forms in the real are all part of an interactive register.

Derrida sets out to deconstruct the concept of mimesis or mimetologism, the possibility of faithful representation of reality. Logocentrism, which he describes as characteristic of Western philosophy since Plato, is the belief in a system of writing that is objective and unmotivated. Others, including the psychoanalyst Jacques Lacan, had pointed out that signifier/signified associations occur in numerous combinations and do not relate to each other as if they are two sides of the same thing. A fixed signified, which relates on a one-to-one basis with a signifier, is replaced in antiplatonic poststructuralist theory by the concept of signification as a never-ending process or a play of signs in which meaning is continually generated. In *Of Grammatology*, Derrida's point is that Western philosophy has imagined a realm unaffected by writing and writing unaffected by the world. Derrida goes back to cuneiform and hieroglyphs and turns to nonphonetic systems of writing in order to develop his own theories. These are systems of writing that cannot be understood by traditional binarisms of the sign, upheld by Western metaphysics. This sort of belief in an unmotivated signification in which the sign has no effect on the *Ding-an-sich* never occurred in Mesopotamia. For the Mesopotamians, writing was an inherent part of creation and was considered in effect an act of creation. Similarly, Derrida (1981a:355) states that "to write means to graft. It is the same word," using an Assyro-Babylonian logic.

5

Ṣalmu: Representation in the Real

The outside is the inside.
—Jacques Derrida (1974:44)

And so art is everywhere, since artifice is at the very
heart of reality.
—Jean Baudrillard (1983:151)

IN *OF GRAMMATOLOGY*, Derrida equated the separation between soul and
body in Western thought to the separation of *physis/tekhne*, real/mimeto-
logic. The conception of the individual person as bipartite is explained
thus as part of the larger ontological binary system of Western metaphysics that distinguishes between a signifier and a stable signified: "It is
not a simple analogy: writing, the letter, the sensible inscription, has always been considered by Western tradition as the body and matter external to the spirit, to breath, to speech, and to the logos. And the problem
of soul and body is no doubt derived from the problem of writing from
which it seems—conversely—to borrow its metaphors" (Derrida 1974:35).
For the Babylonians and Assyrians, the Egyptians, and perhaps other people of the Near East in antiquity as well, the individual was not bipartite
but a multifaceted assemblage of parts.[1] This notion of individuality needs
to be seen in light of Assyro-Babylonian ontological system as revealed in
its view of the processes of signification primarily in writing. Investigating
the ancient conception of such processes further can lead to a better understanding of the ancient function of, and response to, works of art. If
we accept, as I have argued in the previous chapter, that signification for
the Babylonians and Assyrians was not so clearly divided into visual and
verbal as two separate realms but was one greater interdependent symbolic system, then the category of art—the realm of visual signification—
ought to be studied as a facet of this larger symbolic system.

I would therefore like to begin this chapter with a question: what is the status of visual representation in Babylon and Assyria? This is a funda-mental question in art historical research that has yet to be asked in the case of Near Eastern antiquity. The Derridian critique of Western meta-physical presuppositions as inseparable from logocentric thinking has par-ticularly important implications for the study of ancient non-Western cultures since their notions of science and reality were formed apart from the Greek-based ideas of Western metaphysics (Derrida 1974).[2] In study-ing these cultures, our interpretive task is made all the more difficult since we are dealing with a system of thought, a worldview that existed long before ours, yet we have no means of approaching it from outside our own ontological system. Therefore, any analysis of Near Eastern art is hampered at the start not only by the Judeo-Christian and classical tradi-tion of the Assyrian and Babylonian as the generic enemy but also by our current scientific worldview, which is nothing like the pre-Greek, ancient Near Eastern view. The axiomatic notion that representation is a means of imitating real things in the world must be set aside, as much as possible, in dealing with works of art from Near Eastern antiquity, even if this means risking an emphasized alterity with all its consequences. As I have begun to argue in Chapter 3, visual representation functioned according to a system unrelated to mimesis or preceptualism. Therefore, even the term *representation* carries certain meanings that might be considered a natural aspect of image making but have the potential of turning into ob-stacles when applied to a study of Mesopotamian images. However, given the current processes of change in the conceptions of duplication and rep-resentation, under the influence of new technologies, the ancient Near Eastern belief in the power of signifiers and their status as an integral part of the real begins to seem less alien. It is perhaps more akin to the ques-tionings of Platonically based notions of representation that are emerging in our own time.

A second point to be made is that it is not only the concept of repre-sentation that needs to be questioned here. Both categories of the binary division of real/representation are at issue when interpretations of Near Eastern antiquity are made because it is not only representation that had a different status from our own. Even the metaphysical category of the *real* as a separable realm of existence from *illusion* is difficult to maintain in the context of ancient Babylonian ontology. Many things that we might consider to belong to the realm of illusion were seen as part of the real and tangible world in their metaphysical system. In art history we have come to question many of the categories with which we work, such as the separation of objects into art/craft or high art/popular culture, but the separation of artifice/nature is equally problematic and needs to be redefined as a relative and variable division. The Assyro-Babylonian record is a fascinating example of at least one culture in which "artifice is at the very heart of reality."

Ṣalmu

> *Hence we must first bring to view the thingly element of the work. To this end it is necessary that we should know with sufficient clarity what a thing is. Only then can we say whether the artwork is a thing, but a thing to which something else adheres; only then can we decide whether the work is at bottom something else and not a thing at all.*

> —Martin Heidegger, "The Origins of the Work of Art" (1993:146)

Ṣalmu is the Akkadian word used in Assyrian and Babylonian texts to refer to what in our view is a representation. Traditionally, philologists have translated this word variously as statue, relief, monument, painting, and image. More recently, it has been argued that the term *image* is a more accurate translation of *ṣalmu* than one that assumes the word defines a particular type of monument.[3] Irene Winter has further argued against the use of portrait when referring to *ṣalmu* as a representation of a person. In discussing the image of the ruler, she points out that the image is not a natural replica of the king (see figure 7) but a conventionally coded, culturally mediated, idealized representation and is therefore not a portrait in the later Western sense (1989, 1992, 1997). In this discussion I would like to define the function of *ṣalmu* as part of a pluridimensional system of representation. While *ṣalmu* was never meant to be a mimetic visual portrayal of the person, it was at the same time certainly a *natural representation*. If this seems contradictory, it is only because we continue to approach *ṣalmu* from the point of view of the opposition of person/image. *Ṣalmu* is no doubt an image that is culturally mediated and conventionally coded, but it is not in this characteristic that it differs as a mode of representation from its later Western counterpart, the portrait. The latter, it can also be argued, has always been culturally mediated, even in its most seemingly mimetic guise. Richard Brilliant has pointed out, for example, that veristic Roman portraiture and modern photography, two types of portraiture we regard as highly mimetic, both depend on a complex transaction between self-presentation and personal traits as

Figure 7. Statue of Ashurnasirpal II from the Ishtar Temple, Nimrud, 883–859 B.C.
Zainab Bahrani.

well as viewer expectation (1991:56–57). The reason for steering away from
the word portrait when discussing *ṣalmu* should rather be in the implied

separation between sitter and portrait, inherent in its use. The portrait is a copy of the real person (whether one thinks of it as encoded or pure). *Ṣalmu*, on the other hand, has the potential of becoming an entity in its own right, a being rather than a copy of a being (see figure 8).

In the *Sophists*, Plato distinguishes between icons, which are copies of the real, and simulacra, which are phantasms. Copies bear a resemblance to an original. Simulacra are images without this dependance. They are disturbing because they parade as independent beings and not as copies of beings or things. They are contrary to the system in which the image is secondary to the thing represented. For this reason, simulacra have been negatively equated with idolatry in Western aesthetic discourse, especially when religious iconography is at issue.[4] In more recent years the simulacrum has been revived as a philosophical concept primarily as a result of the writings of Gilles Deleuze and Jean Baudrillard and has since become central to critiques of postmodern society. In "The Precession of Images," Jean Baudrillard lists four levels of representation as historically defined in Western thinking, from the pure mimetic reflection to the maleficent simulacrum. He believes that our postmodern world has become a society where hyperreal images or simulacra are what constitute the real (Baudrillard 1983).

At the same time, Gilles Deleuze, in his later work with Felix Guattari, came to argue that our separation of signified and signifier or expression and content is not only arbitrary and conventional, as some earlier theoreticians had recognized, but that the concepts expression and content are actually interchangeable. There is no justification for calling one, and not the other of these, expression or content because their function is essentially the same. In other words, our distinction between expression and content has been learned not only as factual but as essential, being in the essence of things or categories. Instead, it can be argued that both expression and content are extracted from the same "plane of consistency" (Deleuze and Guattari 1987). The current interest of continental philosophy in the questioning and reversal of Platonic philosophical concepts is helpful in rethinking what have become standard interpretations of ancient Near Eastern representational practices, whether visual or verbal. It is clear that ancient Near Eastern boundaries between representation and the real or expression and content are not only unfamiliar to us, but that the very concepts with which we work are alien to that system. Certainly there was, at least at some level, a quality of interchangability between categories that we perceive as logically separate. The simulacrum,

Figure 8. Detail of Ashurnasirpal II statue. Zainab Bahrani.

which in Platonic thinking has such negative connotations as an illusion, a phantasmagoric unbeing, may in fact be far closer to the Akkadian notion of *ṣalmu* representation than the image because it is a sign-representation that takes its place in the realm of the real. That is, rather than being a copy of something in reality, the image itself was seen as a real thing. It was not considered to resemble an original reality that was present elsewhere but to contain that reality in itself. Therefore, instead of being a means of signifying an original real thing, it was seen as ontologically equivalent to it, existing in the same register of reality. The reason that this notion of representation was possible for the Babylonians and Assyrians is that the domain of the real by definition includes a multilayered and complex system of signs that might be described as a metasemiotic real as opposed to metaphysical. What to our modern thinking is illusion, for them was in the realm of empirical knowledge. That is why in divination things are read literally like cuneiform signs embedded into the real. Such thinking, however, is not so different from contemporary semiology:

A garment, an automobile, a dish of cooked food, a gesture, a film, a piece of music, an advertising image, a piece of furniture, a newspaper headline—these indeed appear to be heterogeneous objects. What might they have in common? This at least: all are signs. When I walk through the streets—or through life—and encounter these objects, I apply to all of them, if need be without realizing it, one and the same activity, which is that of a certain *reading*. (Barthes 1988:155)

This statement by Roland Barthes in 1964 would fit neatly into a description of Mesopotamian thinking if it were not for the references to modern objects. For the Mesopotamians, everything encountered could be read as a sign that referred to something beyond its surface appearance. For instance, an enormous amount of omens listed in texts, known by the title *šumma âlu*, records the ominous signs in the most commonplace aspects of the inhabited environment. The ultimate wisdom was to be able to interpret scientifically everything in the world. Thus, *pašir šame u erṣetim,* one who is able to (exegetically) decipher the meaning of the heaven and earth, is an epithet used to describe a god as all knowing. Therefore, visual representations might be encoded, but they are also embedded into the real and have an influence on it as mantic. The relationship between *ṣalmu* and reality is not one that was considered to be unidirectional, as we might describe the functional movement of the mimetic image. According to the concept of mimesis, representation imitates a preexisting reality. It is a process that entails a predetermined hierarchy of real to imitation and depends on the prior assumption of difference between reality and its doubles. Here I will demonstrate why *ṣalmu* does not aspire to mimesis as representation but functions instead according to what might be termed as the structuration of *differánce*, similar to what I have described in the context of the logic of the script. As such, *ṣalmu* is better understood as a form of image that circulates within the real.

The Representational Process

As I have attempted to demonstrate in the previous chapter by means of the writing system, in Babylon and Assyria the relationship of the signified to the signifier is characterized by a constant shifting between the two realms—realms that are integral to the real. If this shifting between the two realms was made possible, at least in part, by the visual shape of things in the case of words (although iconic signifiers were not privileged), then the realm of visual signification must also take into account encountering things in various ways. Therefore, image and name, and the organic body of a person were all ways of encountering that person. A body double (an organic substitute body for the person), a wax or clay effigy, or a statue of durable materials such as stone or bronze can be likened to the iconic or homophonic substitute signifier, which functions by means of resemblance. Likewise, things related to magical substitution (fragments of attire, fingernails, sand taken from one's footprint) as well as offspring or seed are metonymic extensions of the person. Thus, we can see that the process of visual representation or duplication is structurally similar to the system of writing. However, what to the modern viewer may seem like a superficial similarity in mechanisms of representation is perhaps better defined as a structural unity because the textual always contains the pictorial, and the pictorial has a constant effect on the textual in terms of trace, according to the logic of the script. And the reverse is also true. Thus, we need not think of two areas of words and images with functional similarities or parallels. The two areas are structurally the same because they belong to the same system of signification.

   While the post-Greek duality of representation as real/mimetic is parallel to the conception of the individual as consisting of a bipartite entity of soul/body, the Assyro-Babylonian system of representation is better conceived as a pluridimensional chain of possible appearances. The possibility of encountering the same things through different signifiers or substances can thus be kyriologic (working by imitation) or tropic (working by transposition or metaphor):

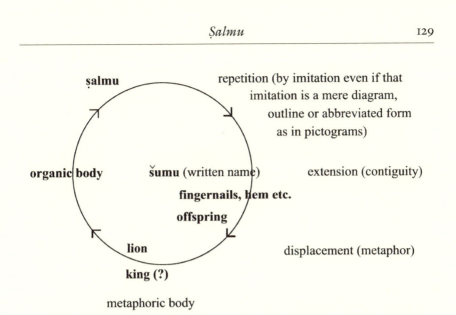

metaphoric body

In Lacanian terms (based on the linguistic theories of Ferdinand de Saussure) the category of extension is a horizontal contiguity that defers. This is a synecdochic process while the category of displacement is a vertical substitution such as metaphor or metonymic displacement. The differentiation made between proper meaning (signs) and transposed meaning (tropes, symbols) in Western language is one that Lacan rejected. All language, every form of signification, is a distortion or transposition. Condensation and displacement, which Freud had defined as the precondition of dream language, are constantly at play in all communication, according to Lacanian psychoanalytic theory (Lacan 1977:146–78). Similarly, in Assyro-Babylonian thought, sign or symbol, proper or symbolic meaning, could not be easily separated. Even the categories outlined here—repetition, extension, and displacement—are difficult to keep neatly in order. *Ṣalmu*, the image, is a repetition that works through resemblance. However, the resemblance did not need to be mimetic, for it was not mimesis that made the image a valid functioning representation of the person. A combination was necessary. Substitution by image required the image, the name, and the utterance of the name, and may have also required further contact with the organic body.

In order to better understand this concept of image, let us reexamine the distinctive practice of human substitution. In a number of Akkadian scholarly texts it is recorded that when the omens predicted a dangerous or unpropitious fate for the king (for example, during an eclipse), a substitute, *šar pūḫi* (Sumerian ki.bi.gar.) was found to take his place. The substitute would then suffer whatever fate had been predestined for the king. This substitute was not a man chosen at random from among the populace, nor was the substitution thought to work on the basis of a physical resemblance to the ruling monarch. A ritual had to be performed through which the human substitute was actually transformed into a valid representation of the king. In this ritual the organic body double is named the king; he is made to wear the clothing of the king. He is further made to listen to the utterance declaring him to be the king, he is made to recite something, and then the words are bound into the hem of his garment (SAS X:12). The organic body double is referred to as *ṣalmu*, but only until the transformation is completed. After the ritual process of substitution, the double is referred to simply as the king.

The process of transformation of double into king seems to have depended on four (or more) requirements: a certain level of resemblance (preferably a man, not an animal), contiguity or contamination (garments), vocal signifier of the utterance of the name, and the inscription (sewn into his garment). The idea that the garment is an extension may seem odd to the modern reader, but in the ancient Near East the fact that this notion was common sensical is easily demonstrated by numerous references to the practice of representing an individual, in juridicial cases, for example, by the fringe of a garment (Finet 1969:101–30; Bottéro 1992:110). Although physical resemblance seems unnecessary, social rank was apparently an issue. There are cases in which a simple person was fictitiously promoted to the rank of royal official solely for the purpose of being a possible candidate as substitute king (Bottéro 1992:147). It is the combination of physical features and performative utterance that are attached to the person or even (at times) ingested by the person that allows the process to work. In one case, in the nineteenth century B.C., it seems that a substitute, Enlil-bani, who was a simple gardener, retained the throne when the king, Erra-imitti, died.

At a smaller scale, a similar practice of substitution is recorded in a ritual for the preparation for battle. In this ritual an enactment of the battle took place before the actual battle as a way of determining its outcome. In the ritual battle tallow figurines were used to portray the enemy ruler and the Assyrian king. However, the king's figurine was a substitute. Instead of using the tallow figurine of the king, a figurine of a leading officer with a name similar to that of the king's name was used to indicate the king because the possibility of a dangerous outcome could not be ruled out as a result of this battle (138). The figurine of the king had to be replaced with the figurine of a substitute, a *ṣalmu*, so that the representation must have seemed both valid as king and farther removed from the king at the same time. At some level the battle itself had a *ṣalmu*-like relationship to the battle enacted through figurines, and this is what enabled a predetermined outcome. Whatever happens to the *ṣalmu* has an effect on the real event at some point in the future.

Ṣalmu is thus clearly part of a configuration that enables presence through reproduction. It is necessary for a valid representation. It is not a statue or a relief or a painting; in other words, it is not a work of art. Nor is it an image that is mediated or otherwise encoded as a direct propagandistic declaration of power. Encoding the body here, if such a word should indeed be used, serves to validate the body double as a substitute for the king for purposes that were considered very real. *Ṣalmu* becomes a real manifestation of the king in this case. Another indication that *ṣalmu* is part of a multifaceted mode of representation is the fact that in texts on monuments—for example, on the Great Monolith of Ashurnasirpal—the monument is referred to as *ṣalmu* in the inscription though it is an object composed of both an image and a text. It is certainly not a portrait as the *Random House Dictionary* defines it: "a likeness of a person, especially of the face, as a painting, sculpture or photograph." Yet it relates to an identity in much closer ways than a portrait.

In his essay "Meditations on a Hobby Horse, or the Roots of Artistic Form," Ernst Gombrich, quoting the *Oxford English Dictionary*, distinguishes between an image and a representation: "an image imitates the external form of an object. To represent, on the other hand, is to 'call up by description or portrayal, or imagination, figure, place likeness of before mind or senses, serve or be meant as likeness of . . . stand for, be specimen of, fill place of, be substitute for' " (1963:1). The focus of Gombrich's essay is the notion of substitution. The hobby horse is a substitute for a real horse and becomes so, according to Gombrich, through function rather than resemblance. The shared quality of ridability, Gombrich argues, is what makes the hobby horse a valid substitute horse for the child. Therefore, as he explains it, substitution does not require resemblance. It is a representation rather than an image because an image, in the dictionary definition, imitates the external form of an object, and it is this resemblance of external form that makes it recognizable as the image of a particular thing. If we consider these classifications, *ṣalmu* therefore, seems to be closer to the category of representation rather than image, yet to confine it into either of these Gombrichian categories (equivalent to his perceptual and conceptual art) can be equally misleading. The *ṣalmu* can be a valid substitute only after a process of transformation that appears to have required contiguity, resemblance, and a performative utterance. *Ṣalmu* as image is itself not a substitute. It only becomes a substitute after the ritual transformation. Unlike Gombrich's hobby horse, it is not through function that the representation can become a substitute, yet like the hobby horse, it does not denote something but is the thing itself.

While he describes the hobby horse as an independent thing, at the same time Gombrich seems to feel that it does stand in for the essence of a real horse to which it refers or represents conceptually. By contrast, the *ṣalmu* has both iconic and indexical relations with (what we might consider) the referent, but the whole essence of being is not the referent of, say, organic body of the king, but an entire semantic web, unfolding horizontally and vertically, including name, seed, body, shadow, and so on, and all their metaphorical and metonymical associations. *Ṣalmu* does not represent an imaginary thing, nor a real thing that is complete and autonomous because in the Assyro-Babylonian view the world is not stable and actual but virtual because it is always in the process of becoming. By using the term *virtual*, I mean to refer to it in Deleuze's sense of the virtual as what is immanent. In his view, as in much poststructuralist or postmodern thought, existence is not a static presence. All existence has the potential for generating the same kind of reproducibility found in the fractal of non-Euclidean geometry. Deleuze uses the analogy of the fractal because it has the potential of endless fissuring and reproduction, and can only be stopped arbitrarily at a particular point, yet it can be assigned a precise mathematical value. Therefore, this is described by Deleuze as "a momentary suspension of becoming," and the traditional philosophical notion of the Thing-in-itself can only be a sum total of the graspings to which it lends itself—its set of potentialities.[5]

According to Deleuze, the double is simulacral, "it is not a reproduction of the same but a repetition of the different" (1988:98). Therefore, simulacra do not represent. They repeat, like the fractal, creating an indiscernibility of the original real and unreal reproduction. Similarly, for the Assyrians and Babylonians, the real is made up of endless signs. Real matter already has images in it so that representations proliferate throughout the universe in a virtual (in other words, immanent) state. At the same time, images or representations are a part of this metasemiotic reality. The semantic web of possible appearances through metaphor or metonymy that makes up this metasemiotic real might be viewed as a conception similar to Deleuze's notion of the virtual. Therefore, *ṣalmu* is better thought of as an ontological category rather than aesthetic concept. To return to the definition of the substitute representation (such as the hobby horse), let us recall that for Gombrich the substitute is a classification for an image that can become a valid representation through similarity in function rather than external resemblance. Substitute images, on the other hand, function on the basis of the belief in the possibility of appearance or presence through the semantic constellation that makes up an identity. Thus, we can say that the link between portrayal and identity was closely related to the workings of the cuneiform script in which each sign could lead in turn, through its phonetic and pictographic values, to an entire constellation of signs that were thought to be linked in an endless process of signification. Image making and portrayal through substitute images were therefore quite literally dependent upon *writing presence*. This presence did not become valid simply by adding an inscription to a statue, as a legend or descriptive text. It functioned on the basis of the belief in the immanent nature of the real.

At the end of his essay Gombrich concludes that the hobby horse is not art. By this he seems to restate his first definition of the difference between perceptual image and representation: unlike the image, the hobby horse does not represent a real horse outside itself. Art, in the Gombrichian definition, imitates reality. The substitute hobby horse is therefore the opposite of art just as Gombrich's definition of conceptual art (discussed in Chapter 3) can exist only in relation to the category of perceptual. *Ṣalmu* is indeed a substitute through representation. It is, like the hobby horse, a thing in its own right, a creation rather than an imitation. But to think of *ṣalmu* in terms of the opposite of perceptual imitation would be to reduce its meaning to this oppositional place and to miss the richness and complexity of its functions.

Representation and the Real

Representation, or a making present, required both word and image (and perhaps other signifiers as well) in order to be a valid presence, but what is the relationship between the word-image representational entity and what in Western philosophy is the Kantian *Ding-an-sich* of the real? Is the latter a priori and the former a secondary manifestation? Here too it seems that, for the Assyrians and Babylonians, the relationship was dialectical in some sense, at least in some cases, because it is clear that each was seen to affect the other. Therefore, a duality of person and portrait, which is our common sensical notion, does not allow for the complexity of the Assyro-Babylonian view:

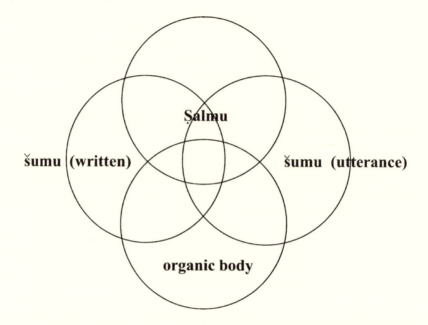

Ṣalmu, according to the diagram I propose, is a mere facet of presence. There is no word for the whole because the whole is only accessible as a concept that can be expressed precisely only in a multiplicity. After the addition of the name, and the utterance, it should be recalled, the word *ṣalmu* is no longer used to refer to the substitute thing, neither to the organic body double nor to the stone monument. The valid representation is *essentially* the same as the person just as *šumu* (name) is essentially an extension and taxonomically the same as offspring. *Ṣalmu* is not simply image as in statue since its material can also be flesh and blood, shadow, or reflection. In substance, therefore, *ṣalmu* and person can be the same while son and name are substantially different but essentially the same, being referred to by the same word. Thus, it would seem that while things and words, people and images are categories that are *essential* as far as we are concerned today, they were by no means categories in Near Eastern antiquity. The world of appearance and the world of essence are the same.

Royal texts often contain a similar phrase when making reference to the setting up of a royal image. The following is an example: "*šiṭir šumiya u ṣalam šarrutiya mahar Šamaš u Aja ukin.*"

This is generally translated as "I set up, before *Šamaš* and Aja, an inscription with my name and an image of me as king." The royal texts are written in the first person in the voice of the king as narrator, and phrases similar to this are always translated as "I fashioned a statue (or stela) showing me as king or "I set up (before the gods) a statue of me as king" (*CAD* vol. S:81). It has already been pointed out that the translation of the word *ṣalmu* as statue, sculpture, relief is incorrect because it means image and should not be used to refer to particular art forms or media. But its mistranslations have been rather heavily influenced by modern notions of art. Thus, the statement "I set up a statue of me as . . ." implies that *ṣalmu* as an image portrays a particular being with a separable identity as a king. Whereas the Akkadian text states that he set up "*šiṭir šumiya u ṣalam šarrutiya,*" which I believe is better translated as "the written [characters] of my name and [visual] image of my kingship," thereby implying an extension that is natural and organic.

Ṣalam šarrutiya, as I translate it, "image or physical manifestation of my kingship," is an analogous reading to the common phrase *ṣalam pagrišu*: "the shape of his body." The contiguous link formed by the use of the possessive construction is important here, as it has quite different connotations from the standard reading of "me as king," which works through displacement rather than extension. There is a reason for my insistence on clarifying and stressing the choice of a particular grammatical construction here. Such a use of the possessive construction is of the utmost importance in magical incantations. Similar modern translations have been made in this genre of texts that I find to be equally misleading, and conversely their clarification can shed some light on the processes of representations that I wish to define. Take, for example, the following incantation:

šiptum šipat Marduk
ašipu ṣalam Marduk

In my reading this translates into:

The conjuration (is) Marduk's conjuration.
The conjurer (is) Marduk's presence/manifestation/substitute.

This reading has different connotations from the standard translation:

> The conjuration recited is the conjuration of Marduk.
> The conjurer is the very image of Marduk.

The Akkadian original is deliberately a repetitive performative utterance that transubstantiates the conjuration into one that Marduk himself is making in his manifestation as organic *salmu* (body double). For the Assyrians and Babylonians, tautology is certainly part of the performative function of speech acts. *Šiṭir šumiya u ṣalam šarrutiya* has a similar repetitive quality in its reference to those signifiers, written name and imaged kingship, which link them directly to the person, as if kingship were as natural a manifestation of the person as his name. And there is little doubt that kingship was a natural manifestation.[6]

In Assyro-Babylonian ontology, omens are written into the real. Omens could be solicited from the livers of sacrificial animals by priests, for example, but they were also inscribed by the gods into the common, everyday world. An observant person could read these messages at any time or place. Catalogs of omens were made, listing vast amounts of possibilities of patterns of flights of birds, of birth deformities, of chance occurrences in cities, and also aspects of the physiognomy of human beings. By the seventh century B.C. at least one hundred tablets, listing ten thousand omens had been cataloged.[7] Thus, hair-growth patterns, moles, and other such physical characteristics were not considered to be accidental but were linked to the fate of the individual. Semantic codes in physiognomy are *in the real*. They are not in any way metaphoric or allegorical references. The difference between material reality and semiosis, which is based on scientific reason in the modern view, was an intertwined area in Assyro-Babylonian thought. This is not even to be explained as a blurring of the real and the imaginary. The real contains what we might call the imaginary within it. A physical body is inscribed as a text with signs from the gods. All bodies are therefore encoded by the gods, not simply the royal body. But the king's body bears the omens of kingship. The king's image could thus be encoded not just in a metaphoric or allegorical way, recalling literary descriptions of the ideal ruler. The physical signs could be read as the divine destiny of kingship, literally written into the body-text. Destiny was inscribed into the real. I do not use that expression in the postmodern rhetorical sense of inscription but as a literal translation of the Akkadian word *šaṭaru*, to inscribe, a verb used in describing omens as they appear in the natural world.[8] Thus, it is more than a matter of ideal body when the king's body is represented. It is a matter of divine destiny.

Ṣalmu is not an objective representation of reality. It is not a represented truth about the person, nor is it a representational lie about the person, as in propaganda. *Ṣalmu*, as mimetic representation, may relate to the object as an excess in that it can act as a repetition, a replacement. But it is not an element that represents the whole. It cannot give access to a referent or signified, the *Ding-an-sich*—at least not uniquely—because the referent can be encountered in many phainomena. *Ṣalmu* is therefore a mode of presencing. The thing or person is accessed through the structuration of *differánce*, which I have described in relation to the logic of the cuneiform script. It is one of several modes and part of a system of circulating presence. In the cuneiform sign the trace or *archi-écriture* is never totally effaced—the difference and deferment always remains present, making any one stable meaning impossible. Not only in the case of the pictogram but in all words, there was a great concern with the constant trace in any manifestation. Substitution through images—which is not only *ṣalmu* but requires *ṣalmu*—is a doubling or a multiplication (as a phainomenon), but it is not a copy in the sense of mimetic resemblance; rather, it is a repetition, another way that the person or entity could be encountered. Yet, like the pictogram, it can never give entire access to the signified or the essential *Ding-an-sich*, or whatever name we choose for this, because a Thing-referent (this term actually indicates only the transcendental object or *gedanken Ding* in Kantian terminology because as a referent it can only be what is behind the signifier but never more) can be encountered through so many signifiers that *the* signifier can never be unique just as the pictogram is never simply iconic and separated from other meaning—synecdochic or metonymic, homophonic, and so on. The other meanings are not supplementary but *essential*. What we see in visual representation, then, is similar to the structure of the script. Each element cannot express a whole. The Thing may be denoted by a pictogram or by syllabic combinations, all of which defer meanings in their differing meanings. Substitution requires both repetition and extension in order to work. The combination results in the valid representation, the portrait, but it is a portrait that is not an icon nor even an index if we use the terminology of Charles Sanders Peirce. It is a simulacrum because it substitutes for the real itself or rather, is part of the real just as omens are not chance occurrences and dreams are not an illusion. The *ṣalmu* of the king is neither model nor copy, nor simply an extension. It is a manifestation of presence that defers the king in differing from him. Therefore, in using the word *image* as a translation for *ṣalmu*, we would do well to remember the Latin imago, which for Romans was not equivalent to the Greek *ikon* but was the stamp of the emperor and directly linked to his physical body.

However, another question remains regarding the image of the king. Is this image an extension or a figuration of a king as a separate entity from a man? That distinction seems to have been made at other places and times in history. The case of the Roman emperor's two bodies—one divine, the other human—presents an example of such a duality. Another is the example of Louis XIV of France (see figure 9), discussed at great length by Louis Marin in his brilliant book *Portrait of the King* (Marin 1981). The latter study is important for my purposes because it has provided a theoretical model for the interpretation of the image of the Assyrian king in recent years. It is a model that can be quite beneficial for understanding the king's image in Assyria or Babylonia, but taken wholesale, in its entirety, it can also create further obstacles in our thinking about the status of the image in Near Eastern antiquity. As is the case with the Roman emperor, there may be similarities, but French baroque portraiture of the king has particularities that are not all applicable to Near Eastern representational practices nor to Assyrian conceptions of kingship. In the following section I will attempt to disentangle some of these aspects of the royal image.

Ṣalam šarrutiya: Image of My Kingship

Louis Marin proposes that we think of *figure* as a process of the image's construction. For Marin, this process is the process of the *figurability* of power. The portrait of the king is the allegory of power, and the king as such is only a king in his image. Beside the image, the king is merely a man. Power is centered in the body of the king as figure. Marin further stresses that representation is not affected by power. Power is only *in* and *through* representation. Therefore, representation does not represent power. It creates power because it is an integral part of the social processes of hierarchy and differentiation. (Here representation refers to any representation and not just to painting.) In the premodern societies of Europe that Foucault designated as "societies of sovereignty," power

Figure 9. Portrait of Louis XIV by Hyacinthe Rigaud, 1701. Giraudon/Art Resource, New York.

became concentrated in the body of the king. Marin describes this as a phenomenology of the monarch because the absolute body of power is incarnated in a singular body. He sees the relationship between power and representation as a chiasmatic relation: power appropriates representation, and the framework of representation produces power. As much as Marin speaks of power or representation as abstract phenomenological concepts, he takes the methods in which they function as being determined within the ontological framework of Europe in the premodern (classical) period. In short, following Foucault, he concludes that these methods are determined by (and determine) the classical episteme. Marin stresses the relationship between royal power and the concept of the one god, for example. The oneness is important here, as it is repeated in the state slogan of seventeenth-century France, "One God, One Law, One Faith," and in other utterances related to political power.[9] Thus, there is a similar unity implied in Louis's famous phrase made in Parliament in April 1655, "*L'état c'est moi.*" Marin proposes that in classical absolutism the king had only one body (unlike the Roman emperor, for example, who often had two: organic body and imago), but this sole body unified three: a physical historical body, a juridico political body, and a sacramental body (the last being the semiotic body in the portrait, which is not just his painted image but his representation as exhibit). Therefore, the king as king is a simulacrum, and it is the play of discourse that makes people believe the reality of this simulacrum. Beyond the image of the king there is no king. There is merely a man.

In Assyria, as elsewhere, the image of the king is also a political symbolic fiction (see figure 10). However, rather than assuming that the fiction of the monarch is constructed according to a universal process, we must ask in this case, what is the specific ontotheological domain in which this symbolic fiction was taken as the real, and how does a specific Assyro-Babylonian discourse or episteme determine or reflect this process of representation or figurabilty. Figurabilty, or "the processes of the images's construction" in Marin's view, "become explicit through pedagogical or ethical discourse." We can deconstruct an image "by exhibiting the psychological and sociological mechanisms—imagination and customs—that create values and essences" (Marin 1989:423). For Marin, these mechanisms are specific to time and place. The first and most obvious difference from the case of European kingship is the conception of the *corpus mysticum*. If the political theology of the transubstantiation of the body of Christ into body of king can be understood within the greater context of early Christian mysticism, then it is a process that must be set aside in

Figure 10. Head of Ashurbanipal, from lion hunt reliefs, Nineveh, ca. 645 B.C. Zainab Bahrani.

thinking about the Assyrian or Babylonian king. Similarly, post-Platonic metaphysics of the earth mirroring the heavens or the king mirroring god are as equally misleading as the idea that representation is a copy of the real. If absolute states with absolute rule existed in both times and places, there are still sufficient differences to call for a questioning of a trans-historical absolutism. One cannot say, for the Assyrian king, despite all his terror, power, and dominance, that Assyria, as absolute state power, is in-carnated in the body of the king as it was in the body of Louis. It is not that the Assyrian king was any less an authoritarian ruler but only that in Assyria there was not that underpinning theological idea of oneness that unified god into king and king into state.

Perhaps in the case of the Assyrian king we might do well to turn to the Assyro-Babylonian ontotheology of divination, a system that was con-sidered to encompass heaven and earth. We know that for the Assyrians and Babylonians signs were literally written into the real, decipherable to those who had the ability to read them. The king's body (as image) was thus likely to be inscribed with the physiognomantic omens of kingship. Therefore, his kingship is certainly divine destiny, but he is not the one god. His body is the mantic body of the king, inscribed by the gods in or-der to determine his fate, his destiny to be ruler. His body is not the place of a transubstantiation of god into king. The Assyrian god is not in the king as the Christian god is in Louis XIV. The king's body is a text of di-vine destiny, not an embodiment of the godly. The Assyrian king may have divine qualities, but he is not the embodiment of Aššur or Šamaš on earth, nor does he mirror a god on earth. The description of the Assyrian king as an embodiment of god and his kingdom as a mirror of the heav-enly kingdom is based on models of kingship borrowed from later periods and is not supported by the ancient texts. Such an interpretation of a mimetologic bipartite mirroring is clearly influenced by post-Platonic metaphysics. Again, the main argument for this interpretation has been the literary construction *šarrum ṣalam šamaš*, "the king is the very image of Šamaš," which appears in ritual texts. However, the Akkadian original makes use of the same possessive construction that I have attempted to clarify above: *šarrum ṣalam Marduk*, which is used in the context of ritu-als: "the king is the manifestation/substitute of Marduk." This construc-tion is necessary as a performative utterance because it allows the person involved in the ritual to have the power necessary for the utterance to suc-ceed. If the king was the embodiment of god on earth as some have ar-gued, then we must deal with the fact that according to ancient texts, so too were numerous other people during religious and magical rituals. The king speaks with the words of the god during a ritual in exactly the same way as any other conjurer so we cannot describe this as a unique privilege of kingship or the king as the singular embodiment of god on earth. A statement such as *šarrum ṣalam Marduk* does not declare the king an embodiment of god on earth. It simply uses the king as a momentary substitute, as an organic body double, for the god and others are known to have fulfilled this function also. To translate *šarrum ṣalam Šamaš* as "the king is the very image" or "the very likeness of Šamaš" is to read into it modern notions of portraiture as a mimetic copy of the original.

For the image of Louis XIV, it is the singularity or uniqueness of the king, related to a theology of oneness, that is of great importance in its function as a royal portrait. Thus, Louis declares, "the state is me," which Marin identifies as a metaphorical utterance. In the case of the Assyrian king the relationship of personality to kingship is metonymic. It is an aspect of the multiplicity of representational elements: name, king, organic body, and so on. All of these work together to make the king present. A performative utterance seems to have transubstantiated name and image into the portrait, but the portrait was never a mimetic copy nor even a propagandistically encoded kingly image. The portrait was a simulacrum that was returned to the real. We must remember that a miracle as a separate event did not exist. The miracle is a Christian magical concept that was important for Louis's court and for his assimilation to god but not for the Assyrian king. Instead, the real and the divine were intertwined in Assyro-Babylonian thought. Miracles are written into the real as mantic, or as *egirru* (omens of everyday occurrences). The king's body is therefore not a sacramental body but an oneiric or a mantic body. If the Assyrian king is constituted in his image as the "image of his kingship," this representation is not an announcement of the divine miracle of god transformed into king but of destiny in the sense of mantic signs embedded into the real.

If we think of the king's representation in Assyro-Babylonian thought as exempla or manifestations of the king, then his infinite power is established through the circulation of the multiplicity of names, images, monuments, and histories. Each of his parts work together toward an incessant presence. However, this is not a virtual real image or presence. It connects to him through synecdochic extension just as his name, son, or seed does. Yet his image as king or rather the image of his kingship is not all and can function only in combination with this name. The combination creates the simulacrum, which is not the *virtual* real but the *veritable* real for the Assyrians and Babylonians. It is not an imitation of the king.

It is a presence of the king and therefore far more powerful. The king's image, as in other times and places in history, is linked to power, but this power is not simply force or propaganda. It is an infinite potency and immortality. The practice of adding texts to monuments, asking that if some future king should restore them, that he should be careful not to erase the name of the original patron is an example of this belief. The king is therefore not the model of the image, even if he is its source because it is a mode of presence. The image is his substance and a real presence just as in the script a thing can be represented by pictogram, syllabic combination, or homophony. The image repeats, rather than represents, the king.

Marin tells us that whereas in the portraits of Alexander the Great, Alexander is the referent of the portrait, "Louis is already before all processes of portrayal a "portrait' " (1981:210). The reverse can be said in the case of the Assyrian king because in his case the portrait is the simulation of the king after all processes of portrayal. It is the representational act that transforms the image into a valid substitute or repetition of the king. For Louis, his identity as portrait is a result of his being already the image of god. He is in this sense already an image, once removed from god, and can thus be thought of as a portrait-being, his entire identity as king itself a portrait. Portraits of Louis are therefore twice removed from the referent. In Marin's words, the portrait of Louis is part of a mimetic series leading back to god, as if in a set of mirrors. The Assyrian king's image, on the other hand, is his offshoot. It is not his mirror image, nor is it a replica of god. It is rather more like the king's nails, hair, the fringe of his garment, or his footprint, directly and physically linked to him in reality. Furthermore, the Assyrian king may have divine qualities, may even be metaphorically likened to a god, but he cannot be syncretically subsumed into a particular god such as Aššur or Šamaš. The success of a king's portrait is also not a question of its level of resemblance to a particular person, for instance, to Ashurnasirpal in flesh and blood. Its success as a portrait of the king is in the recognition of Ashurnasirpal as king in the destiny of his form, in the image of his kingship. In premodern Europe, if the king is deprived of his portrait, he is only a man, for he is king only in his image. In Assyria no one real presence can be sought beyond the representation. There are only different facets of presentation: name, image, seed, organic body. In both societies the king is a concept that exists in an image, but the processes of representation, the differentiations between image and source, are distinctive of each society. According to Marin, the constitution of the portrait as king and the king as portrait is a political fiction based on resemblance. For the West, then, the physical organic individual body and its relation to a portrait functions through a mistake. The sign is taken for the referent, the thing for the being. Louis is mistaken for the king or for the king-sign. It is a matter of Louis's usurpation of the king-sign. Marin goes on to describe the king's portrait as an empty signifier, "a tomb that shelters no body, but that is royal body in its very vacuity" (1981:238). In the framework of Assyro-Babylonian ontology, kingship is not the usurpation of a sign because that usurpation implies a binary division of essence and sign. There is not even an attempted erasure of the representational mechanisms or processes of signification that we would consider necessary for ideological image making. Instead, the very processes are elaborated into a ritual so that the image is no longer a representation but a being in its own right. The system functions through the ontological notion of the word-image-being entity. If this system served the ideology of kingship, so much the better, but it is not a simple propagandistic assertion of absolute power as a way of manipulating public opinion by means of a mediated image. It is a far more subtle and complex expression of power and its predestined place inscribed into the city-state.[10]

Presence and Similitude

In "The Precession of Simulacra," Jean Baudrillard states that simulation is opposite to representation in that "the latter starts from the principle that the sign and the real are equivalent (even if this equivalence is utopian, it is a fundamental axiom). Conversely, simulation starts from the *utopia* of this principle of equivalence"; it "envelops the whole edifice of representation as itself a simulacrum." He identifies the four phases of the image in the following way:

1. It is a reflection of a basic reality.
2. It masks and perverts a basic reality.
3. It masks the absence of a basic reality.
4. It bears no relation to any reality. (1983:11–12)

In the first phase the image is seen as good and truthful. In the second phase it is a distortion and is therefore evil. In the third stage it is of the order of sorcery, and in the fourth it is no longer an image but a simulation. In terms of the present discussion, then, Baudrillard's first stage would include the type of image that is described by some as a pure, unmediated portrait. The second phase is the realm of the propagandistic image. The third and fourth phases are the phases of magic and idolatry. In Babylon and Assyria the king's image functioned as his valid representation, masking his absence in this sense. While the Western notion of portrait, or the mimetic image based on resemblance, affirms the category real, the simulacrum and the Assyro-Babylonian representation blur the division of real and representation.

The distinction drawn by Foucault between resemblance and similitude is perhaps even more useful for understanding why *ṣalmu* is different form Western image. Resemblance, Foucault writes, "presumes a primary reference that prescribes and classes." It has an original element that orders. Similitude "develops in a series that has neither beginning nor end, that can be followed in one direction as easily as in another. . . . Similitude circulates the simulacrum as an indefinite and reversible relation of the similar to the similar" (1982:44). In sum, similitude, as Foucault puts it, serves repetition while resemblance serves representation. In Western metaphysics, as Baudrillard writes, "the very definition of the real becomes: *that of which it is possible to give an equivalent reproduction.* This is contemporaneous with a science that postulates that a process can be perfectly reproduced in a set of given conditions, and also with the industrial rationality that postulates a universal system of equivalency (classical representation is not equivalence, it is transcription, interpretation, commentary)" (1983:146). Baudrillard argues that at the limit of this process the real is not only what can be reproduced but that which is always already reproduced. This exchange between signification and the real constituted the limit of the real for the Babylonians and Assyrians. They seem to have been almost acutely aware of the play of signs within the real. This awareness is reflected in their extensive study of the production of signs by the real, in the science of deductive divination, and in the thousands of omens that were collected and cataloged in antiquity.

The dialectical relationship between signifiers and signifieds in Assyro-Babylonian antiquity can be read along the structure of a chiasmus, but not in the same way or along the same lines as Marin argued for baroque France. In Assyria, if the king is in his image, so too is the image in the king. We know that chiasmatic sentence structures are often used in conjurations and in omen reading as well as in dream interpretation. This is a rhetorical structure that creates a sense of unity between what appear to be opposing elements in a statement. The dual elements are then rhetorically presented as interdependent. Therefore, while today we might find it simple enough that the Assyrian king is the source of his image, we are less likely to realize that this indexical relation also works in reverse. Indeed, the reverse is an integral part of the very process of representation, which creates the valid substitute image. If the image is the index of the king, the king too is the index of the image, each having direct effects on the other. But this integral duality should not be mistaken for a mimetic relationship. Mimesis refers to a mirroring of a real essence, whether it be the person and the image or the heavens and the earth. In Assyro-Babylonian theology, things written in the heavens as astral formations could refer to people and events on earth. For example, Esarhaddon declares that he carved in stone the astral images corresponding to his name, but such correspondences were by no means limited to analogies between heavenly and earthly signs. Any correspondence based on analogy, homophony, metaphor, or metonymy was considered a valid link. Similitude for the Mesopotamians, as Jean Jacques Glassner puts it, "is an essential principle according to which the similar has an effect on the similar" (1995:1818). But again it must be stressed that this network of similitude was by no means mimetologic. Correspondences in the visual realm were as complex and pluridimensional as were the numerous possible readings of the cuneiform signs.

According to the Assyro-Babylonian view, language does not simply state facts, nor is it produced by the real. It is language or signification in its broadest sense, including the pictorial, which creates the real. Since the fundamental nature of cuneiform writing is the fact that it made use of signs from two languages, Sumerian and Akkadian, every sign essentially had at the very minimum two possible readings. A correspondence of one sign to one referent is therefore completely alien to this system. More commonly, the myriad of possible readings, the semantic constellation surrounding each sign, was at the center of all intellectual thought in Babylon and Assyria. In the previous chapter I have explained how cuneiform writing can be defined as an image-text. The Babylonians and Assyrians observed that the distinction between writing and pictures as modes of signification is always unstable. I argue that when we speak of language or script as a coded system of signs that are conventionally determined, it should not merely be on the level of the sign that we become aware of difficulties in cross-cultural interpretation, for it is not merely in the sign that meaning is generated in culturally specific ways. Object, sign, signifier, and signified are all concepts that need to be rethought in attempting to access Assyro-Babylonian practices of signification, and such a rethinking is just as necessary in studying the processes of visual representation as it is in understanding the system of writing. Nature and artifice were completely merged into one universal, interactive order. The real was in itself an edifice of representation.

6

Decoys and Lures:
Substitution and the Uncanny
Double of the King

In our relation to things, in so far as this relation is
constituted by way of vision, and ordered in the figures
of representation, something slips, passes, is transmitted,
from stage to stage, and is always to some degree,
eluded in it, that is what we call the gaze.
—Jacques Lacan (1986:73)

The Other is an expression of a possible world in a
perceptual field.
—Gilles Deleuze (Deleuze and Guattari 1994:18)

IN HIS STUDY of colonialist novels of the nineteenth and early twentieth
century, Abdul Rahman JanMohamed has shown how it is a genre that
does not so much depict a world at the outer limits of civilization as cod-
ify and preserve the structures of its own mentality: "Such literature is essentially specular: instead of seeing the native—it uses him as a mirror that
reflects the colonialist self image" (JanMohamed 1985:59.) On the surface,
this literature is seemingly a description of particular places and peoples,
but it also contains an integral subtext that is the valorization of Europe. Through the rhetorical strategies of metonymic displacement and
fetishization a metaphysical alterity of the colonial subject is established:
"Socially or ideologically determined aspects of culture are described as
characteristics inherent in the race or the blood of the people, and at
times all specificity is transmuted into a magical essence" (1985:60). Jan-
Mohamed presents Isak Dinesen's novel *Out of Africa* as an example of
such writing in which, he points out, the native in the flesh, the mountains,

and the trees of Africa is described as being one. Africa, in this way, is collapsed into a single essence.

Essentialist metonymy and synecdoche are likewise two of the main representational forms of art historical commentaries on non-Western art. Art historians writing from a colonized India, for example, repeatedly referred to "the decadence" in Indian art and the profusion of its ornament as reflecting the nature of the inhabitants of the subcontinent. Similarly, the past and present of these alien areas of the world could be collapsed into one reflection of the same metaphysical or magical substratum. As Homi Bhabha points out, the space of the other is always occupied by an *idée fixe* in colonial discourse: "It is a form of knowledge and identification that vacillates between what is always in place, already known, and something that must be anxiously repeated" (Bhabha 1994:66). Through art historical writing, representational practices became yet another place where the relation to the other could be constituted. In Chapter 1 I have charted rather broadly the relationship between colonial discourse and the development of an institutionalized art historical narrative. Here I would like to investigate more specifically how alterity is located within this dimension of academic knowledge. As a case in point I will examine the practice of mutilating images of kings in the Near East. In this chapter I will analyze this practice and the current discussions of it in scholarly literature. Not only have stereotypes been utilized in the interpretation of this practice, but a privileging of one type of ancient text over all others has also aided in its perception as a senseless act of violence and thus serves the purposes of the Orientalist model by validating two of its main abstractions: Oriental violence and Oriental despotism (Said 1978:4).

The presupposition underlying the interpretations made in this chapter is that while certain aspects of perception may be universal constants in the psychic apparatus and are part of the human cognitive system, aesthetics and attitudes toward images are culturally constructed and can be understood only through contemporary textual evidence that relates specific acts, attitudes, and rituals involving images. The mutilation of royal images is, of course, not unique to the ancient Near East. It is a concept that crosses cultural and chronological boundaries. But the Near Eastern attitude toward the ruler's image must be understood in the context of ancient Near Eastern culture and not through any cross-cultural comparative models, as there are too many differences despite the similarity to the practices known from Egypt, Byzantium, and numerous other places and times (Freedberg 1989).

Here I will investigate the assault and abduction of statues in the context of Near Eastern culture and ontology, using primarily Assyro-Babylonian textual evidence. Therefore, when I make reference to psychoanalytic discussions of fetishism or the uncanny, I have utilized only what seems relevant to ancient Near Eastern culture and ontology. In using the term *fetish* I do not intend it to be equated with the concept of the fetish as a defamiliarized or camouflaged substitute for something repressed or any worshiped inanimate object. The term is meant to indicate figurines used in magic rituals, but these figurines were never defamiliarized, displaced signifiers of the person in question. They were more iconic in that they referred directly to the signified. They were seen simply as valid "re-presentations" of the persons portrayed.

In what follows I will discuss works of art from two Near Eastern cities where the deliberate attack on monuments took place. The first group of objects comes from Nineveh, in northern Iraq, and is now in the British Museum, London. The second group is from Susa, in southwestern Iran, and is now in the Louvre Museum, Paris. All the objects discussed have been studied firsthand for evidence of deliberate damage made by sharp tools or weapons, and this damage has been compared to normal erosion of surfaces on the same monuments. This is intended to be a complete catalog of mutilated objects neither from the Near East nor from these particular sites. The Near Eastern monuments that appear to have been deliberately damaged are many, and their enumeration is beyond the scope of this study. The objects discussed here are presented only as a manifestation of the practice of assaulting images, as I am more interested in understanding the thought processes behind such attacks than in listing every extant example.

Nineveh

Nineveh was the Assyrian capital sacked by Medes and Babylonians in 612 B.C. in the battle that ended the mighty Assyrian empire. Both the Medes from Iran and the Babylonians from southern Iraq had been under the yoke of this empire and had unsuccessfully revolted against Assyrian rule in the past. When Assyria was finally defeated, they took their revenge. Reliefs from two palaces in Nineveh were mutilated. Sennacherib (ruled 704–681 B.C.), who had chosen this city as his capital, built the Southwest Palace here, the Palace without a Rival. Its walls were decorated with carved stone reliefs representing his valor and glory. Among the scenes depicted was the siege and destruction of Lachish. On one relief panel showing the enthroned Sennacherib receiving the booty from this defeated city (see figure 11), the face of the king has been gouged out deliberately with a sharp tool. An epigraph above his head was similarly attacked, and the name and title of the king were removed. A close examination makes it clear that the only deliberately damaged face among the many represented was that of Sennacherib.

Sennacherib's grandson, Ashurbanipal (ruled 669–627 B.C.), added to the decoration of the Palace without Rival a series of carved reliefs that depict his army's defeat of the Elamites at the battle of Til-Tuba in 653 B.C. One such relief depicts the introduction of a new ruler to the defeated Elamites by an Assyrian officer. Here the face of the Elamite king, a puppet of the Assyrians, was attacked (see figure 12). Again, a comparison with the remainder of the relief's surface and the representations of other people on it shows that this was deliberately done. The real king of the Elamites, Teumman, had been killed in the battle, and another panel represents an Assyrian soldier cutting off his head (Roaf 1990a:pl. 190b). This soldier's face has been mutilated as well. Teumman's head was sent to Nineveh for display and is shown on a relief from Ashurbanipal's new palace at Nineveh, hanging on a tree in the garden where Ashurbanipal feasts with his queen, Ashur-Sharrat (see figure 13). On this relief the faces of both king and queen have been mutilated as well as the king's right hand.

In all these representations particular people were singled out while the surrounding attendants, soldiers, and prisoners were left unharmed. This implies that in the days following the capture of Nineveh, when it was still occupied by the invading army, one or more people went around the palaces identifying specific people by reading the inscriptions or through their regalia and other attributes, and set about gouging out their faces. The act was not done in the frenzy of battle. Clearly some forethought had to have preceded it. A decision had to be taken, and a scribe or other literate person had to be ordered to identify particularly odious people in the representations.

Susa

The city of Susa in southwestern Iran has provided the best example in the archaeological record of the practice of assaulting and abducting im-

Figure 11. Sennacherib viewing the booty from Lachish, Nineveh, Southwest Palace, ca. 700 B.C. Zainab Bahrani.

Figure 12. Assyrian officer presenting the new Elamite king, Nineveh, Southwest Palace, ca. 650 B.C. Zainab Bahrani.

Figure 13. Ashurbanipal banquet, Nineveh, North Palace, ca. 645 B.C. Permission of the British Museum.

ages. In 1158 B.C. the Elamite ruler of Susa, Shutruk-Nahunte, raided Babylonia and brought back statues and monuments as booty gathered from various Babylonian cities. Numerous pieces of mutilated victory, religious, and political stelae and royal statues formed this booty (see figures 14–18). Among the stolen works were objects that were already of great antiquity in 1158 B.C., such as the so-called *Law Code of Hammurabi*, which was erected in the eighteenth century B.C. and had been standing at the same site in the marketplace of Sippar for over six hundred years when the Elamites came to take it (see figure 14). The most ancient ruler's image stolen was an almost life-size diorite statue of which only the lower half remains (see figure 15). An inscription added by Shutruk-Nahunte declares that he had destroyed the city of Akkad and had taken this statue, which he identified as king Manishtushu. This ruler had been dead for more than a thousand years, but his statue was still on display in his capital city, Akkad.

Perhaps the best-known monument among the booty was the victory stele of Naramsin (see figure 18). By the time Shutruk-Nahunte arrived in Babylon, Naramsin had already become the legendary ruler *par excellence*. During his reign he had expanded his land into a vast empire, allegedly spanning from Iran to Cyprus, and subsequently he had deified himself. His stele had stood in the Babylonian city of Sippar for over a thousand years and was admired not just for its antiquity but venerated as a monument of a powerful ancestral king. The relief represents Naram-Sin's conquest of the Lullubi, an Iranian mountain people. The Lullubi ruler, on the upper right side of the relief, is shown pleading for mercy, and Naramsin, wearing the horned crown of the gods, is standing with one foot placed on a dead enemy.

There are two inscriptions on the monument: one is well preserved and was inscribed by Shutruk-Nahunte on the surface of the mountain. In it he describes how he took the relief from Sippar, brought it to Elam, and dedicated it to his god, Inshushinak. The other, the original Akkadian inscription above Naramsin's head, is almost entirely lost, but enough remains for recognizing a memorial of a victory over a foreign enemy.[1] It has always been assumed that the deterioration of the Akkadian inscription was caused by the erosion over time. However, a close inspection shows that the general erosion on the lower part of the stele is different in nature from the condition of the surface layer in the area of the inscription, and the possibility cannot be ruled out that this text was deliberately erased by Shutruk-Nahunte.

Figure 14. Codex Hammurabi, 1792–1750 B.C. Permission of the Louvre Museum, © photo RMN: Hervé Lewandowski.

Figure 15. Manishtushu, king of Akkad, ca. 2260 B.C. Permission of the Louvre Museum, © photo RMN: Hervé Lewandowski.

Figure 16. Head of Babylonian king, possibly Hammurabi, ca. 1750 B.C. Permission of the Louvre Museum, © photo RMN.

Figure 17. Enthroned ruler of Eshnunna in eastern Iraq, ca. 2000 B.C. Permission of the Louvre Museum, © photo RMN.

Figure 18. Victory stele of Naramsin, 2254–2218 B.C. Permission of Pierre and Maurice Chuzeville/Louvre Museum.

The case of the Naramsin stele would not be unique. Practically every Babylonian royal monument found at Susa had its inscription erased, to be replaced by Shutruk-Nahunte's own inscription, and had been damaged. Inscription panels on royal statues have clearly been scraped off, at times leaving one or two cuneiform signs or traces of signs where the original Akkadian inscription had once been. Elamite inscriptions were added on, declaring that Shutruk-Nahunte was responsible for taking these monuments.

Were these objects taken by the Elamites and carried the four hundred kilometers back to Susa for their economic or aesthetic value? Were they smashed in the general violence of war? Obviously, the assault and theft of the Babylonian monuments by the Elamites were no mere whim. Most of the statues and stelae were carved out of heavy stone at a monumental scale, and altogether they must have been a tremendous weight to carry the long distance to Elam. If the reasons behind the attack were just political violence, then mutilating the statues and leaving them behind would have sufficed. And if they were taken for their intrinsic or economic value, such as the Nazi army's theft of French paintings, for example, no damage would have been done at all. I believe that the Elamite theft was a deliberate act of abduction that required these monuments to be under their control. In the following section I will present various facets of Assyro-Babylonian thought that lead to this interpretation after a review of the currently maintained view on the subject.

Scholarship

The scholarship on the practice of assailing images is limited to three brief articles that were all heavily influenced by modern Western values regarding the arts and by preconceptions about the Near East. The unusually violent nature of Near Easterners, especially Assyrians and Babylonians, stressed in several handbooks, was considered enough to explain this behavior until Carl Nylander pointed out that the damage visible on some works of ancient art was not random or accidental. He identified the mutilated condition of the bronze head of an Akkadian ruler (see figure 19), found at Nineveh, as an act of political iconoclasm (Nylander 1980:329–33). The statue's left eye was gouged out, the upper bridge of its nose had been chiseled, the point of its nose was flattened, and both ears had been cut off. This condition had been regarded as the result of plunder by robbers

Figure 19. Bronze head of Akkadian ruler, possibly Naramsin, Nineveh, ca. 2254–2218 B.C. Scala/Art Resource, New York.

looking for the precious inlays of the eyes, but Nylander pointed out that the damage was due to a deliberate attack that he attributed to Medes. Nylander said that this was not a magical act of annihilation of identity but an act of political propaganda. He went on to explain this by the fact that the Near East, both in antiquity and today, "abounds in examples of gruesome mutilation as political expedient."[2] This a priori vision of the Near East determined Nylander's conclusion that this was a propagandistic act, similar to punishments that are presumably common in the Middle East today. No discussion of the alleged abounding examples was thought necessary. Scholars took it on his authority and on preestablished notions of Oriental violence that this was a correct conclusion.

Nylander's interpretation was accepted by Thomas Beran, who briefly listed other examples of mutilated Near Eastern statues (Beran 1988). Most recently a contribution to the exhibition catalog, *The Royal City of Susa,* by Prudence Harper found this practice so abhorrent that the author attempted to exonerate the Elamites from the responsibility for the damage to Babylonian monuments found at Susa and tried to shift the blame elsewhere (Harper et al. 1992:159–62). Harper suggested that the defacement of these monuments either took place in Babylonia before the Elamites brought them carefully to Susa or during a later attack on Susa by the Assyrian king Ashurbanipal. Her argument was heavily based on the Elamite text added to the stele of Naramsin. Harper relied on a mistaken translation of this text, which maintains that Shutruk-Nahunte declared that he "protected the stele and brought it to Elam."[3] However, the inscription merely says that he *took* the stele, an assertion repeated on all the inscribed pieces of booty. The Elamite ruler neither protected the stele of Naramsin nor treated it exceptionally. The monument was handled in exactly the same way as the remainder of the booty. Harper took this alleged protection of the stele as an indication that the original Akkadian inscription was not removed deliberately and so perhaps neither were the original inscriptions on the other monuments.

Harper's desire to shift the blame onto Ashurbanipal's troops disregards what is well known of Assyrian culture: it is highly unlikely that the Assyrians would have damaged statuary of Akkadian rulers. The Assyrians are known to have venerated such images of kings, whom they considered to be their own ancestors (Hallo 1983:1–17). It is also doubtful that the damage was done before the monuments were carted off to Susa by the Elamites. If the royal statues had been assailed in an earlier conflict or had been damaged accidentally, the Babylonians would have seen to their repair. Such ancient restorations are visible on several earlier statues and are recorded in texts. The idea of leaving a venerated statue of a god or king in mutilated form standing in a city or temple square goes against every tenet of Assyro-Babylonian belief and would be seen as unpropitious at the very least. Therefore, even if the royal Akkadian and Babylonian statues had been disfigured prior to the arrival of the Elamites on the scene, the Babylonians would have repaired them, and the Elamites would have damaged them, albeit for a second time. The Assyrians were capable of destroying foreign images, but for exactly that reason they were incapable of destroying their own venerated kings. Harper's desire to preserve the innocence of the Elamites implies that she sees the mutilation and theft of statues as an act of violence that she is reluctant to associate with them. Nylander, Beran, and Harper echo the voices of the Greeks after perhaps the best-known act of Near Eastern assault and abduction of statues and monuments, that of the sacking of the Athenian acropolis in 480 B.C. Ever since Herodotus and Lycurgus, the incident has been presented in Western scholarship as the prime example of the barbarity of the East. Handbooks on Greek art or history do not attempt to disguise their disdain for this act of philistine depravity, and scholars of the Near East have inherited this view. Aligning themselves with the ancient Greeks, they describe the mutilation and theft of statues as a barbaric act of violence.

The Curse: An Eye for an Eye

The cuneiform inscriptions that were carved onto images provide some clarification of the practices in question, but the contents of these texts have not been taken into consideration. These inscriptions, which, to the ancients, were an integral part of a statue or relief, have even been thought of as an aesthetic eyesore and a nuisance, and are often dismissed as bearing no relation to the image by art historians.[4] The propagandistic value of texts on Assyrian reliefs that record the valorous or pious deeds of kings has been stressed, but these and other inscriptions on works of art are clearly more than just political rhetoric. The images of rulers are not systematically studied in combination with their inscriptions because they are thought to constitute two different records. However, the conjunction of text and image is one of the hallmarks of Near Eastern art, both ancient and Islamic. The text on a statue or relief is an integral part of it and as such merits our serious consideration, not as a parallel source of information beside the image but as part of the internal logic of that image.

Deconstructive critics have identified how the categorization of writing into an opposition of serious/non-serious (for example in truth/fiction, history/propaganda) relegates certain forms of writing to marginal categories that are irresponsible (Culler 1983:115–28). The inscriptions on Mesopotamian royal monuments are seen as one of the false genres. They are considered formulaic and meaningless. Mario Liverani has shown how the Assyriological method of categorizing texts into main texts and their variants forces the majority to become apparatuses of a few and does not allow us to consider the contents seriously (1981). He used the example of royal titularies, which are one of the forms of writing most commonly referred to as meaningless formulae, and showed how the words chosen for the king's epithets, far from being formulaic, had a great deal to do with events in his reign. But in art history even scholars who recognize the importance of the text see it as an accessory or adjunct to the real artistic product. In a recent book on Sennacherib's palace the author devotes several pages to Liverani's discussion of titularies, with which he wholeheartedly agrees but does not extrapolate the concept to the remainder of the text nor to other texts in the same palace (Russell 1991). All royal inscriptions are seen as propagandistic declarations of power meant for a human audience, literate or illiterate. Because of his preconceptions regarding the inscriptions, the author did not recognize the magical aspects of the text that were spelled out clearly, such as the incantations written to keep the bull colossi from walking off (see figures 20 and 21) (Luckenbill 1927:178). According to this commonly held view, invocations to the gods served as yet another record of the king's accomplishment, and the only power that writing had was in displaying the political authority of the king (see, for example, Russell 1991:7–33, 241ff). The focus on only one facet of royal art and inscriptions is a fixation and hierarchization that can be read in terms of racial stereotype. While royal inscriptions are certainly propagandistic, many other factors went into their composition besides the consciously political. Reading all royal texts as nothing more nor less than propagandistic utterances of the king is extremely reductive and works to verify the preconception of another Orientalist abstraction: Oriental despotism. This abstraction is no less a stereotype because Near Eastern royal texts and art had propagandistic value. The stereotype is not a false representation of reality but an arrested, fixated form of representation

Figure 20. Human-headed winged bull, Khorsabad, ca. 710 B.C. Permission of the Louvre Museum, © photo RMN.

Figure 21. Lamassu, human-headed winged lion, Nimrud palace, gate guardian, ca. 865 B.C. (Gift of John D. Rockefeller, Jr., 1932, 32.143.2). Courtesy of the Metropolitan Museum of Art.

that gives access to an essential identity that needs no proof (Bhabha 1994:75).

It is considered a transcendental truth by many art historians that a text is not part of an image, but this is in fact a Western concept articulated in the aesthetic theory of Immanuel Kant. According to his idea of the *parergon,* anything that is not part of the form or design of the object, such as drapery or surface decoration, is part of the extrinsic framing of the work of art. Writing on objects would then also lie outside the object proper.[5] Kant's aesthetic theory forms the basis for the Western discipline of art history, but this is a theoretical choice that is anachronistic and foreign to the art of Iraq and Iran.

The separation of text and image into two different categories is alien to the Near East. The script was seen as an integral part of the image in Near Eastern art, or in Kantian terms it was within the frame of the work of art. This concept was employed for complicated stylistic, iconographic, and cryptic schemes throughout the history of Islamic art and thrives in the art of the modern Middle East. Therefore, in this case perhaps the application of a Middle Eastern concept of script, rather than a Western one, would be more fruitful in the study of inscriptions on images in the Near East. This entails reading texts closely, even hermeneutically, as part of the image, and considering the power of writing, which is not necessarily only the power of rhetoric but what has often been seen in the Middle East as a mystical or magical quality in script and the process of writing.

At least by the beginning of the twenty-fourth century B.C., curses come into use in southern Iraq that are almost invariably placed on every royal image. Yet they have never been discussed by art historians. These curses are not formulaic. They vary according to the monument they are intended to protect. They explicitly mention the dangers specific to that particular monument and invoke an appropriate punishment upon the attacker. In the case of damage to portraits of kings, they invoke the sterilization and ending of the progeny of the would-be attacker:

> Whosoever should deface my statue
> and put his name on it and say
> "It is my statue" let Enlil, the lord of this statue,
> and Šamaš tear out his genitals and drain out
> his semen. Let them not give him any heir. (Buccellati 1993:70)

Curses are also used for the purpose of repelling attacks on inscriptions, most particularly on the royal names in these inscriptions (see, for example, Luckenbill 1926:42). Often both curses are inscribed together onto images, the first to protect the image, the second to protect the name. The persistent use, spanning two millennia, of similar curses when the image or the name of the ruler is displayed raises the obvious question. Is this just a traditional ending to a royal inscription that is repeated from habit, without being given much thought? Or is it an essential and necessary prophylactic device against a real threat and therefore construed as an equally real counter threat?

The punishment invoked by the curse is usually one that is most fitting for the crime, according to Near Eastern thought. For example, a foundation inscription of Adad-nirari I (ruled 1305–1274 B.C.), recording the building of a quay wall on the river Tigris, curses the one who would neglect or destroy the wall and its foundation inscriptions, thereby causing a flood, with a curse that his land become like a ruin left by a deluge (Grayson 1987:14–23). Similarly, a stone foundation tablet recording the construction of a new capital by Tukulti-Ninurta I (ruled 1243–1207 B.C.) is particularly concerned with the overthrow of the kingdom of the one who would destroy, neglect, or abandon that new city (Grayson 1987:270–71). In an entirely different realm is the curse recently found on the tomb of the Assyrian queen Yaba, wife of Tiglath-Pileser III (ruled 744–727 B.C.) (Damerji 1991). It curses the person who would disturb her tomb with eternal unrest and wandering, an appropriate revenge for disturbing the dead. That all these curses were taken seriously in antiquity can be seen from the inscriptions of rulers who rebuilt or restored the works of earlier kings in which they always swear that they did not disturb the earlier remains and restored only what was necessary.

The significance of the invoked curses becomes clear if we go back to the well-known Near Eastern paradigm of an eye for an eye which made its prebiblical appearance in the law code of Hammurabi. Curses on statues call for the ending of the progeny of the attacker and his sterilization, thereby not only ending his existence but making any survival through his offspring impossible. This is an eye for an eye punishment. When an image that is meant to stand for all time is destroyed, the ending of the attacker's progeny is an appropriate revenge. The Sumerians, Babylonians, and Assyrians were all obsessed with posterity, with leaving a record of themselves. This is reflected in literature, for example, in the epic of Gilgamesh, where the hero king searches in vain for immortality after the death of his friend Enkidu, only to find that he can achieve it by recording his deeds on a monument. To the Mesopotamians there were three ways of achieving immortality: recording great deeds, erecting images to stand for all time, and the simpler and more basic method of having children. Therefore, the ending of the progeny, the sterilization of an attacker of a statue, was an appropriate and parallel punishment for the destruction of an image meant to immortalize the represented person.

Likewise, the reverse was possible. A real offense by a mortal could be avenged by the destruction of his or her image, as is surely stated in the following text of Ashurbanipal: "The statue of Hallusu king of Elam, the one who plotted evil against Assyria, and engaged in hostilities against Sennacherib, king of Assyria, my grandfather, his tongue (lit. mouth), which had been slandering I cut off, his lips which had spoken insolence, I pierced, his hands, which had grasped the bow to fight against Assyria I chopped off" (Luckenbill 1927:363). Hallusu's image was being made to suffer specific punishments appropriate to his sins against Assyria even though by that time he had long been dead.

Animism and the Uncanny

As I have argued in the previous chapter, ancient texts imply that in ancient Iraq the king's image represented himself, the specific person, not just as a representation or even a symbol, but as a substitute, a double. Statues of kings were regarded as real things. This view is supported by other practices that reflect the animistic perception of Babylonians and Assyrians—namely, the consecration of cult statues and the use of fetishes in magic.

The ancient practice of holding magical religious rites in order to bring inanimate images to life is perhaps best known from the texts recording the ritual of the consecration of cult statues. The gods were anthropomorphic, and their cult statues were treated as living beings. After their creation, cult statues were subjected to a magic ritual known as the Mouth Opening Ceremony that breathed life into the statue, named it as a specific deity, and thus brought it to life (Jacobsen 1987). The statue, which had by then become a god, was no longer referred to as ṣalmu, the Akkadian word for image or statue. It was bathed and fed on a daily basis as if a living being (Oppenheim 1977:183–98). It owned entire wardrobes of clothes and objects of adornment that were regularly changed, repaired, and cleaned. Every item of clothing that the god might require was made available. Even articles of underclothing that would never be seen by worshipers but that would have been necessary if the god were to be completely dressed were supplied.

Images of kings were given a similar treatment, and such statues were also conceived of, and treated, as living beings.[6] A Mouth Washing Ritual that formed part of the Mouth Opening Ceremony is also known to have been used on royal images. Statues of kings acquired omnipotence and a totemic power. Oaths were taken before images of ruling kings, and offerings were made to them.

Deconstructive criticism has identified the opposition of conscious/unconscious as one that has privileged the former at the expense of the latter, and it has made extensive use of Freudian and Lacanian theory in the investigation of the unconscious aspects of subjects that heretofore have been marginalized. Art historians too have been primarily concerned with the conscious, ideological reasons for Near Eastern royal portraits, and it is a methodological given in Near Eastern scholarship that images of kings, like their texts, are nothing more nor less than overt propaganda. However, while the propagandistic aspects of royal images should not be ignored, it is worthwhile, considering the psychological processes and the ontological beliefs behind the animistic perception of these images, as it is described in the ancient textual record.

Animism, magic, and omnipotence of thought are all closely related to the uncanny and form the basis for magic rituals in many cultures (Freud 1912–13:79). The uncanny as defined by Freud has several aspects. It can refer to the familiar and to the concealed, but it refers most particularly to moments of instability or ambivalence when boundaries are crossed. This last aspect encompasses the incidents of ambiguity between animate/inanimate, dead/living, real/imaginary, original/copy. This blurring of boundaries plays a part in animism and combines with omnipotence of thought. According to today's terminology, it enables a signifier to take over the functions of the signified. The perception of an image as a living being entails a moment of confusion and ambivalence and is therefore an aspect of the uncanny. Freud pointed to the *Doppelgänger*, the double, as the most common image of the uncanny. Through its splitting and fragmentation of the person, it both points to and denies mortality at the same time (Freud 1919:244). In this sense, representation in portraiture is a doubling or a reproduction of the represented. It can immortalize the sitter through reproduction, just as progeny does, according to Freud and Lacan (Lacan 1986:119). As I have argued in the previous chapter, this presence or repetition via the image is even more complicated in Assyro-Babylonian thought. An image of a person, whether mirror image, shadow, or artificial representation, therefore, might have been originally an insurance against the destruction of the ego, doubling as a form of preservation against extinction. But from being this assurance of immortality it became the medium for death or the site of the announcement of death's approach (Freud 1919:234–36).

The Ritual of Substitution

The perception of the royal image as the uncanny double of the king can be better understood in light of the Assyro-Babylonian belief in imitative or homeopathic magic. The practice of making substitute figurines for use in the cult or in black magic rites is well documented. Small bitumen, wax, wood, or clay figures were used to signify a person. Figurines made of wax, bitumen, and wood were burned, those of clay dissolved in water, in order to procure a specific effect on the person represented. The figurines were also pierced, buried, or subjected to other maltreatment in order to harm the intended victim. They could be buried to suppress the sexual potency or virility of a man. Alternatively, images of the beloved could be used in the case of unrequited love in a ritual at the temple of the goddess of love, Ishtar, in the hope of gaining the affections of the person in question and might even be used for the improvement of one's sex life (Biggs 1967:10, 28).

The ultimate expression of the belief in imitative magic was the ritual of the substitute king. When danger to the king's life was predicted in the omens, a living person was made his double and became the king's substitute through an elaborate ritual. He was given the king's name, his clothes and insignia, and was placed on his throne while the king went into hiding. Then the substitute bore the wrath of the gods and suffered the evil that had been intended for the king, leaving the real king unharmed (Bottéro 1992:138–55). The living substitute is referred to in the texts by the Akkadian term *ṣalmu* (see Chapter 5).

The use of substitute effigies was not limited to occasional black magic. To the ancient Babylonians and Assyrians, what we see as a distinction between magic, theological, or ontological thought was blurred and at times converged also with the field of science or medicine. Thus, following a prescribed treatment of an image could produce a beneficent as well as a maleficent result, depending on what was required, and such rituals could fall under the expertise of priest, physician, witch, or warlock.

An integral part of all substitution rituals was the act of naming. The image was first fashioned and then given a specific person's name in order to function as a valid substitute for the person in question. Physical resemblance was not always required. The utterance of the name was the main factor that worked the magic (Daxelmüller and Thomsen 1982:55). Usually the name was also inscribed onto the image. The name was so consequential because Babylonian theological thought held the basic doctrine that the naming of a thing was tantamount to its existence and that a thing did not exist unless it was named. Thus, the opening lines of the Babylonian Epic of Creation describe a time before creation, when nothing had yet been named. This equation of the act of naming with creation made the power of naming indispensable in substitution and imitative magic. This association of the name with existence explains the standard curses concerned with the removal of the name. The contiguity of the signifier with the signified made the removal of the name a means of obliterating the identity of the named person. Similarly, the firm belief in substitution led to seeing the damage to a person's image as a means of harming the person. The removal of the name from the image could also invalidate that image as an immortalization of the represented.

The destruction or damage of the image, therefore, was not feared as a political act that merely brings disgrace to the ruler through his portrait. The image became a substitute, and the portrait's destruction became an uncanny embodiment of death's threat to the ruler.

Assault and Abduction

The Near Eastern practice of the destruction and seizure of cult images in battles is well attested in ancient texts beginning from the third millennium B.C. onward and is also known from the archaeological record (see figures 22 and 23). The loss of the image of the god was seen as the loss of divine favor, and this favor could not be regained without the return of the statue (Hallo 1983:13). Numerous inscriptions refer to the abduction of the deity statues from enemy cities throughout the Near East. The texts refer to the statues as gods, and sometimes these gods are named specifically (see, for example, Luckenbill 1927:30). Divine protection was also considered to increase with the number of gods (statues) in a city.[7] The presence or absence of a deity from a city and that deity's protection depended on the presence or absence of the cult image. The best-known records of this practice are the events related to the movements of the cult image of the Babylonian god Marduk.

Figure 22. Removal of the gods, Nimrud, palace of Tiglath Pileser III, ca. 730 B.C. Zainab Bahrani.

Figure 23. Detail of cult statue from the removal of the gods, Nimrud, ca. 730 B.C.
Zainab Bahrani.

In 1594 B.C. Marduk, along with his consort, Ṣarpanitum, was taken from Babylon to Anatolia after the Hittite attack that ended what is generally designated as the Old Babylonian Dynasty. An early Kassite king, Agum-Kakrime, son of Tashshigurumash, who is thus far known only from one text, claims to have returned Marduk to Esagila, his temple in Babylon. Agum-Kakrime explained that he had acted upon an order from the gods and from Marduk himself, who had decided that the time had come for his return to Babylon. The king apparently received this information through a consultation (by divination) with the god Šamaš and was also given directions for the correct treatment of the gods during the time of their restoration and until their shrine had been properly restored by means of consulting the oracles of Šamaš.[8] The gods were placed on cedar thrones until the time came to move them back into the temple. Various craftsmen were hired to restore the statues, their clothing and jewelry as well as the sanctuary itself. After the sanctuary had been restored and ritually purified by priests, the gods were brought in and a festival took place as a celebration of their return. There, Marduk remained, protecting his people and his city by means of his presence until the Assyrian king Tukulti-Ninurta (1243–1207 B.C.) carried him off to Assyria. Marduk remained in Assyria until the reign of Ninurta-Tukulti-Aššur (circa 1133 B.C.), when he again returned to Babylon (Luckenbill 1926:49–50; Grayson 1975: IV:1–13).

In the middle of the twelfth century B.C., the Elamite ruler Kudur-Nahunte, son of Shutruk-Nahunte, invaded Babylonia, attacking first Nippur and then Borsippa and Bablyon. Kudur-Nahunte had claimed the vacant Babylonian throne on the basis of his descent from a Kassite king of Babylon through the female line. When his claim was rejected by the Babylonians, he invaded Babylon and carried away its cult objects. The god Nabu was taken from Nippur, and Marduk was taken from Babylon. When this happened, all the sacred rites of the temples stopped, they had been cut off, and "were deathly still" the text tells us (Foster 1993:287). While Kudur-Nahunte had attacked Babylonia and taken its gods as a result of disagreements regarding the rightful succession to the throne, some wars at least were fought primarily as image wars. Nebuchadnezzer I, who ruled Babylonia from 1124 to 1103 B.C., marched against Elam specifically for the sake of returning Marduk to his rightful place, or at least this is what a series of texts written during his reign claim. We are told that after first setting out for Elam, Nebuchadnezzer was forced to turn back due to an outbreak of plague among his men, and it was only after returning a second time, during the summer, that they were able to surprise the Elamites in their attack and to successfully return Marduk to Babylon.

The return of Marduk during the reign of Nebuchadnezzar resulted in the usual great festivities, but it also instigated a period of literary production celebrating the event, and Marduk's glory, in a way that is perhaps unsurpassed in other periods of Babylonian or Assyrian history.[9] Poetry, myths of origin, and scholarly acrostic hymns that required hermeneutic readings were all written in his honor, and in the honor of Nebuchadnezzar, in both Akkadian and Sumerian versions. Again we are told in one of these texts that it was Marduk himself who had resolved to go to "the new city," and it was Marduk who finally decided to return to Babylon following the entreaties of Nebuchednezzar:

> [His] prayers went up to Marduk, Lord of Babylon,
> "Have mercy on me, in despair and pros[trate],
> "Have mercy on my land, which weeps and mourns,
> "Have mercy on my people, who wail and weep!
> "How long, O lord of Babylon,
> will you dwell in the land of the enemy?
> "May beautiful Babylon pass through your heart,
> "Turn your face towards Esagila which you love!"
> [The lord of Babylon] heeded Nebuchadnezzar['s prayer],
> [ ] befell him from heaven,
> "I command you with my own lips,
> "[A word of] good fortune do I send you:
> "[With] my [help?] you will attack the Westland.
> "Heed your instructions, [ ]
> "Take me [from El]am to Babylon.
> "I, [lord of Bab]ylon, will surely give you Elam,
> "[I will exalt] your [kingship] everywhere."[10]

The text explains that it was always Marduk who made the decisions and that his presence was necessary for the prosperity of Babylon. Another text dating to the same time, known as "The Marduk Prophecy," is a speech made by the god himself in which he relates his wanderings and travels, how he lived among the Hittites and returned to Babylon, how he was then taken to Assyria, and his second return to Babylon before setting off for Elam (B. Foster 1993:304–7). His twenty-four-year stay in the land of Hatti is explained as having been for the benefit of expediting trade there for the Babylonians. In Assyria he claims to have blessed the land by his presence. He delivered lands into the power of Assyria. While in Elam, Marduk prophecies that a powerful king will arise and renew his mar-

velous temple, the E-kur-sagila in Babylon, and will lead him in procession back to his sanctuary. The future of Babylon is revealed as one of
goodness and wealth. The god therefore chose to go to other cities. Assyria could even prosper due to his presence, but it was always Babylon
that was his rightful home, and it was Marduk himself who decided to return although it was the destiny of Nebuchadnezzar to lead him home.
While away from Babylon, Marduk is described as having abandoned his
city. Babylon thus became impotent while the land in which he dwelt, Aššur, for example, gained more power. Taking the cult statue of an enemy
land was therefore not an act of barbaric plunder but one of taking the
enemy's source of divine power into captivity and thus suppressing its
power.

   Similarly, the deportation of royal monuments was an act of magical
and psychological warfare. It cannot simply be explained as random plunder and looting. In the following historical text, after a description of the
vengeance meted out to Hallusu's image for his offenses against Assyria,
Ashurbanipal records the abduction of the statue of king Tammaritu of
Elam: "The statue of Tammaritu, the latter, who at the command of Aššur and Ishtar from Elam had fled (who, in the past) had laid hold of my
feet and performed a vassal's service I took from Elam to Assyria" (Luckenbill 1927:363). This clearly implies that Tammaritu, who had fled, was
taken into captivity in effigy. The image replaced the king. Its capture replaced his capture. Therefore, the statue was the king's substitute. There
are even records of cases where a person was brought to trial in absentia
with only his/her effigy present in court (Abusch 1987:87). Thus, having
Tammaritu's statue was a valid substitute for taking Tammaritu himself,
and having control of his image gave Ashurbanipal control of Tammaritu.
This animistic perception of images explains the practice of abducting
statues and the dread of having one's image removed and placed in the
hands of the enemy. Consider the very real fear recorded in this curse
from the *Great Monolith* of Ashurnasirpal II (ruled 883–859 B.C.) that
stood at the entrance of the Ninurta Temple at Nimrud (see figure 24):

As for one who does not act according to this inscription of mine (but) alters
the ordinances of my text; (who) destroys this monument (lit. image), discards
(it), covers it with oil, buries it in dust, burns it with fire, throws it in water, puts it
in the path of beasts or the track of animals; (who) prevents scholars from seeing
and reading the ordinances of my inscription, bars anyone access to my inscription
in order that it might not be seen and read; (who) because of these curses, in-
structs and incites a stranger, a foreigner, a malignant enemy, a prisoner, or any

Figure 24. *Great Monolith* of Ashurnasirpal II, Ninurta Temple, Nimrud, 883–859 B.C. Permission of the British Museum.

living being so that he destroys, chisels away, changes its wording to something else; (who) makes up his mind and decides to destroy this monument (lit. image) of mine and to alter my ordinances and therefore commands a scribe or diviner or anyone else, "Destroy this monument! (lit. image). Its dictates are not to be observed!" and whoever heeds his statements; (who) conceives anything injurious and orders (it to be done) to my works and my monument (image); (who) says, "I know nothing (of this)" and during his sovereignty diverts his attention elsewhere with the result that this monument (image) is destroyed and smashed (or) the wording of its text altered; or (who) seeks (to do) evil against this monument (image) of mine: may Aššur, the great lord, the Assyrian god, lord of destinies, curse his destiny; may he remove his works; may he pronounce an evil curse for the uprooting of the foundations of his sovereignty and the destruction of his people; may he inflict his land with distress, famine, hunger, and want.[11]

The specific maltreatment of the image that concerned Ashurnasirpal, including its possible burial, burning, throwing into water, or being trampled by animals, is exactly paralleled by treatments of fetishes in black magic rituals that are known from Babylonian witchcraft texts. We can see clearly in this curse that the king was taking precautions against any possible harm coming to himself through his own image in the event that it might fall into unfriendly hands. The curse threatens with a revenge similar to the original transgression, not only when the assailant attacks the image himself but also when he uses a foreigner, a prisoner, or an enemy to act out the crime in order to avoid the curse. This is not a unique occurrence. Several inscriptions on statues state that the curse still applies should the attacker use an intermediary to do the work. That such a possibility is taken seriously shows the firm belief in substitution: the assailant thinks he will avoid retribution by using a substitute, a person of no importance, while the owner of the statue points out that the same curse applies should the attacker use a substitute because the real culprit is he who commissioned the attack.

Another dimension of the practice of assaulting and abducting images that can be understood in the context of Near Eastern ontology is the truly fearful consequences implied for both king and kingdom when the king's image was damaged. The Babylonians and Assyrians believed that the entire world, the heavens and earth and everything in them, consisted of potential signs that were omens or messages from the gods. Thus, the appearance of the stars, the movements of birds, the incidents of abnormal or multiple births all predicted a specific fate or future event (Bottéro 1992:125–37). The appearance of a desert plant in a city, for example, meant that that city would become a desert, would be abandoned.

Such signs were also seen in the bodies and physical features of human beings. The appearances of moles or skin discolorations could predict a specific fate for the person in question or for the entire community (Oppenheim 1977:221). Thus, the following omen reflects no mere superstition but a religious belief: "If the image of the king of the country in question, or the image of his father, or the image of his grandfather falls over and breaks, or if its shape warps, (this means that) the days of the king of that country will be few in number" (Pritchard 1969:340). The omen makes it very clear that if the image of the king is damaged, deliberately or accidently, the king will die. The belief in such a result occurring from the damage of a king's statue is another reason for the curses on kings' images, protecting them from malicious acts and abduction. The same fear can explain the dreaded removal of an image as the possibility of its being abducted and falling into the hands of an enemy who could maltreat it.

The fear of having one's image destroyed or name effaced was beyond just the loss of an object of aesthetic or intrinsic value, or degradation through a political act. The fear was of a supernatural maleficent result that affected the subject, even beyond the grave. This fear was the reason for the placement of the curse, which is concerned with the ending of the attacker's progeny, because the ending of his progeny was seen as a parallel punishment for the destruction of an image. Progeny and images both ensure immortality, and their destruction means the cessation of existence. Through the named image two results could be procured. The first is positive and the reason for its creation. It stood in the stead of the king "for all time," thus immortalizing him, not just symbolically but literally. Then a dilemma occurred, and in Freud's words, "from being an assurance of immortality it became the uncanny harbinger of death" (Freud 1919:236). If the first, beneficial result could be procured from the image, then the second, harmful result could be achieved by damaging it. The solution to this dilemma was the addition of the curse. The curse would, it was hoped, counteract the threat to the image by invoking a similar fate upon the attacker. Thus, royal images were not stolen and mutilated in a moment of barbaric looting. They were taken into captivity and punished as if live beings because of a complex religious and philosophical worldview in which representation by image was a real, not a symbolic, substitution, and having control of a person's image was one more way of having control of that person.

This is a system of representation in which the image becomes a substitute or even a simulacrum. As a presence in its own right, it is not, nor does it need to be, a mimetic image. Plato, who found mimesis disturbing, warned against the dangers of confusing the image for the true original. According to Aristotle, we identify what is represented because it contains features of the actual object within it. Identifying the representation as such is through an intellectual process he said, and we derive pleasure from the recognition of the representation as representation and not the original. However, there are instances and cultures where the image came to stand in as a valid substitute for the thing represented and where there is a need for the distinction between the two to be blurred or even effaced. This is what has generally been referred to as sympathetic magic and what Freud described as an instance of the uncanny. This is when a sublation of the signified into the signifier occurs, and the effacement of the distinction between them allows the representation to take on the full meanings of what it represents. In ancient Iraq such distinctions are not simply blurred but invalid. The practices described above are not simply a matter of (what anthropology describes as) sympathetic magic because uncanniness was somehow in the very nature of the image as image. For the ancient Greeks, representation was not to be confused with the real. Mimesis was a resemblance or mimicry of the original and not part of it. For the Assyrians, Babylonians, Elamites, and perhaps others in the ancient Near East, the image always retained something of the original within it and could even take the place of the represented, occulting it to an extent but at the same time being its presence. Yet despite these differing viewpoints between Greeks and Near Easterners regarding the function of imagery, both cultures were gravely concerned with the dangers inherent in representation, whether visual or verbal.

Writing is also a form of image making, and scholarship regarding Near Eastern art and aesthetics is no less concerned with a political power of images. Through the use of metaphorical substitutions and metonymies of presence a particular identity comes to be understood as the true mimetic image and an embodiment of the East. In *Colonizing Egypt,* Timothy Mitchell (1988) stresses the importance of the power of image in the exhibitionary order of colonialism, in scientific texts, in display, and in the colonized geographical space itself. In *Mimesis and Alterity,* Michael Taussig describes colonial writing as the "colonial mirror of production," referring to the magic of mimesis as an inherent part of colonial discourse (1993). Traditional art historical scholarship regarding the Near East can be thought of in similar terms in its descriptions of "culture-as-sign" (to use Homi Bhabha's phrase). Because it is invested with what is construed as the spirit of the real or the essence of the Orient, this textual representation of the ancient Near East becomes like the substitute used in Babylonian sorcery. The elocutionary force of the utterance of naming, necessary for empowering the substitute in Babylonian witchcraft rituals, is here established through the performative voice of the scholar. Having authority over the image is also a form of control because the spirit is in the representation, the image can in fact become even more powerful than that which it represents, and like the double of the king, the image can occult the represented. Colonial discourse's method of capturing its subject by means of its image is thus not unlike the ancient Near Eastern practice of the abduction of statuary.[12] Both practices are a form of political magic in which the power of images is of paramount importance.

7

Presence and Repetition:
The Altar of Tukulti-Ninurta

I have revealed to Atrahasis a dream, and it is thus that
he has learned the secret of the gods.
—*Epic of Gilgamesh* (Ninevite version), XI, 187

The dream is a rebus.
—Sigmund Freud, *The Interpretation of Dreams*
(1959:1)[1]

IN THE ASSYRO-BABYLONIAN TRADITION, visual representation was considered to be part of an entire semantic constellation. Like the ideogram in
the script, the visual sign had the potential of referring to a chain of referents, linked to it and to one another by a logic that may escape the contemporary viewer but that could be deciphered in antiquity through
hermeneutic readings. Such readings were obviously not accessible to a
general public, most of whom were most likely nonliterate; however, the
potential of signs referring to other signs in a continuous chain of meanings was a knowledge not limited to the literate. The ominous nature of
things was a subject of concern for all in Babylonian and Assyrian society.
It seems clear from numerous texts that signs in the environment could
be read and deciphered by people other than the scholarly elite or the
priesthood. For omens related to the destiny of king or country, court diviners and the priesthood studied the signs, using their scholarly knowledge of astronomy and hermeneutics. But the reading of omina in the
environment was also a part of the daily lives of people in general, as we
know from textual references to *egirru* (omens of chance utterances) or
to dreams and dream interpretation.

Like other signs in the world, visual images could never be seen as
the relationship between one signified and one signifier. An image was a

pluridimensional sign that carried latent meanings beyond the one manifest on the surface. Since many works of art were made without any intent of presentation to mortal viewers, the polyvalence inherent in their imagery was not always a code intended for a particular audience, whether literate or nonliterate, although one can imagine that the system was at times deliberately manipulated for the purposes of generating a required meaning. In the previous chapters I have attempted to unfold my argument that this polyvalence was considered to be in the very nature of the image-sign. The audience or intended viewer was not of the greatest import in many cases because the work of art was put in a position where it was only to be viewed by the king, his courtiers, or temple officials. In these cases whatever meanings were generated through the imagery had much less to do with the good opinion of the chance viewer than they did with the power of the image as a means of creating an incessant presence. In attempting to catalog ancient Near Eastern images by means of an iconography of one-to-one relationships of signifiers and signifieds, of symbols and gods, for example, we have perhaps limited our readings unnecessarily in a way that the Babylonians and Assyrians would not have done. Taking one canonical work of art as an example, I will attempt to demonstrate why a less restrictive methodology may lead to a more nuanced understanding of Assyro-Babylonian works of art. Rather than depending solely on iconography and philology, my reading also makes use of deconstructivist and semiotic theory. In doing so, I will not apply semiotics as an organizational model but simply take it as a point of departure for considering aspects of signification that cannot be articulated through traditional iconographic or philological studies. Since I have already argued for the polysemous nature of Assyro-Babylonian signification through a systematic study of the cuneiform script and rituals using images, this insistence on polysemous meaning is based on the ancient textual evidence itself. Because semiotic theory allows for a consideration of polysemy of meaning, it provides useful tools for our attempts to understand Assyrian representations, and these should expand, rather than replace, more traditional methods. At the same time, the approach I take also incorporates the postprocessual archaeological theory of the retrieval and interpretation of ancient materials as a "mode of presencing." Contrary to the fears of their opponents, making use of postmodern archaeological or visual theories does not mean disregarding the scientific data from excavations. However, it does require that we consider our own place in relation to the compiling and interpreting of that data, a stance that is particularly needed in the case of Assyrian antiquity.

Ne-me-ed ᴰnusku:
The Form and Function of the Seat of Nusku

The so-called altar of Tukulti-Ninurta is an alabaster monument carved in relief with an uncommon scene that has notoriously escaped the interpretational logic of art history (see figure 25). It is a canonical monument, appearing in all surveys of the arts of the ancient Near East, and is discussed as an important example of Assyrian art. The representation on the altar is celebrated not only as an instance of narrative in visual art but also as an early example of an Assyrian relief glorifying the power of the king.[2] The object was discovered by the German expedition led by Walter Andrae, in the city of Aššur (Qal'at Sherqat). It was uncovered, along with two other similar objects in Room 6 of the Ishtar Temple, a sanctuary rebuilt by the Middle Assyrian king Tukulti-Ninurta I (1243–1207 B.C.). Currently it is in the Staatliche Museen, Vorderasiatisches Museum in Berlin (VA 8146, ASS19869).[3] The two other altars with which it was found were not carved with figural scenes although an example of a pedestal carved with a scene, unlike this one but dating to the reign of the same king, is known from another context. That pedestal is now in the Archaeological Museum in Istanbul (Ass 20069). According to the excavator, Walter Andrae, the three pedestals uncovered in Room 6 were not found in their original positions. Because their backs were undecorated, he postulated that they were designed to be placed against a wall. However, they were found by the excavators in the center of the room. At a certain point the door of Room 6 had been sealed off, and the room was no longer used after that time. Andrae therefore suggested that the pedestals had originally been in the main cult room, or *cella,* of the temple positioned with their undecorated backs against the wall and were moved to Room 6 only for storage when they were no longer in use. At that time they were placed into the room without consideration of carved versus uncarved sides or consideration of their accessibility to the viewer. Andrae believed that these three pedestals, as well as the one other pedestal now in Istanbul, were all originally in the temple's *cella.* The Istanbul example had been found at the side of the temple's main door (Muscarella 1995).

Figure 25. The altar of Tukulti-Ninurta, from Ashur, 1243–1207 B.C. Permission of the Vorderasiatisches Museum, Berlin.

All of the information we have from the archaeological context therefore suggests that (with the exception of one) the pedestals were not in the view of the general public. One carved pedestal was excavated at the entrance of the temple and may have been more in the public view. The example under discussion here, however, was unlikely to have been seen by many, even if, as Andrae suggested, it had been originally placed in the *cella* and only later moved to the sealed Room 6 as a form of ritual burial of sacred objects. In a temple context, however, placement of decorated and undecorated sides of an object may in fact have worked in ways quite different from what we might expect. Access to the *cella* of a temple was limited to a few elite people. It was not a public space. If a god was to be the viewer, the carved figural scene may very well have been placed in a particular position in relation to other cultic objects or statuary rather than human beings.[4] The undecorated side that Andrae assumed to have been placed against the wall may well have been positioned facing any other direction in the room. The fact is that we have no information about the standard placement of such objects. When they are found in a good archaeological context (which is an event rare enough in itself), we are led into re-creating the history of their movements within the space in order to make the objects and their reception fit into our conceptions of the presentation of works of art: displayed, museum style, to an audience of mortal art connoisseurs. Or (as I have argued in Chapters 2 and 6) we are taught to believe that all Assyrian works of art were always in the public view because this is how the Assyrian kings ideologically manipulated public opinion. The Assyrian context of art is likely to have been quite different from the forms of display with which we are most familiar, especially in the positioning of temple images. In the case of works of art made to be placed in a temple, questions of reception and audience, visibility and decorativeness, become all the more problematic.

The object under discussion here is commonly referred to as the altar of Tukulti-Ninurta. However, it is perhaps better described as a cult pedestal on which an image or deity symbol could be placed.[5] It is formed in one piece as a pedestal standing on a double plinth rectangular base and measures 22 11/16 inches (57.7 cm.) inches height, 22 11/16 inches (57.7 cm.) in width. The "altar" or pedestal proper is a rectangular object with a semicircular projection at either end of its upper part. A thirteen-petaled rosette is carved within each of these terminals. On one side of the pedestal the surface is recessed and surrounded by a projecting linear border, within which is the scene carved in a relatively low relief. The opposite side was left uncarved.

The image shown on the sculpted side depicts two male figures in profile, one standing and the other kneeling. The figures seem to represent the same person, bearded, wearing the same mantle and tunic, the same earring and bracelet, and holding the same scepter. The hand gestures of the two figures, with forefinger and thumb extended, are also the same, as are the details of their physiognomy. The figures are identified as representations of Tukulti-Ninurta himself, based on the royal attribute of the scepter. He appears to be shown twice, first approaching and then kneeling in front of a monument. The monument that Tukulti-Ninurta approaches in the carved relief image is a representation of the same monument on which it is represented. It is a pedestal. On top of this represented pedestal stands a rectangular object with what appears to be a vertical stick placed at its center. The object has been interpreted as either the door of a temple or a tablet and stylus. It is generally assumed to be the symbolic representation of the deity, who is being worshiped by the kneeling Tukulti-Ninurta.

The lower part, in the form of a double plinth, bears an Akkadian inscription stating that it is a pedestal dedicated by Tukulti-Ninurta to the god Nusku. Unfortunately, the last part of the inscription has worn away, leaving us with only partial information. Most art historical discussions of this pedestal record these basic facts of the inscription. For the purposes of this study, however, I am proposing that a closer investigation of the inscription, even as it survives in its partial form, can lead to a new interpretation of the monument if studied in conjunction with the imagery of the relief. By a closer investigation I do not mean a purely philological and historical study of the text. Philology is no less compromised in its interpretations than the study of visual images although archaeologists often seem to believe in the anterior authority of the word. Instead, what I am proposing is to read the text in a way that considers such things as polysemy, the structuration of *différance,* and the notion of trace, or *archi-écriture,* that I have discussed earlier in relation to the development of the script.

The sequential approach and kneeling of the king's figure has been seen as an innovative step in the development of a narrative art. Since narrative has been considered a more sophisticated type of image making in art history, the object's canonical status, its appreciation as a work of aesthetic refinement, hinges on this interpretation to a great extent.[6] The inscription at the base is generally read as a helpful means of historical documentation. It tells us that Tukulti-Ninurta was the patron, at least that it was made during his reign. It tells us that the pedestal was made for (belongs to) the god Nusku. But as helpful as the inscription is for this factual data, it has also been regarded as a source of confusion because the symbol of the god Nusku on other works of art that bear inscriptions identifying this deity is a lamp, and this is appropriate because Nusku is primarily known as the god of light. Instead, the symbol on the pedestal of Tukulti-Ninurta looks very much like the tablet and stylus represented elsewhere as belonging to the god Nabu, the god of writing. In other words, though the scene depicted is described art historically as a narrative, recording a movement in time, the text in the inscription does not narrate the event in the scene. Text and image are incompatible. This is considered to be a typical problem of Near Eastern art in general. Where inscriptions occur with images, most of the time the one appears to have little or no relation to the other. Such incompatibility has led to a series of laments in art historical scholarship, often going so far as to describe the writing as an intrusion into the work of art proper. At times this lack of correspondence between word and image has even been seen as something of a blunder on the part of ancient artists or has led to speculations that sculptor and scribe were different people. The problem, however, is as much in our interpretive methods as it is in the ancient record, if not more so. We expect that the inscription will work as a legend, as a form of explanation of that image. I suggest instead that perhaps it is this perceived inadequacy of the text to the image itself that can help us to better understand the altar of Tukulti Ninurta. Rather than viewing it as an obstacle, this perceived disjuncture can be used as a point of departure for our study. If we do not approach the text as a descriptive legend, the possibility of other readings in conjunction with the image emerge.

Image Text

In ancient Near Eastern art history, studies of images and texts have assumed that the comparative method is the only possible means of analysis—that is, the comparison of iconography to texts as narrative whether the texts are inscribed on the image or separate and simply found to be similar in content. Since in the early days of our discipline this approach was found not to be very fruitful, the alternative approach became the repeated declarations regarding the futility of the matter of the relation of texts and images altogether. As a result most studies have focused on either texts or images but not both. Images were often analyzed in the minutest detail, but their inscriptions were avoided and relegated to philological analyses in separate volumes. This approach is still common practice in many studies, especially in such publications as museum catalogs, even though a number of scholars have argued for the integration of the study of art and texts, and have shifted the focus of research in that direction. Among them, Irene Winter has particularly insisted that "the visual needs to be studied with the full analytical arsenal available to us—art historical, archaeological, anthropological, and textual—and on its own terms" (1997:359). I would emphasize Winter's argument even further by adding that "on its own terms" in Assyro-Babylonian culture by definition includes the textual as an aspect of the work. I stress that the text is part of the logical constitution of the monument as understood by the Babylonians and Assyrians. In my reading of the royal inscriptions on the images of the king in Chapter 6, I have attempted to analyze the text as part of the internal logic of the image itself. Reading the text on royal images as a serious mode of writing rather than a repetitive apparatus allows for a rethinking of the perception of statuary in antiquity and a far more complex understanding of the power of such images than has been allowed them

by traditional scholarship. Here again I view the inscription on the altar of
Tukulti-Ninurta not as a separate source of information for the visual image but as part of the signifying logic of the monument as a whole, a
monument which I take to be comprised of both text and image.

The inscription reads:

> Cult platform of the god Nusku, chief vizier of Ekur, bearer of
> the just scepter, courtier of the gods Aššur and Enlil, who
> daily repeats the prayers of Tukulti-Ninurta, the king, his
> beloved, in the presence of the gods Aššur and Enlil and a
> destiny of power [for him] within Ekur . . . may he
> [pronounce . . . the god Aš]ur, [my] lord, . . . forever . . .

The transliteration is as follows:

1. *né-me-ed* ᵈ*nusku* SUKKAL.MAH *šá é-kur na-ši* GIŠ.GIDRU
2. *eš-re-ti mu-zi-iz* IGI ᵈ*aš-šur ù* ᵈBAD *šá u-me-šàm-ma*
3. *te-es-le-et* ᵐGIŠ.*tukul-ti-*ᵈ*nin-urta* MAN *na-ra-mi-šú*
4. *i-na* IGI ᵈ*aš-šur ù* ᵈBAD [*ú*]-*š*[*á-n*]*i-ú-ma ù ši-mat*
5. *kiš-*[*šu*]-*t*[*i-šu*] *i-na* ŠÀ *é-k*[*ur*] . . . x-*šú*
6. *šu-me* . . . *li-ta-*[*asqar*] . . . [ᵈ*aš*]-*šur*
7. EN-[*ia*] . . . *a-na da-*[*riš*] . . . (Grayson 1987:279–80).

In the standard lexical lists of ancient Near Eastern iconographic studies,
Nusku is the god of light. But of course Nusku is not limited to one function since the majority of gods were generally thought to possess more
than one characteristic or power. The inscription on this monument does
not refer to Nusku as the god of light but as the Sukkalmah, chief vizier,
of Ekur, and the bearer of the just scepter. In this capacity he is the one
who intercedes with the supreme gods Aššur and Enlil on behalf of
Tukulti-Ninurta. The dedication of the pedestal, then, is a dedication
to Nusku in his guise as an interceding deity and not to Nusku as an abstraction light. Nusku is described in the pedestal inscription as *naši*
GIŠ.GIDRU, "bearer of the scepter." GIŠ.GIDRU is the Sumerian logo-
gram for scepter. The addition of the Akkadian adjective *ešreti* makes it a
scepter of justice or rightness. The Akkadian reading for the combination
GIŠ.GIDRU is *ḫattu*, and *ḫattu* can also be read as GIŠ.PA in Sumerian.
The latter part of this combination, the sign PA, also occurs in the Sumerian rendition of Nusku's name, PA.TUG. While these readings are nar-
rowed down by philologists into the one that best fits the context, in

Assyro-Babylonian hermeneutic thinking the possibility of other readings were latent in such cuneiform signs (see Chapter 4). Nusku is therefore the bearer of the scepter in his name, which in Assyro-Babylonian ontology cannot be separated from his essence. Nusku actually bears the scepter in his name identity. GIDRU is another reading for PA. Nusku is in fact referred to as naši GIŠ.PA; both readings were therefore equally applicable (*CAD* vol. 6:154).

The stick or stylus in the god's symbol can perhaps be read as a direct reference to Nusku, as *naši* GIŠ.GIDRU. Some scholars have attempted to identify the iconography of the symbol on the pedestal as the "bright rod of light" of Nusku. Such an interpretation is reached as a result of the belief in a one-to-one iconographic relationship between deities and their symbols so that Nusku is simply god of light. Instead, we would do well to look at other characteristics of the god Nusku. Nusku is also a god of dreams. I suggest that the reference to his being the vizier of Ekur may be better explained through this part of his identity. As all Near Eastern scholars know, Ekur is the name of a temple in Babylonia, but in theological writing it was also a term used to refer to the bond between heaven and earth, an epithet that is often used for temples. In my reading of this statement, Nusku is therefore the vizier of the bond between heaven and earth, and not of a particular temple. I suggest that as the vizier of this bond, and the courtier of Aššur and Enlil, Nusku's role as a dream god rather than as god of light is appropriate. This suggestion is not so out of keeping with standard philological interpretation. It differs only in insisting on the Assyro-Babylonian awareness of the latency of possible meanings carried in cuneiform signs. In what follows I will attempt to demonstrate that such latency of meaning (or what I have previously described as trace) exists in the visual imagery of the monument and in the relationship of that visual imagery to the cuneiform text.

The second aspect of this text, which seems to be emphasized in the cursory references made in art historical studies, is Nusku's intercession and prayer on behalf of Tukulti-Ninurta. Here a closer reading shows that it is not simply a formulaic statement of prayer. It repeats the visual image. However, it repeats the visual not by describing it through narrative means but by doubling its structure. What is fascinating about this particular monument is that this very structure is in itself a structure of repetition. The text states that Nusku daily *repeats* the prayers of Tukulti-Ninurta in front of Aššur and Enlil. This entreaty is a repetition. The text uses the word *repeats* (*ušaniuma*) The akkadian verb also means to double, deriving from *šanū*, second, other, or double (*CAD* vol. 17:388–409). Nusku intercedes and repeats (doubles) the prayers of Tukulti-Ninurta in the presence of the gods Aššur and Enlil. Nusku's words become Tukulti Ninurta's words to the gods. This is in effect a direct reversal of conjurations made by mortals, discussed earlier in Chapter 5: *šipatum šipat Marduk* ("the conjuration is Marduk's conjuration"). In that conjuration the words used by the mortal become Marduk's words; they are transformed through a performative utterance into the words of Marduk. They are not a mimetic reflection of Marduk's words but Marduk's actual words, and it is precisely this transformation that enables the success of the conjuration. The reversal here in Tukulti-Ninurta's pedestal is important. What happens on earth in terms of substitute utterance can also happen in heaven. Ann Guinan uses the term *binary opposition* in her discussion of the interpretive code of the *Šumma ālu* omen series, a group of omens to be found in urban life. Guinan suggests that the key to reading such omens is opposition but stresses that contiguous connections are the most important aspect of the omens since they occur in pairs or groupings (1989). Thus, Guinan's use of the term *binary* can be augmented. Each omen may use binary oppositions in the relationship of protases and apodoses, however pairs of omens are chiasmatically linked, in a rhetorical structure that creates a natural bond, a bond that works through a relationship of reciprocity rather than simply as binary opposition. For example, Omen I reads as follows: "If a city is situated on an elevation, as for the inhabitants, the mood of the city will be depressed." Omen II continues, "If a city is situated in a depression, the mood of that city will be elevated."[7] However, both possibilities clearly belong together in a chiasmatic relationship. It is along the rhetorical structure of the chiasmus, a structure that occurs in conjurations and in dream interpretation, that the decipherment of mantic signs seems to work. It is also the structure of the chiasmus that we can see at work in the altar of Tukulti-Ninurta.

An aspect of the text on this monument that the usual summaries gloss over is the latter part of the statement regarding intercession. References to this text in scholarship briefly describe it as a prayer of entreaty for Nusku to intercede on behalf of Tukulti-Ninurta, but the inverse ending is not noticed. It is stated in this ending (albeit in fragmentary condition now) that Nusku is also to bring a propitious destiny to Tukulti-Ninurta. Nusku not only intercedes for the king in the presence of Aššur and Enlil. He repeats the utterance of destiny decreed by Aššur and Enlil in the presence of Tukulti-Ninurta.

Destiny, as I have already discussed in Chapter 5, was written by the gods into the signs of the real. One method that the gods had of indicating one's destiny to that person was by means of dreams. Dreams are signs sent by the gods that had to be deciphered through a hermeneutic reading exactly like the signs of the script. The dream signs were considered to be pictograms that could be read and studied for traces of hidden messages. As Bottéro puts it, the dream is a vision that is read as an oneiromantic pictogram (1992:113). When deciphered by a Barû (priest dream interpreter), the dream indicates destiny. As the god of dreams, Nusku brings these visual pictograms of the gods to the sleeping person. Nusku thus repeats an inverted process of repeating statements in his aspect as vizier messenger. He is the bearer of the words of the gods to Tukulti-Ninurta just as he is the bearer of the words of Tukulti-Ninurta to the gods. The chiasmatic structure of this relationship is clear.

From the Assyrian Dream Book, as well as other references to dreams from earlier periods, we know that vision is used in relation to dreams in the Akkadian language as it is in contemporary Semitic languages. One does not have a dream. One sees a dream. The dream *comes*. The dream is described as entering and leaving the dreamer's presence. It is an apparition that will double into a destiny. If the dream predicts an undesirable fate, rituals are followed that can change the course of events. Tablets I, X, and XI of the Assyrian Dream Book contain such rituals or incantations against the destiny or consequence of the dream. There are also references attesting to the existence of other such texts. In Aššur, textbooks were written that Barû priests were made to study during their apprenticeship. Among the rituals recorded was a series titled "MAŠ.GE.ḪUL.SIG.GA" ("to make evil dreams pleasant"). From the Neo-Babylonian period a tablet from Sippar lists a catalog of conjurations for dreams, "Against the seeing of dead people," "To remember what has been forgotten," "Against evil signs" (Oppenheim 1956:295–307). Among the rituals listed in the Assyrian Dream Book tablets is a prayer addressing the god Nusku as dispenser of dreams:

In front of the Lamp he shall . . . a bundle of reeds. The hem of the right side of his (garment) he shall cut off and hold it in front of the Lamp. He shall say as follows: "You are the judge, judge (now) my case: This dream which during the first or the middle or the last watch of the night was brought to me and which you know but I do not know—if (if its content predict something) pleasant, may its pleasantness not escape me—if its contents (predict something) evil, may its evil not catch me—(but) verily (this dream) be not mine! Like this reed is plucked (from the bundle) [and] will not return to its (original) place and this hem will not return to [my] garment after it has been cut off, this dream which [was brought] to me in the first or the middle or the last watch of the night shall verily be not mine!" In front of the . . . he shall break the reed in two [   ]." (Oppenheim 1956:298)

This ritual incantation is for one who does not remember a dream. If the dream is forgotten, then the destiny predicted by it remains unknown, and the correct conjuration against such a destiny, in the case that it might be unfavorable, might not be followed. The incantation also states that if the fate is favorable, then may that pleasant destiny indeed not escape the dreamer. Other rituals to Nusku against evil dreams are also known, and they are also related to destiny through oneiromancy (1956). Since the inscription on the altar of Tukulti-Ninurta includes an entreaty for an auspicious destiny of power for the king, an interpretation of the prayer and the pedestal as a whole as a dedication to Nusku as dream god seems appropriate. Other aspects of the pedestal and its imagery may be explained as befitting a magical-religious object associated with oneiromancy.

Monuments and Mantic

According to the Assyrian Dream Book, the dream is an image. Such a conception of dreams is also well known from Assyro-Babylonian literature in general, just as it is described in psychoanalytic writings regarding dreams from our own time. I am suggesting here that the altar of Tukulti-Ninurta is an oneiromantic monument. And that due to its concern with oneiromancy it can be read as a visual-verbal representation about images, about representation itself. The signifying structure of the monument can thus be likened to a dream. The characteristics of a dream are that it is a pictogram, having both visual and verbal polysemic characteristics, and as a mantic pictogram, the numerous possible meanings of which can be accessed, *the dream is a double* (ṣalmu) of the destiny which it predicts (such a conception is suggested by a number of prayers related to dream destiny). The altar of Tukulti-Ninurta is likewise an object that represents itself. There is a clear doubling or repetition in several of the representational elements in this monument.

The shape of the pedestal is repeated in the carved relief; the king is shown twice, along with all the details of his attire. We can further imagine that the god symbol carved in the relief was also doubled in some form upon the actual pedestal. And we should keep in mind that the living presence of the king as he stood or knelt before the pedestal was yet another tangible repetition, doubling the representation by his organic body, just as the pedestal itself doubles the pedestal represented in the relief image. The king is within the space of the representation and extraneous to it at the same time. These are two forms of presence or visibility. In the inscription we have yet another type of repetition in the name of the object itself, "pedestal of Nusku," and the name of the king, Tukulti-Ninurta. Thus, the whole monument seems to make a statement about repetition or doubling. We might even read it as a treatise on tautology; the tautology we know to have been a necessary device in religious magic is performative. The inscription indicates the importance of repetition in presenting the king's prayers to the gods in heaven, doubling his prayers on earth. The image also refers to repetition by doubling the shape of the object, the image of the king, and certain elements of the inscribed text. The monument thus creates a referential circle of meaning, or better yet, we can think of the reciprocal reference between elements in terms of the same chiasmatic structure that occurs in conjuration, hermeneutical interpretations, and oneiromancy. A bond is thereby created between text and image, and between representation and the real.

The king stands and kneels before the pedestal, on which is placed the symbol of the god: a blank, uninscribed tablet and a stylus. Perhaps we can still read the symbol as the tablet and stylus but not as those associated with Nabu. The symbol of a tablet and stylus is not incongruous with the identity of Nusku because what has been identified as a stylus may stand for GIŠ.PA or GIŠ.GIDRU, the identity of Nusku as dream bearer, and the tablet may be the tablet of destiny on which the pictograms or the signs of the dream-destiny will appear. The king as observer waits for the signs to appear on the tablet of destiny. The pedestal on the representation is also blank, left uncarved. There is something enigmatic about the image that has often made me think of some of the paintings of René Magritte, where a rather large and incongruous object appears in an otherwise very normal looking landscape.[8] In the altar of Tukulti-Ninurta the king is shown in profile; the depicted altar is frontal. This disjunction of narrative space creates a sense of the incongruity of the depicted altar. The large tablet and stylus (or scepter) on the pedestal are, of course, most likely to be explained iconographically as divine symbols. But they also have an uncanny effect in the depicted reality of the image. They are rather large in comparison to the king and the pedestal, and have an almost supernatural quality like a phantasm that has entered into a more natural scene. It is almost as if the tablet with a stylus symbol is in itself a symptom, an inadvertently emitted sign, like an *egirru* or other chance omen that is a phantasmatic appearance in the midst of reality. The nature of omens is that they uncannily have a place in the real but at the same time stand out as something strange or incongruous. Perhaps the tablet with a stylus is also a sign of the omen of destiny to be brought by the dream. If so, then we can read it as another example of repetition within the monument, the tablet with a stylus as a mantic sign of oneiromancy itself, in which representation has an effect on destiny.

Concepts such as mantic or destiny are by definition unrepresentable. They can be represented only through their own system of signs. As visual images, then, such concepts are trapped within their own system of signification just as Freud described the functions of the dream as the unconscious depicted through the language of the conscious. The unconscious, he said, cannot be described. Its existence cannot be empirically known. It can be depicted only through the rhetoric of the conscious by means of metaphors and analogies, and so on. In an uncanny parallel to the readings of the dream pictograms by the Barû, Freud himself used the metaphor of the mystic writing pad for the space of the psyche and described dream images as pictographs or hieroglyphs (as opposed to phonetic writing) to be deciphered by the psychoanalyst. As a representation of the possible space of the appearance of oneiromantic signs of destiny, the tablet and stylus may also refer to the blurred boundaries between the realms of real and supernatural, and how that boundary is traversed by representation.

Picturing the Real

In an often-quoted essay Michel Foucault describes *Las Meninas* by Diego de Velasquez as a painting that is "the representation of Classical representation, and the definition of the space it opens up to us" (see figure 26) (Foucault 1970:16). Historically, the subject of the painting is the group of figures in a room of the palace. They are all identifiable by name as members of the court of Philip IV of Spain, including the painter Velasquez himself. That historical identification of the depicted figures does not limit the painting to being a group portrait. This seems like an obvi-

Figure 26. *Las Meninas* by Diego de Velázques, 1660. Alinari/Art Resource, New York.

ous enough statement, yet when we look at the art of the ancient Near East, we are usually unwilling to broach any interpretation beyond the correlation of object and king's reign.

In my rereading of the altar of Tukulti-Ninurta as an integral visual-verbal monument, I have attempted to call into question its generic identification as a political portrait of the king. This monument was not intended for public display. There is no mortal spectator in this case, yet it is a royal portrait because it is a valid image-presence of Tukulti-Ninurta, representing him incessantly to Nusku, who will in turn represent him in the presence of the gods Aššur and Enlil. Power remains a concern for Tukulti-Ninurta because potency, life, and destiny are linked, but this is not a propagandistic display of power. This monument is not simply about a particular king. It is a complex image about the visible and the readable as representations forming the real, constituting the bond between the realms of gods and mortals.

In *Las Meninas* the signs and forms of representation, and the relationship of representation to its model, to its author, Velasquez, and to its spectator, are distributed all over the painting. In the altar of Tukulti-Ninurta we can also see a depiction of representation itself. The relationship depicted, however, is not one of representation to its model according to the rules of mimesis, but perhaps what we can read here is the specifically Assyro-Babylonian notion of the constitutive nature of the relationship between representation and the real. In his study of *Las Meninas*, Foucault describes the canvas behind which the self-portrait of Velasquez is seen as "stubbornly invisible." The easel and painting on it are shown from the back so that we are left with the potential of representation on it, but we cannot see the picture. This canvas, which does not show its image to the viewer, stands as if a signifier of signification itself. The tablet and stylus object, whether or not it is a tablet and stylus, similarly stands as an enigma in the Tukulti-Ninurta relief. But in *Las Meninas* it is Velasquez who seems to be in control of the image as the artist-creator. Instead, in our relief Tukulti-Ninurta awaits the signs, as the ideal viewer awaits the Velasquez painting on the depicted, reversed canvas. Tukulti-Ninurta's gaze is directed at the blank tablet and gestures at it as if it were a void in which a sign will appear. The tablet with a stylus is therefore like an uncanny void in the real, an opening or a space in the real through which the representation, which creates a real destiny, can appear.

In *The Critique of Pure Reason*, Kant defined concepts as distinct from sensations or that which makes up the material content of our knowledge. Concepts are therefore rules or tools for the ordering and classification of knowledge. The *Ding-an-sich* is a totally independent real while the transcendental object is a real thing as we access it. What Kant did not see, but what is emphasized by more recent philosophy and what seems to have been understood by the Babylonians and Assyrians, is that *das Ding* is a mirage, that it cannot have independence from the transcendental object. It is like the curtain in the famous story of Zeuxis, where the painter is tricked into looking for something beyond the depicted curtain. Nothing stands beyond the representation. There is no *das Ding*, no separate real, no difference between phenomena and noumena in the philosophy of Babylon and Assyria.

W. J. T. Mitchell uses the term *hypericon* to refer to a summary image that encapsulates an entire episteme (1994). Like Velasquez's *Las Meninas* and Magritte's celebrated pipe images in *Les deux Mystères*, the altar of Tukulti-Ninurta is a representation about an episteme and ontology, about repetition and doubling, about representation itself. Canonically, it has been included in our scholarship as a masterpiece of Assyrian art because it is an early stage of narrative, depicting the portrait of a powerful king. Reading it outside these Western parameters, however, may allow us to appreciate it as an engaging work of art in itself. We can perhaps come to value this image for what it reveals about the concepts of representation at work in its own cultural context rather than as a step toward the development of a visual narrative that finds its most complete expression among the Greeks. The altar of Tukulti-Ninurta is quite the opposite of a narrative because it displays itself as representation instead of effacing representational structures as narrative scenes do. That effacement is what makes narrative a successful means of representation, convincingly mimetic in its depiction of the real. But neither is the image on the altar the posited opposite of mimetic narrative: a symbol or a magically animated fetish. The altar of Tukulti-Ninurta is a complex work of art that seems to refer deliberately to the instability between representation and authenticity, and to declare (in keeping with the Babylonian epic of creation) that far from miming reality, it is representation that creates the real.

8

Conclusion:
Image, Text, and *Différance*,
or from Difference to *Différance*

It is because of *différance* that the movement of
signification is possible only if each so-called "present"
element, each element appearing on the scene of
presence, is related to something other than itself,
thereby keeping within itself the mark of the past
element, and already letting itself be vitiated by the
mark of its relation to the future element, this trace
being related no less to what is called the future than to
what is called the past, and constituting what is called
the present by means of this very relation to what
it is not.
—Jacques Derrida (1982:13)

IN THE PLATONIC WESTERN TRADITION, reality and representation have
been seen as two logically and ontologically disparate things. One belongs
in the realm of the essential real; the other is simply an imitation or an
illusion and is thus secondary to the real. The first enjoys an originary
superior identity—it is a real essence—while the second depends on resemblance to the first. In sum, the thing being represented must fall
ontologically outside of the representation itself. Another important Platonic distinction lies in the types of representation: between the categories of images that are copies and classified as having an iconic function,
and simulacra or phantasms that do not reflect an originary reality or
identity but become independent beings in their own right. Such distinctions have been the focus of philosophical investigations in recent years. It
has been argued that an identity, far from being essential or stable, depends on *différance*: a differing and deferring of presence. This Derridian
motif of *différance* as the continuous play of absence and presence has

certain similarities to the Assyro-Babylonian conception of the processes of representation in both script and visual image. Likewise, the philosophy of difference developed by Gilles Deleuze depends on the conception of the cosmos as the ceaseless becoming of a multiplicity of interconnected forces. Because that multiplicity disallows the possibility of a stable or nondynamic entity, the universe must be understood in terms of difference rather than identity.[1] This view of the universe as dynamic and polysemous also has similarities to the Assyro-Babylonian conception of the world as saturated with multivalent signs.

In this book I have argued that visual representation in Babylon and Assyria functioned according to the rules of a metaphysical system that was unrelated to Platonism. For reasons that are similar to those determining the nonphonetic nature of the script, this is a representational mode that is not mimetic, nor does it aspire to mimesis. To evaluate or attempt to understand ancient Near Eastern images in terms of external resemblance and levels of naturalism is to impose an anachronistic and alien conception of art as mimesis upon them. Mimetic representation works on the assumption that a naturalistically rendered image can be the accurate record of a perception of the real or essential thing. For the Assyrians and Babylonians, the visual image, *ṣalmu*, was not the record of a perception, nor could it ever be a complete or absolute portrayal of an essential identity in itself. There was always an awareness of the lack of plenitude in any representation, whether visual or verbal. Expressing an identity of an essential thing, what we would call the *Ding-an-sich* of Kantian philosophy, involved an awareness of the circulation of presence and absence or difference. For the Mesopotamians, the *Ding-an-sich* was not separable from the processes of thought, of rhetoric and representation. Ontology and semantics were one reigning discourse.

I have started from the theoretical positions of postprocessual archeology and poststructuralist historical criticism, both of which stress the necessity for greater awareness of the role of interpretation or translation as part of the process of accessing the distant past. The position of the historian or archaeologist thus becomes one of a translator of culture. A translator will necessarily use the language of his/her own time and place to explain the past. I have used the language of Western philosophy to explain and theorize Babylonian ontology. However, I have pointed out that the traditional Western Platonic system of metaphysics, as well as the critique of this system by recent continental philosophy or poststructuralism, both fall short in an encounter with the Near Eastern record. While I

have found poststructuralism and other postmodern theories of representation useful for rethinking the Assyro-Babylonian notions of signification, I have used these simply as a point of departure from Platonism and
not as a model to be applied to the ancient record. Instead, I have
pointed out the limits of poststructuralist theories when confronted with
cuneiform script and the concept of *ṣalmu*. In Chapter 3 I have argued in
some detail that mimesis is not a useful means of understanding the ancient Near Eastern image. I have further argued that the categories of
semiology are not only inapplicable but actually have a tendency to collapse if applied to the Assyro-Babylonian material. Likewise, I have
demonstrated that the notion of the simulacrum as it is utilized in the
philosophy of Gilles Deleuze or Jean Baudrillard is problematized by the
Assyro-Babylonian notion of *ṣalmu*. As I have shown in Chapters 3 and 5,
for postmodern thinkers such as Baudrillard the simulacrum is part of a
scale of representation from mimetic to nonmimetic. I have argued instead that *ṣalmu*, while seemingly closer to the simulacrum, must be
thought of as outside this system of opposition to mimetic image. I have
argued that we must get out of this formulation altogether if we are to
reach a better understanding of the notion of *ṣalmu* because the metaphysical divide between representation/real is one that fails when applied
to *ṣalmu*. What this incompatibility means is that the Assyro-Babylonian
record should force us to reformulate the questions that we ask about
representation itself because it provides evidence of a tradition that
throws the proverbial wrench into the works of what we had thought was
a universal, transhistorical, or commonsense definition of signification.

In the portrayal of individual people (which is not portraiture in the
modern English sense of the word) the valid substitute image required a
series of links to the represented, including most particularly the inscription and the utterance of the name. Otherwise, the image remained simply a partial signifier and could not qualify as substitute. Substitution
through image worked through the combination of as many signifiers as
possible conjured up in one location. This process can be seen as a desire
for a cumulation or an accumulation of presence, the fullest possible measure of plenitude. The result, however, was neither icon nor portrait. It
was a being in its own right, a repetition rather than a mimetic image, indexically linked to the essence of the person represented but being just as
much the real essence as the person proper. There is thus no vertical hierarchy of original and copy as in the processes of mimesis. For the Babylonians and Assyrians, the image was a liminal or uncanny presence within

the realm of the real rather than a representation of the real or the presence of an absent original.

In this logic the portrayal in *ṣalmu* functioned according to the same system of substitution known as the institution of substitute kingship. The carved statue had similar characteristics as the organic body double in this ritual exchange. The body double did not mirror the king. Such a vertical hierarchy would have defeated the purpose of the ritual. The king could not remain the original with this substitute functioning as a copy. The very logic of the ritual depends on a horizontal repetition of the essence of the king, where the *ṣalmu* cannot be a mere copy but appears as an entity in its own right. In referring to this ritual we often forget that for the Mesopotamians, this substitution was real. Portrayal by image, I have argued, is better understood according to this system. Rather than continuing to think of it according to the verticality of mimesis, where the hierarchy of real to representation is a given, I propose that Assyro-Babylonian image making is better understood in terms of a horizontal repetition. I have found that this seems to be the case, at least in the representation of individual people as portraits, where the aim of the image seems to be similitude rather than resemblance.

In a sense, such a representation of a person is ambivalent because it remains split. It is a partial presence of the person represented and indicates the absence of that person at some level although at the same time that absence is only a temporal deferment, never a total absence. This representation lacks the duality of sign: referent that we might have considered the most fundamental given opposition in the definition of the term *art* or in the function of image making. Especially in the case of portraits, the Assyro-Babylonian image must never be read mimetically as affirming reality. It is not an illusion of the person in any sense nor a resemblance of the person. It is better thought of in terms of a metonymy of presence in which the presence is never a plenitude or unique because it always carries a measure of absence. Rather than approaching it in terms of mimesis, a mimesis that is distinctive of a post-Greek metaphysics and closely linked to the notion of a possible pure phoneticism, this function of the image can be read or understood as part of a system of circulation of presence, difference, and deferment.[2]

The cuneiform system of writing, which functions on the basis of a chain of substitutions, can also be better understood according to this system of the circulation and deferment of presence and *différance*. The script, in its developed Akkadian form, operates according to a constant deferral and difference of meaning. It thus locates meaning in cuneiform signs through temporalization. When a particular value was read in the sign, it nevertheless did not erase the latency of other possible meanings. It is often said that the pictographic aspect of the script was never overcome and that in this, cuneiform writing failed or reached its limitation. The constant lament in scholarship that the script never became fully phonetic has placed unfortunate limits on our understanding of the complex and fascinating nature of this writing system. The reason that the script did not aspire to total phoneticism is that the trace of other words was constantly carried in each particular cuneiform sign. But contrary to popular belief, cuneiform was not participating in an evolution toward the perfect phonetic script. For the Assyrians and the Babylonians, no script could ever be completely phonetic because mimesis as the reflection of a separate spatiotemporal real was impossible. In Assyro-Babylonian thought it was the concept of a pure and uncontaminated indication of things in the world through abstract signs, separable into another realm, which was the illusion. The script and the world were part of the same system of the universe. It was this conception of things, this version of ontology, that allowed the development of the most distinctive Assyro-Babylonian science, the science of divination.

Divination depended on the belief that everything in the world could be read semiologically and rhetorically, according to the system of the cuneiform signs. And the divinatory key can be shown in numerous cases to work in an exact parallel to the circulation of presence and difference, a circulation that can be recognized in the cuneiform script and in the concept of substitute images. There is thus a literal intertwining of image and script because the script always bore the trace of pictograms and images just as things in the world likewise bore the rhetorical traces of cuneiform signs. Everything carried layers of meaning that could be retrieved, at least partially, in exegetical decipherment (*pašaru*), according to the tropes and figures of rhetoric through metonymy, synecdoche, and metaphor. We can sum up, therefore, by stating that for the Assyrians and Babylonians, signification in image or cuneiform script, absence and presence, representation and repetition were all linked and constantly shifting. As a system of representation it can best be understood as a constant circulation of presence and deferment, where what is present is *différance* rather than a plenitude of identity or a copy of the real. Mimesis is a concept that affirms the real by maintaining boundaries between the categories of reality and representation. Far from affirming the real by being its copy or attempting to reflect its thingness, the Assyro-Babylonian notion of representation or image destabilizes the real by being transphenomenal (in Kantian terms). The relationship is therefore horizontal and reciprocal as well as mutually determining. For the Assyrians and Babylonians, the image was understood ontologically rather than epistemologically. Reality itself was imagelike and significant, being constituted by signs encompassing the world with all its subjects and objects.

The separation of subject and object, which may seem self-evident and natural in modern thinking, is a separation into the categories of a Platonically informed worldview. In philosophical terms this is a view based on vertical thinking. Vertical philosophy separates the world of appearance from the world of essence, a distinction that was not so clear in Assyro-Babylonian thought. We might, as many have done before us, lament this state of affairs as something lacking in the Mesopotamian mind or intellect. Numerous historical texts describe this as a failure of an otherwise sophisticated culture to develop a true philosophy or metaphysics. As an alternative we might instead consider how such a view of the relationship between representation and reality can lead to a rethinking of the a priori notions with which we work in the field of art history and archaeology. Such a shift in approach turns away from evaluating all works of art according to the standards of perceptualism or mimesis and allows a more nuanced understanding of ancient Near Eastern imagery, contextualized in Near Eastern ontology and philosophy. In other words, I argue that a better description or analysis of ancient Near Eastern cultural practices is one that takes into account the ancient view of these practices. I have therefore argued that to contextualize representational practices in Near Eastern ontology and philosophy is a means of getting closer to the Assyro-Babylonian conception of representation.

This approach is certainly not without its own limitations, however. It involves methodological presuppositions that also require a great deal of attention and clarification. Most important among these might be the need to question how we as scholars re-create this native context and how we apprehend indigenous notions of representation, an issue I discussed in some detail in Chapter 3. Clearly our own identities, sociohistorical contexts, and ways of seeing the world come to play a part in our constructions of that past. As Johannes Fabian puts it, we can only translate the experience of others according to "our own measure of being-in-time" (1983). However, the ancient record itself must be taken seriously. This is what I have attempted to do through a close reading of the system of cuneiform script and investigation of the uses and treatment of images. At the same time I have stressed the need for an approach to the ancient record that reveals the role of the cultural translation and sees the historian as an active agent in the writing of history. This does not mean that I believe the past to be irretrievable or that the historical record is simply invented by the historian and archaeologist but that I see this academic practice as a process of translation.

In the first part of this book, I argued that an awareness of the cultural project of imperialism is vital for writing a post-Orientalist history of Mesopotamia or of the Near Eastern world. I further insisted that a postcolonial historiography can be politically meaningful only if it considers the discourse of the present in light of the modes of knowing or structures of reference established in the period of colonialism. I believe that as scholars involved in retrieving original context of works of art or indigenous notions of aesthetics we cannot imagine ourselves irrelevant to the interpretations we present. Every observer, as Claude Lévi-Strauss puts it, is self-evidently his/her own instrument of observation. For postcolonial histories, the challenge, then, is not in finding or setting up the true essence of a misunderstood past or alien culture as a symbol of identity. It is in redefining the relationships through which knowledge is constructed and bringing forth a critical intervention aimed at transforming the conditions of cultural translation and the enunciation of cultural difference. In terms of the study of non-Western cultures or societies, what this means is that one cannot stand aside as an impartial observer, scientifically collecting data. As an observer, one always becomes part of the observation. The division of subject and object of study is blurred. My insistence on the role of cultural translation is not unique. It is a stance that is congruent with postprocessual archaeological theory and poststructural anthropology and one that I argue has particular relevance for the study of Mesopotamia because of the Orientalist stereotypes that continue to inform the theoretical paradigms of this discipline.

For those of us starting from a point outside the Western tradition, the perspective we assume in relationship to Western scholarship, in aesthetics and in history, can be a perspective only from a displaced, disjunctive position. We can lament this marginality and scramble for a place within the hegemonic mainstream of the discourse, or we can instead utilize the agency of this disjunctive position for questioning what passes as commonsensical and universal. This strategy of utilizing the agency of being marginal is what Gayatri Chakravorty Spivak has defined as *strategic essentialism* (1988:206). In a discussion of subaltern studies and the deconstruction of historiography, Spivak argues that the subaltern "is necessarily the absolute limit of the place where history is narrativised into logic" but that subaltern historiography also remains heterogenous to hegemonic history. This definition of subaltern identity in relation to the hegemonic system may seem like a denial of agency to the marginal, but Spivak points out that the effect of the subject as marginal or subaltern cannot be before the hegemonic narrative itself. To see that identity of marginal or subaltern as preceding the hegemonic narrative is a historiographic metalepsis where the effect precedes the cause. If subalternity is an effect of the hegemonic system rather than being prior to it, then it can be used as a means of insurgency from within the system itself. Likewise, other scholars whose cultural backgrounds are not Euro-American, such as Edward Said, Homi Bhabha, and Jacques Derrida, have read against the grain of the Western tradition, working from within the system in order to call it into question. My own approach has been similar to theirs in that I address this system from within in order to call it into question. In this sense I do not address the disciplinary traditions of Near Eastern archaeology or of art history from an Oriental position. Such a view would entail a belief that this identity of (a constructed notion of) Oriental is essential in scholars from the East. But this notion of an Oriental essence is exactly what Edward Said's critique of Orientalism set out to dismantle in the first place. The argument is then not that scholars from Asia do not exist outside the imagination of the West but that Western stereotypes of what their position as an Oriental scholar ought to be are simply that— stereotypes. As a non–Euro-American scholar, one is often left in the position of a subjective aporia. As Spivak points out, either the marginal or subaltern is seen to express an essential subjectivity that is otherwise disavowed as a valid concept in the postmodern academy, or they are totally unrepresentable and have no voice. If they speak, they are said simply to parrot Western discourse. This means that postmodern academic discourse itself becomes colonized as a properly Western realm while it can be shown, without a great deal of effort, that much of what has come to be called Western postmodern theory has been formulated or inspired by scholars from the Middle East, South Asia, and Africa. I therefore take it that one cannot speak of postmodern theories as being Western or Eastern, and I do not see myself as working in a purely Western tradition, even if my critiques do involve postmodern theories. Postmodern critiques of hegemonic discourse or grand narratives cannot be said to be a purely Western development in that case because much postmodern theory that has been developed as counterhegemonic insurgence from within this system has been the work of scholars from other parts of the world. Strategic essentialism strategizes the position of marginal as a means of challenging hegemonic narratives of history. This is a strategy of working from within, as Spivak makes clear, but as a strategy, it cannot be called Western. Likewise, in deconstruction one reads from within the text but against the grain (Derrida 1974:24). Spivak further argues that subaltern historiography is by definition and necessity deconstructive. It is both an interruption and a displacing of discursive fields.

This strategic essentialism as formulated by Spivak is by no means an all-seeing sphere of marginality with a perspective that can reach the transcendental truth. However, it is by definition a position that is askew, disallowing any possibility of seeing things according to their assigned "proper" place. Therefore, as much as I have set out to challenge a dominant discourse, I have no claims to becoming the living agent for Near Eastern antiquity. That past is mediated by my own relationship to it. Yet this is by definition a relationship that is rooted in its own cultural specificity. In this book I have attempted to open up new avenues for understanding what is defined as ancient Mesopotamia, its culture, and its representations. I have attempted to change the form of the questions we ask this material by insisting that we move away from mimesis. I have argued that this difference is not simply a different system of representation but that as a system of representation it implies a different conception of reality as well. By means of the ancient record, I have tried to show that *ṣalmu* is an ontological category and not an aesthetic genre. I have put forth other questions regarding signification and the uses of images, even when I could not answer them myself. I hope that these questions will initiate further discussion that will lead to a better understanding of this remarkable ancient civilization, as well as our own relationship to it, in "our own measure of being-in-time."

Notes

Chapter 1

1. Bernal (1987). See the response by various scholars of antiquity in Lefkowitz and MacLean Rogers (1996), especially the contribution of Mario Liverani, "The Bathwater and the Baby," pages 421–27, which cautions against the total dismissal of Bernal's arguments by archaeology. See also Howe (1998:193–211) for a summary of the arguments and responses to Bernal. For an excellent discussion of the ideologies of classical archaeology, see Shanks (1996), especially pages 53–91.

2. For a critique of Said's *Orientalism* and a call for an understanding of colonial discourse that moves away from monolithic distinctions, see Bhabha (1983); Clifford (1988); Lowe (1991); Ahmed (1992); Behdad (1994).

3. Keith Moxey and Robert Nelson have both already pointed out the unnatural quality of the canonical divisions of art history and their inclusion of non-Western areas. See Moxey (1995), Nelson (1997).

4. Boardman (1994:13–14). On the other side of the methodological spectrum, see Schnapp (1994:40).

5. M. Liverani, "Ancient Near Eastern History from Euro-centrism to an 'Open' World", lecture delivered in Copenhagen, 1995. I am very grateful to Mario Liverani for providing me with a copy of the manuscript of this lecture.

6. Hegel (1956). For further discussion on the interest in decay, see Liverani (1994); Larsen (1996).

7. This is an aspect of universal developmentalism still in use today, exemplified by the work of such scholars as Bernard Lewis. See Chapter 2.

8. See *The Art Journal*, vol. 54, no. 3, Fall 1995, which is dedicated to this subject; also Preziosi (1989); Bal and Bryson (1991); Moxey (1994).

9. See the discussion of the notion of aesthetics in Ingold, (1996), where opponents and proponents of transcultural aesthetics categories both present their arguments.

10. Price (1989) argues that primitive art ought to be evaluated by the same critical standards as Western art because art from non-Western cultures is not different from Western art; Coote and Shelton (1992) argue for transcultural categories of aesthetics; Gell (1998) makes the argument that if Western aesthetic theories of art apply to "our" art, then they should apply to everybody else's art and should be so applied (see page 1). Yet at the same time, these writers consider the cultural context and the ethnographic process to be important considerations in the assessment of this art.

11. See, for example, the arguments in Coote and Shelton (1992) and Ingold (1996).

12. See H. Foster, "The Artist as Ethnographer," in H. Foster (1996b:171–204).

13. This approach has been the subject of much controversy in art history in the past five years. See the responses of various art historians to the "Visual Culture Questionnaire" circulated by the editors of the journal *October* and published in *October*, volume 77 (1996), and the discussion in Moxey (2001:103–23).

14. The relation of such displays to colonial discourse has been discussed recently, but it is important to see that such production of cultural difference continues in museum galleries today. See Bal (1996); Seeden (1994).

Chapter 2

1. For the application of the Freudian concept of the uncanny to historiographic analysis, see especially de Certeau (1988); Bhabha (1994).

2. See *Lisan al Arab*, a Mediaeval Arabic dictionary, for an extensive entry on the word *Iraq* (in Arabic). For a short entry in English, see *Encyclopaedia of Islam*, vol. 2 pt. 1 (H–J) (Leiden: E. J. Brill), 1938, pages 515–19.

3. The al Idrisi map dates to A.D. 1154 (A.H. 960) and is preserved in a copy of A.D. 1553. It is mistakenly dated A.D. 1456 in Whitfield (1994:28). I would like to thank Doris Nicholson of the Bodleian Library, Oxford, for bringing this to my attention.

4. The issue of the religious or biblical impetus for the archaeological endeavor in Mesopotamia is of great importance and has been discussed by Kuklick (1996). Kuklick's study reveals this to be even more distinctive of American archaeologists than of Europeans. It should be pointed out here, however, that postcolonial criticism generally takes the stance that the religious interest, and missionary work in particular, was part and parcel of the colonial enterprise and was a crucial aspect of the civilizing mission of imperialism. See Comaroff and Comaroff (1992).

5. Cooper (1992:133). For similar arguments, see also Larsen (1996) and my review of this book (Bahrani 1999).

6. Gramsci (1987:12, 56, 261). For a discussion of the development of the concept of hegemony in the Marxist tradition, and particularly in the thought of Antonio Gramsci, see Mouffe and Laclau (1985); Anderson (1976–77).

7. See Williams (1973) for the concept of the deflection of oppositional emergent cultures by the hegemonic center. See also Said (1983).

8. Similar critiques have been made regarding the assimilation of postcolonial theory into what Stephen Slemon calls "an object of desire for critical practice: as a shimmering talisman that in itself has the power to confer political legitimacy onto specific forms of institutionalized labor." See Slemon (1994). See especially the valuable critiques of Shohat (1992) and McClintock (1992).

9. These are three of four master tropes defined and analyzed by White (1973). See also Ricoeur (1984) for the function of mimesis in historical writing.

10. Fergusson (1850:363–64). Similar statements were made by Lord Curzon and by Henry Frankfort and are pointed out by Roaf (1990b).

11. The meaning of the term *ideology* and the processes through which ideology functions are not addressed by this scholarship. Thus, the theoretical literature on ideology is largely dismissed by Near Eastern archaeology. See, for example, the post-Marxist theories of Althusser (1971); Laclau (1977); Mouffe and Laclau (1985); and more recently Žižek (1994; 1989). For a discussion of the complexity of this notion from the point of view of postprocessual archaeology, see Hodder (1992).

12. For such a survival in the field of history, see Leveque (1987), in which volume one of his history of the ancient world is titled *Des despotismes orientaux à la cité Greque.*

13. The current usage of the term in the English language according to the *Oxford English Dictionary* refers to very close, accurate resemblance.

Chapter 3

1. Piaget (1973) said that a child's mode of relating to the world is metaphoric or symbolic as opposed to rational adult thought.

2. The exception to the silence on this point is the work of Keith Moxey in a series of articles; see especially Moxey (1995, 1994). See also Nelson (1997). Preziosi's study, *Rethinking Art History* (1989), had already questioned the poetics and rhetoric of art historical disciplinary practices.

3. This theory of subjectivity as a constitutive splitting that involves alterity derives from Jacques Lacan, who described the nature of the subject as being effectively split from the moment of the formation of subjectivity. In other words, "splitting" is constitutive of the subject (Lacan uses the sign $ to indicate the subject). Therefore, alterity is originally the decentered other place of our own splitting. See "The Mirror Stage" (Lacan 1977:1–7).

4. For the realm of the visual, this point is argued by Marin (1981:18–42); Bryson (1983, 1992); Moxey (1991; 1994:1–19, 41–50) following Althusser's thesis in "Ideology and the Ideological State Apparatuses" (1971).

5. Summers (1991) points to this equation of conceptual with non-Western art.

6. For example, Goodman (1976) assumes that all images have to do with reference, with resemblance or lack thereof. According to this notion, all representations are thus things that refer to other things.

Chapter 4

1. The hymn, which is of the reign of Ashurbanipal (668–627 B.C.), is found in Ebeling (1915–23: nos. 105 and 361) and translated in Falkenstein and von Soden (1953:247–48). Derrida's source, however, is Gernet (1963).

2. I borrow this phrase from the work of W. J. T. Mitchell, especially, his *Picture Theory* (1994). However, Mitchell's work is not concerned with Near Eastern traditions or other forms of signification developed outside the Euro-American arts.

3. In this chapter I will mostly draw upon the writings of Jacques Derrida and Tzvetan Todorov, although neither of these writers actually address the cuneiform system of writing as such. Derrida makes reference to cuneiform as a system of writing and refers to Gelb's book (Derrida 1974:323, n. 4), but without any detailed discussion. Although Julia Kristeva devotes a chapter to cuneiform in her book *Language the Unknown* (1989), her survey remains in the traditional historical style and makes no attempt at a grammatological investigation. Jean-Jacques Glassner's excellent new study, *Écrire à Sumer: l'invention du cunéiforme* (2000), came out after this book had gone into production and unfortunately could not be taken into consideration.

4. Fergusson (1874:55–64) explains that the Turanians were the first to people the world. See also Young (1995:129) for Egyptological arguments to the same effect.

5. For a good overview of "the Sumerian problem," see D. Potts (1997:43–47), who also provides further references for the debates of early Sumerology.

6. For a good review of this problem, see Michalowski (1990), who also points out that numerous sign systems existed in antiquity before writing, including such things as Potter's marks and stamp seals, as well as tokens, but that none of these are precursors to writing. Instead, they are parallel systems of communication (58). Schmandt-Besserat's work was published in numerous journals culminating in her book *Before Writing* (1992).

7. The issue of the extent of literacy in Babylon and Assyria is discussed by Wilcke (2000), who argues that a greater amount of the population was literate than we have been willing to accept. However, Wilcke does not hazard a guess as to what percentage of the population that would mean. Postgate (1992:69) also argues that literacy had reached a very high rate in the Old Babylonian period. But see also Michalowski (1995), who believes that literacy was always highly restricted in the ancient Near East.

8. For the theory of the effects of literacy on society, see the work of the structuralist anthropologist Jack Goody (1977, 1986, 1987). Bottéro's arguments were developed prior to these publications; see especially, "Symptômes, signes, écritures" (1974).

9. For the discussion of the function of this monument, which is generally referred to as the Codex Hammurabi or the Laws of Hammurabi but is most likely not a code of laws, see chapter 10 in Bottéro (1992:156–84).

10. See von Soden (1972:842–43) for the Akkadian verb *pašarum* although the translation here is my own.

11. It is remarkable that most early commentators on the script referred to these pictograms as pictures of things, directly representing those things, without differentiating between parts and the whole. As far as I am aware, it is again Bottéro who first made this distinction.

12. For the faculties of knowledge in the philosophy of Immanuel Kant, see his *Critique of Pure Reason* (1781); for introductions to his work, see Deleuze (1984). For Kant on fine art, see *Critique of Judgement* (1790) and discussions of this work in Kemal (1986, 1992). Heidegger's discussion of the realm of being is in his *Being and Time* (1962).

Chapter 5

1. For notions of identity, the individual, and body and soul in ancient Egypt, see Hornung (1992). For the notion of the individual as a multifaceted assemblage of parts, see Bahrani (2001:96–120), which discusses the relationship between the body, identity, and portraiture.

2. I am referring particularly to Derrida's stance that the episteme of Western science, linguistics, and philosophy is founded upon the notion of the possibility of a pure phonetic writing, see Derrida (1974:27–73, especially 30).

3. Morandi (1988:105–6); Winter (1992:36, n.5; 1997:364–65); Bahrani (1995: 378–79, n. 46). For the traditional philological translation, see *CAD*, vol. S.

4. For an overview of the term in Western writings, see Michael Camille (1996). See also the discussion in Gilles Delueze (1990).

5. For a good explanation of Deleuze's concept of the virtual, see the introduction to his work in Massumi (Massumi 1992: 20ff; 34ff). This conception of the virtual is not to be confused with the common contemporary usage of the word *virtual*, derived from computer technologies.

6. Irene Winter has translated *ṣalam šarrutiya* as image "in the office of my kingship." She adds that by this inscription "we are told literally that this is not a personal, but an *official image*" (her emphasis). But the word *official* occurs nowhere in the text. *Šarrum* in Akkadian means king. *Šarrutu* means kingship royalty. The suffix *-iya* is the suffix applied for creating any possessive construction. I therefore find the translation "official image" or even the posited "personal image" as its opposite unconvincing, and if such a distinction is to be made for Mesopotamian representation, it needs to be done on the basis of other information from antiquity and not on this statement. However, Winter's argument against the use of portrait should be heeded, and her description of the image of the king as "coded for ideal qualities and attributes of a ruler" is important in any discussion of royal images (1997:374).

7. For the series *šumma ālu*, see Nötscher (1928, 1929, 1930); Gadd (1925–27); Guinan (1989). For physiognomatic *omina*, see Kraus (1939). For *egirru*, see *CAD* vol. E. See also Oppenheim (1974); Leichty (1997) for aspects of divination.

8. *CAD*, vol. 17, part 4: 221ff. esp. 229: "if a fog is written into the city . . ."

9. Marin claims to have been influenced by Kantorowicz's earlier study, which demonstrates the fundamental role played by the theology of the corpus mysticum in the European theory of royalty and its political and juridical processes: *The King's Two Bodies* (1957).

10. It should be noted however, that the city-state is not collapsible into the

king. The unification of king and state we see in Europe is perhaps more closely paralleled by the unification of the city god's statue and city-state in ancient Near Eastern practices. The absence or presence of this city god (statue) determined the welfare of the city and all its inhabitants (see Chapter 6).

Chapter 6

1. For the inscription, see Scheil (1900:53 pl. 2) for the Akkadian text and Scheil (1901:40 pl. 2) for the Elamite text. The stele was first published in de Morgan (1900:106, 144 pl. 10).

2. Nylander (1980:331). It must be said that it was an uncharacteristic statement on the part of Nylander, who has often stressed how prejudices interfere in our view of Persian art. He is one of only a handful of scholars who have ever considered how modern attitudes might affect our views of the Near East. It is perhaps because of this awareness that he was the first to recognize that such destruction was not random, and my research owes much to his seminal article.

3. This translation was seemingly introduced by the art historian Amiet (1976:128). Philologists specializing in the difficult Elamite language translate the word in question as "to take" rather than "to protect." See König (1965:76, 22); Hinz and Koch (1987:568).

4. For this attitude to the inscriptions on Near Eastern art, see, for example, Strommenger (1964:28, 42) and Schapiro (1969).

5. Kant (1790:67–68). See also Derrida's critique in *The Truth in Painting* (1987).

6. Meier (1937–39); Civil in Reiner and Civil (1967); Renger and Seidl (1980–83); Spycket (1968); Oppenheim (1977:183–98); Winter (1992).

7. See Hallo (1983:13–14). Indications of this belief in the power of images can be seen in Babylonian Chronicle I iv:34–36 (Grayson 1975:109; Luckenbill 1927:33–34, §66–67).

8. B. Foster (1993:273–307) provides a discussion and translations of texts; III.9, 11, 12, 13; IV, 16.

9. For the literary production and the religious changes that resulted at this time, see Lambert (1964:3–13; 1967:126–27); B. Foster (1993:351–52) provides an extensive bibliography on the Epic of Creation and Marduk's supremacy.

10. This translation is from B. Foster (1993:301, III, 15, e: lines 4–19). I am grateful to Ben Foster and to CDL press for the permission to quote it here.

11. Grayson (1991:253–54, A.0.101.17). I have inserted the word *image* instead of Grayson's broader choice, *monument*, as the ideogram used in the original text, ALAM, which refers to Akkadian *salmu*, meaning image as opposed to Akkadian *naru*, meaning inscribed monument or stele.

12. I am indebted to the work of Michael Taussig (1993) for the parallel between image magic and colonial writing. My discussion of the practices of assault and abduction of images was inspired by David Freedberg (1989).

Chapter 7

1. Also quoted by Lacan (1977:159). See also 277ff of *The Interpretation of Dreams,* where Freud describes the dream content as a pictographic script.

2. See Baffi Guardata and Dolce (1990:203), who view the altar as a religious monument used by Tukulti-Ninurta for the celebration of his power.

3. Andrae (1935:57–67 pls. 12, 30). For a recent discussion of this object see Muscarella (1995).

4. For the location of sculpture within temples, see the discussion on the placement of the statues of Gudea in Winter (1989). This is a useful discussion of the issue in general, even if it deals with an earlier period.

5. It should be noted that there is no correct designation for this object, and categorizing it as either pedestal or altar is perhaps too limiting in description. It is likely that there was an overlapping of these categories in antiquity. The current favored use of pedestal is supported by iconographic evidence from similar objects represented in seals and other relief carvings that depict a deity symbol on top of such monuments. However, we should be wary of reading iconography as if it were a direct reflection of daily life.

6. For the most eloquent argument regarding the superiority of narrative as an artistic form, see Gombrich, (1960:116–45) "Reflections on the Greek Revolution." This attitude has pushed several ancient Near Eastern scholars into the position of arguing for the origins of narrative in the East. Although narrative was no doubt a common form of visual representation in Near Eastern antiquity long before Greece, the constant battle for its origins in the East can turn into another confirmation of classically determined categories as proper art.

7. Guinan refers to it as "an antithetical unit whose ominous signs are linked by opposition" (1989:231).

8. See especially *The Voice of the Winds* of 1928 and *The Castle in the Pyrenees* of 1961. In the first painting three large, seemingly metallic orbs float over a field. In the second a boulder upon which stands a castle floats over a seashore. For illustrations, see, for example, Meuris (1994:57, 146).

Chapter 8

1. For an introduction to the philosophical work of Gilles Deleuze and Felix Guattari, see Mengue (1994); Massumi (1992); Bogue (1989).

2. For the association of what Derrida terms Graeco-Western metaphysics and phoneticism, see Derrida (1974, 1982).

Bibliography

The following abbreviations are used in the bibliography:

CAD   *The Assyrian Dictionary of the Oriental Institute of the University of Chicago.* A. L. Oppenheim, E. Reiner et al., eds. Chicago: University of Chicago Press, 1956–.

MDOG   Mitteilungen der Deutschen Orient-Gesellschaft. Berlin, 1898–.

RLA   *Reallexikon der Assyriologie und Vorderasiatischen Archäologie.* E. Ebeling et al., eds. Berlin and Leipzig, 1932–.

SAS   State Archives of Assyria. The Neo-Assyrian Text Corpus Project of the Academy of Finland in Co-operation with Deutsche Orient-Gesellschaft, K. Deller, F. M. Fales, S. Parpola and N. Postgate, eds. Helsinki: Helsinki University Press, 1987–.

WVDOG   Wissenschaftliche Veröffentlichungen der Deutschen Orient-Gesellschaft, Leipzig and Berlin, 1900–.

Abusch, I. Tzvi. 1987. *Babylonian Witchcraft Literature.* Case Studies. Atlanta: Scholars Press.

Adorno, Theodor, and Max Horkheimer. [1944] 1972. *Dialectic of Enlightenment.* Trans. J. Cumming. New York: Herder and Herder.

Ahmed, Aijaz. 1992. *In Theory.* London: Verso.

Althusser, Louis. 1971. Ideology and the Ideological State Apparatuses. In *Lenin and Philosophy and Other Essays.* Trans. B. Brewster. Pp. 121–73. London: New Left Books.

———. 1972 *Montesquieu, Rousseau, Marx.* Trans. B. Brewster. London: Verso.

Amiet, Pierre. 1976. *L'Art d'Agadé au musée du Louvre.* Paris: Éditions des musées nationaux.

Anderson, Perry. 1976–77. The Antinomies of Antonio Gramsci. *New Left Review* 100: 5–78.

Andrae, Walter. 1935. *Die jüngeren Ischtar-Temple in Assur.* Leipzig: WVDOG 58.

Asad, Talal, ed. 1973. *Anthropology and the Colonial Encounter.* London: Ithaca Press.

Baffi Guardata, Francesca, and Rita Dolce. 1990. *Archeologia della Mesopotamia l'età Cassita e Medio-Assira*. Rome: Bretschneider.

Bahrani, Zainab. 1995. Assault and Abduction: The Fate of the Royal Image in the Ancient Near East. *Art History* 18 (3): 363–382.

———. 1998a. Conjuring Mesopotamia: Imaginative Geography and a World Past. In *Archaeology under Fire*, ed. L. M. Meskell. Pp. 159–174. London: Routledge.

———. 1998b. Al sharq "al khariji": Bilad ma bain al nahrain fi al zaman wa al makan. *Al Hayat*. August 13:7 (in Arabic).

———. 1999. Review of *The Conquest of Assyria*, by Mogens Trolle Larsen. *Journal of the American Oriental Society* 118 (4): 115–16.

———. 2001. *Women of Babylon: Gender and Representation in Mesopotamia*. London: Routledge.

Bakhtin, Mikhail. 1986. *Speech Genres and Other Late Essays*. Ed. C. Emerson and M. Holquist, trans. V. W. McGee. Austin: University of Texas Press.

Bal, Mieke. 1996. *Double Exposures: The Subject of Cultural Analysis*. London: Routledge.

Bal, Mieke, and Norman Bryson. 1991. Semiotics and Art History. *Art Bulletin* 73 (2): 174–208.

Bann, Stephen. 1984. *The Clothing of Clio: A Study of the Representation of History in Nineteenth-Century Britain and France*. Cambridge: Cambridge University Press.

Barker, Francis, ed. 1983. *The Politics of Theory*. Colchester: The Universtity of Essex.

Barthes, Roland. [1964] 1988. *The Semiotic Challenge*. Trans. R. Howard. New York: Hill and Wang.

Baudrillard, Jean. 1983. *Simulations*. Trans. P. Foss, P. Patton, and P. Beitchman. New York: Semiotext(e).

Behdad, Ali. 1994. *Belated Travellers: Orientalism in the Age of Colonial Dissolution*. Durham, N.C.: Duke University Press.

Behrens, Hermann, ed. 1989. *DUMU-E2 DUB-BA-A: Studies in Honor of Åke Sjöberg*. Philadelphia: University Museum.

Belting, Hans. 1987. *The End of the History of Art?* Chicago: University of Chicago Press.

Benjamin, Walter. 1979. *On the Mimetic Faculty: Reflections*. Trans. E. Jephcott, ed. P. Demetz. New York: Harcourt Brace Jovanovitch.

Beran, Thomas. 1988. Leben und Tod der Bilder. In *Festgabe für Karlheinz Deller*, ed. G. Mauer and U. Magen. Pp. 55–60. Neukirchen-Vluyn: Neukirchener Verlag.

Berenson, Bernard. 1948. *Aesthetics and History*. New York: Pantheon Books.

Bernal, Martin. 1987. *Black Athena*. New Brunswick, N.J.: Rutgers University Press.

———. 1994. The Image of Ancient Greece as a tool for Colonialism and European Hegemony. In *Social Construction of the Past: Representation as Power*, ed. G. C. Bond and A. Gilliam. Pp. 119–28. London: Routledge.

Bhabha, Homi. 1983. Differences, Discrimination and the Discourse of Colonialism. In *The Politics of Theory*, ed. F. Barker. Pp. 194–211. Colchester: Univesity of Essex.

———. 1994. *The Location of Culture*. London: Routledge.

Biggs, Robert. 1967. *ŠA.ZI.GA: Ancient Mesopotamian Potency Incantations*. Locust Valley: J. J. Augustin.

Blier, Suzanne Preston. 1987. *The Anatomy of Architecture: Ontology and Metaphor in Batammaliba Architectural Expression*. RES Monographs in Anthropology and Aesthetics. Cambridge: Cambridge University Press.

———. 1995. *African Vodun: Art, Psychology and Power*. Chicago: University of Chicago Press.

Boardman, John. 1994. *The Diffusion of Classical Art in Antiquity*. London: Thames and Hudson.

Bogue, Ronald. 1989 *Deleuze and Guattari*. London: Routledge.

Bohrer, Frederick. 1989. Assyria as Art: A Perspective on the Early Reception of Ancient Near Eastern Artifacts. *Culture and History* 4: 7–33.

———. 1992. The Printed Orient: The Production of Austen Henry Layard's Earliest Works. In *The Construction of the Ancient Near East*, ed. A. Gunter. Pp. 85–105. Copenhagen: Academic Press.

———. 1994. The Times and Spaces of History: Representation, Assyria, and the British Museum. In *Museum Culture*, ed. D. J. Sherman and I. Rogoff. Pp. 197–222. Minneapolis: University of Minnesota Press.

———. 1998. Inventing Assyria: Exoticism and Reception in Nineteenth-Century England and France. *Art Bulletin* 80 (2): 336–56.

Bottéro, Jean. 1974. Symptômes, signes, écritures. In *Divination et Rationalité*, ed. J. P. Vernant. Pp. 70–196. Paris: Éditions du Seuil.

———. 1985. *Mythes et rites de babylone*. Geneva: Slatkine-Champion.

———. 1988. Magie. In *RLA* 7 (3/4): 200–234.

———. 1992. *Mesopotamia. Writing, Reasoning and the Gods*. Trans. Z. Bahrani and M. Van De Mieroop. Chicago: University of Chicago Press.

Breckenridge, Carol. 1989. The Aesthetics and Politics of Colonial Collecting: India at World Fairs. *Comparative Studies in Society and History* 31: 195–216.

Brilliant, Richard. 1991. *Portraiture*. London: Reaktion Books.

Bryson, Norman. 1983. *Vision and Painting: The Logic of the Gaze*. New Haven, Conn.: Yale University Press.

———. 1991. Semiology and Visual Interpretation. In *Visual Theory*, ed. N. Bryson, M. A. Holly and K. Moxey. Pp. 61–73. Oxford: Polity and Blackwell.

———. 1992. Art in Context. In *Studies in Historical Change*, ed. R. Cohen. Pp. 18–42. Charlottesville: University of Virginia.

Bryson, Norman, Michael Ann Holly, and Keith Moxey, eds. 1991. *Visual Theory*. Oxford: Polity and Blackwell.

———. 1994. *Visual Culture: Images and Interpretations*. Hanover: Wesleyan University Press.

Buccellati, Giorgio. 1993. Through a Tablet Darkly. In *The Tablet and the Scroll*, ed. M. Cohe. Pp. 58–71. Bethesda, Md.: CDL Press.

Camille, Michael. 1996. Simulacrum. In *Critical Terms for Art History*, ed. R. Nelson and R. Schiff. Pp. 31–44. Chicago: University of Chicago Press.

Çelik, Zeynep. 1992. *Displaying the Orient: Architecture of Islam at Nineteenth-Century World's Fairs*. Berkeley and Los Angeles: University of California Press.

Chamberlain, J. Edward, and Sander Gilman. 1985. *Degeneration: The Dark Side of Progress*. New York: Columbia University Press.

Chard, Chloe. 1995. Nakedness and Tourism: Classical Sculpture and the Imaginative Geography of the Grand Tour. *Oxford Art Journal* 18 (1): 14–28.

Clifford, James. 1983. On Ethnographic Authority. *Representations* 2: 118–46.

———. 1988. *The Predicament of Culture: Twentieth Century Ethnography, Literature, and Art*. Cambridge, Mass.: Harvard University Press.

Clifford, James, and George E. Marcus, eds. 1986. *Writing Culture: The Poetics and Politics of Ethnography*. Berkeley and Los Angeles: University of California Press.

Comaroff, John, and Jean Comaroff. 1992 *Ethnography and the Historical Imagination*. Boulder, Colo.: Westview Press.

Cooper, Jerrold S. 1992. From Mosul to Manila: Early Approaches to Funding Ancient Near Eastern Studies Research in the United States. In *The Construction of the Ancient Near East*, ed. A. Gunter. Pp. 133–59. Culture and History 11. Copenhagen: Academic Press.

———. In press. Babylonian Beginnings: The Origin of the Cuneiform Writing System in Comparative Perspective. In *First Writing*, ed. S. Houston. Cambridge: Cambridge University Press.

Coote, Jeremy, and Anthony Shelton. 1992. *Anthropology, Art, and Aesthetics*. Oxford: Oxford University Press.

Crinson, Mark. 1996. *Empire Building: Orientalism and Victorian Architecture*. London: Routledge.

Culler, Jonathan. 1983. *On Deconstruction: Theory and Criticism after Structuralism*. Ithaca, N.Y.: Cornell University Press.

———. 1988. *Framing the Sign: Criticism and Its Institutions*. Norman: University of Oklahoma Press.

Damerji, Muayyad Said. 1991 The Second Treasure of Nimrud. In *Near Eastern Studies*, ed. M. Mori. Pp. 9–17. Wiesbaden: Harrassowitz.

Daxelmüller, Christoph, and Marie-Louise Thomsen. 1982. Bildzauber im alten Mesopotamien. *Anthropos* 77 (1/2): 27–64.

de Certeau, Michel. 1980. Writing vs. Time: History and Anthropology in the Works of Lafitau. *Yale French Studies* 59: 37–65.

———. 1988. *The Writing of History*. Trans. T. Conley. New York: Columbia University Press.

de Man, Paul. 1996. *Aesthetic Ideology*. Ed. A. Warminski. Minneapolis: University of Minnesota Press.

de Morgan, Jacques. 1900. *Descriptions des objets d'art; Mémoires de la Délégation en Perse*, vol. 1. Recherches archéologiques. Première série. Fouilles à Suse en 1897–1898 et 1898–1899. Paris.

Deleuze, Gilles. 1984. *Kant's Critical Philosophy*. Trans. H. Tomlinson and B. Habberjam. Minneapolis: University of Minnesota Press.

———. 1988. *Foucault*. London: Athlone Press.

———. 1990. *The Logic of Sense*. Trans. Mark Lester. New York: Columbia University Press.

———. 1994. *Difference and Repetition*. Trans. P. Patton. New York: Columbia University Press.

Deleuze, Gilles, and Felix Guattari. 1987. *A Thousand Plateaus: Capitalism and Schizophrenia*. Trans. B. Massumi. Minneapolis: University of Minnesota Press.

———. 1994. *What Is Philosophy?* Trans. H. Tomlinson and G. Burchell. New York: Columbia University Press.

Derrida, Jacques. 1974. *Of Grammatology*. Trans. G. Chakravorty Spivak. Baltimore: Johns Hopkins University Press.

———. 1978. *Writing and Difference*. Trans. A. Bass. Chicago: University of Chicago Press.

———. 1981a. *Disseminations*. Trans. B. Johnson. Chicago: University of Chicago Press.

———. 1981b. Economimesis. Trans. R. Klein. *Diacritics* 11: 3–25.

———. 1982. *Margins of Philosophy*. Trans. A. Bass. Chicago: University of Chicago Press.

———. 1987. *The Truth in Painting*. Trans. G. Bennington and I. McLeod. Chicago: University of Chicago Press.

Dirks, Nicholas. 1992. *Colonialism and Culture*. Ann Arbor: University of Michigan Press.

Dirlik, Arif. 1994. The Postcolonial Aura, Third World Criticism in the Age of Global Capitalism. *Critical Inquiry* 20: 328–356.

Eagleton, Terry. 1990. *The Ideology of the Aesthetic*. Cambridge: Basil Blackwell.

———. 1991. *Ideology*. London: Verso.

Ebeling, Erich. 1915–1923. *Keilschrifttexte aus Aššur religiösen Inhalts*. Leipzig: J. C. Hinrichs.

Fabian, Johannes. 1983. *Time and the Other: How Anthropology Makes its Object*. New York: Columbia University Press.

———. 1990. Presence and Representation: The Other and Anthropological Writing. *Critical Inquiry* 16: 753–72.

Falkenstein, Adam, and Wolfram von Soden. 1953. *Sumerische und akkadische Hymnen und Gebete*. Zürich: Artemis Verlag.

Fanon, Frantz. 1963. *The Wretched of the Earth*. Trans. C. Farrington. New York: Grove Press.

———. 1967a. *Toward the African Revolution*. Trans. by H. Chevalier. Harmondsworth: Pelican.

———. 1967b. *Black Skin, White Masks*. Trans. C. Markmann. New York: Grove Press.

Fergusson, James. 1850. *The Palaces of Nineveh and Persepolis Restored: An Essay in Ancient Assyrian and Persian Architecture*. Delhi: Goyal Offset Printers.

———. 1874 [1865]. *A History of Architecture in All Countries*. London: John Murray.

———. 1974 [1881]. *Archaeology in India*. Delhi: KB Publications.

Finet, André. 1969. Les symboles du cheveu, du bord du vetments et de l'ongle en Mésopotamie. In *Eschatologie et cosmologie: Annales du centre d'etude des religions*, vol. 3, ed. A. Abel, et al. Pp. 101–30. Brussels: Editions de l'Institute de Sociologie. Université Libre de Bruxelles.

Firth, Raymond. 1951. *Elements of Social Organization*. London: Tavistock.

Forge, Anthony. 1967. The Abelam Artist. In *Social Organization: Essays Presented to Raymond Firth*, ed. M. Freedman. Pp. 65–84. London: Frank Cass.

———. 1973. *Primitive Art and Society*. London: Oxford University Press.

Foster, Benjamin. 1993. *Before the Muses: An Anthology of Akkadian Literature*. Bethesda, Md.: CDL Press.

Foster, Hal. 1983. *The Anti-Aesthetic: Essays on Postmodern Culture*. Port Townsend, Wash.: Bay Press.

———. 1995. The Artist as Ethnographer. In *The Traffic in Culture: Refiguring Art and Anthropology*. Berkeley and Los Angeles: University of California Press.

———. 1996a. The Archive without Museums. *October* 77: 97–119.

———. 1996b. *The Return of the Real*. Cambridge, Mass.: MIT Press.

Foucault, Michel. 1970. *The Order of Things: An Archaeology of the Human Sciences*. New York: Vintage.

———. 1972. *The Archaeology of Knowledge and the Discourse on Language*. Trans. A. M. Sheridan Smith. New York: Pantheon.

———. 1982. *This Is Not a Pipe*. Trans. J. Harkness. Berkeley and Los Angeles: University of California Press.

Frazer, James. 1911. *The Golden Bough. Part I: The Magic Art and the Evolution of Kings*. London: Macmillan.

Freedberg, David. 1989. *The Power of Images*. Chicago: University of Chicago Press.

Freud, Sigmund. 1912–13. *Totem and Taboo*. Standard Edition of the Complete Psychological Works. Vol. 13. Trans. J. Strachey. New York: Basic Books.

———. 1919. *The Uncanny*. Standard Edition of the Complete Psychological Works. Vol. 17. Trans. J. Strachey. New York: Basic Books.

———. 1959. *The Interpretation of Dreams*. Standard Edition of the Complete Psychological Works. Vols. 4–5. Trans. J. Strachey. New York: Basic Books.

Gadd, C. J. 1925–27. *Cuneiform Texts from Babylonian Tablets in the British Museum*. Vols. 38–40. London: British Museum.

Gelb, I. J. 1952. *A Study of Writing: The Foundations of Grammatology*. Chicago: University of Chicago Press.

Gell, Alfred. 1992. The Technology of Enchantment and the Enchantment of Technology. In *Anthropology, Art, and Aesthetics*, ed. J. Coote and A. Shelton. Pp. 40–63. Oxford: Oxford University Press.

———. 1998. *Art and Agency: An Anthropological Theory*. Oxford: Oxford University Press.

Gernet, Jean. 1963. *L'Écriture et la psychologie des peuples*. Paris: Armand Colin.

Glassner, Jean-Jacques. 1995. The Use of Knowledge in Ancient Mesopotamia. In *Civilizations of the Ancient Near East*, ed. J. Sasson. Pp. 1815–24. New York: Scribners.

———. 2000. *Écrire à Sumer: L'invention du cunéiforme*. Paris: Éditions du Seuil.

Gliddon, George R. 1848. *Ancient Egypt*. Philadelphia: Peterson.

Gliddon, George R., and Josiah C. Nott. 1854. *Types of Mankind; or, Ethnological Researches Based upon the Ancient Monuments, Paintings, Sculptures and Crania of Races, and upon Their Naural, Geographical, Philological and Biblical History*. London: Trubner.

Goguet, Antoine-Yves. 1758. *De l'origine de loix, des arts, et des sciences, et de leurs progrès chez les anciens peuples*. Edinburgh: George Robinson.

Gombrich, Ernst. 1950. *The Story of Art*. London: Phaidon.

———. 1960. *Art and Illusion: A Study in the Psychology of Pictorial Representation*. London: Phaidon.

———. 1963. *Meditations on a Hobby Horse and Other Essays on the Theory of Art*. London: Phaidon.

Goodman, Nelson. 1976. *The Languages of Art: An Approach to a Theory of Symbols*. Indianapolis: Hackett.

Goody, Jack. 1977. *The Domestication of the Savage Mind*. Cambridge: Cambridge University Press.

———. 1986. *The Logic of Writing and the Organisation of Society*. Cambridge: Cambridge University Press.

———. 1987. *The Interface between the Written and the Oral*. Cambridge: Cambridge University Press.

———. 1997. *Representations and Contradictions: Ambivalence towards Images, Theatre, Fiction, Relics and Sexuality*. Oxford: Blackwell.

Gramsci, Antonio. 1987. *The Prison Notebooks*. Trans. Q. Hoare and G. Nowell Smith. New York: International Publishers.

Grayson, A. K. 1975. *Assyrian and Babylonian Chronicles*. Texts from Cuneiform Sources 5. Locust Valley, N.Y.: J. J. Augustin.

———. 1987. *Assyrian Rulers of the Third and Second Millennia* B.C. Toronto: University of Toronto Press.

———. 1991. *Assyrian Rulers of the Early First Millennium* B.C. Toronto: University of Toronto Press.

Guinan, Ann. 1989. The Perils of High Living: Divinatory Rhetoric in Summa Alu. In *DUMU-E2-DUB-BA-A: Studies in Honor of Åke Sjöberg*. ed. H. Behrens. Pp. 227–36. Philadelphia: The University Museum.

Gunter, Ann, ed. 1990. *Investigating Artistic Environments in the Ancient Near East*. Washington, D.C.: Smithsonian Institution.

———. 1992. *The Construction of the Ancient Near East*. Culture and History 11. Copenhagen: Academic Press.

Hall, Edith. 1989. *Inventing the Barbarian: Greek Self-Definition through Tragedy*. Oxford: Oxford University Press.

Hall, Stuart. 1996. When Was the Post-Colonial? Thinking at the Limit. In *The*

Post-Colonial Question, ed. I. Chambers and L. Curti. Pp. 242–60. London: Routledge.

Hallo, William W. 1971. *The Ancient Near East: A History.* New York: Harcourt Brace Jovanovich.

———. 1983. *Scripture in Context.* Winona Lake, Ind.: Eisenbrauns.

Harper, Prudence Oliver, et al., eds. 1995. *Assyrian Origins: Discoveries at Ashur on the Tigris.* New York: Metropolitan Museum of Art.

Harper, Prudence Oliver, Joan Aruz, and Françoise Tallon, eds. 1992. *The Royal City of Susa: Treasures from the Louvre Museum.* New York: Metropolitan Museum of Art.

Hegel, Georg Wilhelm Friedrich. 1956. *The Philosophy of History.* Trans. J. Sibree. New York: Dover Publications.

———. 1975. *Aesthetics.* Trans. T. M. Knox. Oxford: Oxford University Press.

Heidegger, Martin. 1962. *Being and Time.* Trans. J. Macquarrie and E. Robinson. New York: Harper Collins.

———. 1993. *Basic writings.* Ed. D. Farrell Krell. New York: Harper Collins.

Heinimann, Felix. 1945. *Nomos und Physis: Herkunft und Bedeutung einer Antithese im griechschen denken der 5 Jahrhunderts.* Basel: F. Reinhardt.

Herder, Johann Gottfried von. 1966. *Outlines of a Philosophy of the History of Man.* Trans. T. Churchill. New York: Bergman.

Herodotus. 1954. *The Histories.* Trans. Aubrey de Sélencourt. Harmondsworth: Penguin.

Hinz, Walter, and H. Koch. 1987. Elamisches Wörterbuch, Teil I, Berlin: Archäologische Mitteilungen aus Iran. Ergänzugnsband 17.

Hodder, Ian. 1982. *Symbolic and Structural Archaeology.* Cambridge: Cambridge University Press.

———. 1986. *Reading the Past.* Cambridge: Cambridge University Press.

———. 1992. *Theory and Practice in Archaeology.* London: Routledge.

Hodder, Ian, et al., eds. 1995. *Interpreting Archaeology: Finding Meaning in the Past.* London: Routledge.

Holly, Michael Ann. 1990. Past Looking. *Critical Inquiry* 16: 371–95.

Hornung, Erik. 1992. *Idea into Image: Essays on Ancient Egyptian Thought.* Princeton, N.J.: Timken Publishers.

Howe, Stephen. 1998. *Afrocentrism: Mythical Pasts and Imagined Homes.* London: Verso.

Immerwahr, Henry. 1966. *Form and Thought in Herodotus.* Chapel Hill: Western Reserve University Press.

Ingold, Timothy, ed. 1996. *Key Debates in Anthropology.* London: Routledge.

Jacobsen, Thorkild. 1987. The Graven Image. In *Ancient Israelite Religion*, ed. P. D. Miller. Pp. 15–32. Philadelphia: Fortress Press.

Jameson, Fredric. 1991. *Postmodernism or the Cultural Logic of Late Capitalism.* Durham, N.C.: Duke University Press.

———. 1998. *The Cultural Turn: Selected Workings on the Postmodern.* London: Verso.

JanMohamed, Abdul R. 1985. The Economy of Manichean Allegory: The Function of Racial Difference in Colonial Literature. *Critical Inquiry* 12 (1): 59–87.

Jenkins, Ian. 1992. *Archaeologists and Aesthetes*. London: British Museum Publications.

Kant, Immanuel. [1781] 1934. *Critique of Pure Reason*. Trans. N. Kemp Smith. London: Macmillan.

———. [1790] 1952. *Critique of Judgement*. Trans. J. Creed Meredith. Oxford: Oxford University Press.

Kantorowicz, Ernest H. 1957. *The King's Two Bodies: A Study in Mediaeval Political Theology*. Princeton, N.J.: Princeton University Press.

Kemal, Salim. 1986. *Kant and Fine Art*. Oxford: Clarendon Press.

———. 1992. *Kant's Aesthetic Theory*. London: Macmillan Press.

Kinney, Leila, and Zeynep Çelik. 1990. Ethnography and Exhibitionism at the Expositions Universelles. *Assemblages* 13: 35–59.

Knox, Robert. 1862. *The Races of Men: A Philosophical Enquiry into the Influence of Race over the Destinies of Nations*. London: Renshaw.

König, F. W. 1965. Die Elamischen Königsinschriften. Graz: Archiv für Orientforschung Beiheft 16.

Kohl, Philip, and Clare Fawcett, eds. 1995. *Nationalism, Politics, and the Practice of Archaeology*. Cambridge: Cambridge University Press.

Kraus, F. R. 1939. Texte zur babylonischen Physiognomatik. Berlin: Archiv für Orientforschung Beiheft 3.

Kristeva, Julia. 1989. *Language the Unknown: An Initiation into Linguistics*. Trans. A. M. Menke. New York: Columbia University Press.

Kuklick, Bruce. 1996. *Puritans in Babylon*. Princeton, N.J.: Princeton University Press.

Labat, Rene. 1963. L'écriture cunéiforme et la civilisation mésopotamienne. In *L'Écriture et la psychologie des peuples*, ed. J. Gernet. Pp. 73–92. Paris: Armand Colin.

Lacan, Jacques. 1977. *Écrits: A Selection*. Trans. A. Sheridan. New York: Tavistock.

———. 1986. *The Four Fundamental Concepts of Psycho-Analysis*. Trans. A. Sheridan. Harmondsworth: Penguin Books.

Laclau, Ernesto. 1977. *Politics and Ideology*. London: Verso.

Lafitau, Joseph-François. [1724] 1974. *Customs of the American Indians Compared with the Customs of Primitive Times*. Trans. W. Fenton and E. Moore. Toronto: Champlain Society.

Lambert, W. G. 1964. The Reign of Nebuchadnezzar I: A Turning Point in the History of Ancient Mesopotamian Religion. In *The Seed of Wisdom: Essays in Honour of T. J. Meek*, ed. W. S. McCollough. Pp. 3–13. Toronto: University of Toronto Press.

———. 1967. Enmeduranki and Related Matters. *Journal of Cuneiform Studies* 21: 126–38.

Larsen, Mogens Trolle. 1996. *The Conquest of Assyria: Excavations in an Antique Land, 1840–1860*. London: Routledge.

Lavin, Sylvia. 1992. *Quatremere de Quincy and the Invention of a Modern Language of Architecture*. Cambridge, Mass.: MIT Press.

Layard, Austen Henry. 1849. *Nineveh and Its Remains: With an Account of a Visit to the Chaldean Christians of Kurdistan, and the Yezidis or Devil-Worshippers; and an Enquiry into the Manners and Arts of the Ancient Assyrians*. London: John Murray.

———. 1849–53. *The Monuments of Nineveh*. London: John Murray.

———. 1853. *Discoveries in the Ruins of Nineveh and Babylon; with Travels in Armenia, Kurdistan and the Desert: being the Result of a Second Expedition Undertaken for the Trustees of the British Museum*. London: John Murray.

———. 1894. *Early Adventures in Persia, Susiana, and Babylonia: Including a Residence among the Bakhtiyari and Other Wild Tribes before the Discovery of Nineveh*. London: John Murray.

Layton, Robert. 1981. *The Anthropology of Art*. Cambridge: Cambridge University Press.

Lefkowitz, M.R. and G. MacLean Rogers, eds. 1996. *Black Athena Revisited*. Chapel Hill: University of North Carolina Press.

Leichty, Erle. 1997. Divination, Magic, and Astrology in the Assyrian Royal Court. In *Assyria 1995*, ed. S. Parpola and R. Whiting. Pp. 161–64. Helsinki: The Neo-Assyrian Text Corpus Project. University of Helsinki.

Leveque, Pierre. 1987. *Les premières civilisations*. T.1: *des despotismes orientaux à la cité grecque*. Paris: Presses Universitaires de France.

Lévi-Strauss, Claude. 1963. *Structural Anthropology*. New York: Basic Books.

Lewis, Bernard. 1994. *The Shaping of the Modern Middle East*. New York: Oxford University Press.

———. 1996. *The Middle East: A Brief History of the Last 2,000 Years*. New York: Scribners.

Liverani, Mario. 1981. Critique of Variants and the Titulary of Sennacherib. In *Assyrian Royal Inscriptions*, ed. F. M. Fales. Pp. 225–57. Rome: Istituto per l'Oriente, Centro per l'antichità e la storia dell'arte del vicino Oriente.

———. 1994. "Voyage en Orient": The Origins of Archaeological Surveying in the Near East. In *The Near East and the Meaning of History*. Pp. 1–16. Studi Orientali 13. Rome: Bardi.

———. 1996. The Bathwater and the Baby. In *Black Athena Revisited*, ed. M. R. Lefkowitz and G. MacLean Rogers. Pp. 421–27. Chapel Hill: University of North Carolina Press.

———. 1997. The Ancient Near Eastern City and Modern Ideologies. In *Die Orientalische Stadt: Kontinuität, Wandel, Bruch*, ed. G.Wilhelm. Pp. 85–107. (Internationales Colloquium dre Deutschen Orient-Gesellschaft 9–10 Mai 1996 in Halle/Saale). Saarbrücker Druckerei und Verlag.

———. 1998. *Uruk la prima città*. Rome: Laterza.

Lowe, Lisa. 1991. *Critical Terrains: French and British Orientalism*. Ithaca, N.Y.: Cornell University Press.

Luckenbill, Daniel David. 1926. *Ancient Records of Assyria and Babylonia*. Vol. 1. Chicago: University of Chicago Press.

————. 1927. *Ancient Records of Assyria and Babylonia*. Vol. 2. Chicago: University of Chicago Press.

MacKenzie, J. M. 1995. *Orientalism: History, Theory and the Arts*. Manchester: Manchester University Press.

Mahan, A. T. 1902. The Persian Gulf and International Relations. *National Review* (September): 26–45.

Makiya, Kenan. 1993. Put an End to Saddam, Just Make Him Lose Face. *Houston Chronicle*. January 31.

Marcus, G., and D. Cushman. 1982. Ethnographies as Texts. *Annual Review of Anthropology* 11: 25–69.

Marcus, G., and F. Myers, eds. 1995. *The Traffic in Culture: Refiguring Art and Anthropology*. Berkeley and Los Angeles: University of California Press.

Marin, Louis. 1981. *Portrait of the King*. Trans. M. M. Houle. Minneapolis: University of Minnesota Press.

————. 1989. The Body of Power and Incarnation at Port Royal and in Pascal. In *Fragments for a History of the Human Body*, ed. M. Feher. Pp. 421–47. New York: Urzone.

Massumi, Brian. 1992. *A User's Guide to Capitalism and Schizophrenia*. Cambridge, Mass.: MIT Press.

McClintock, Ann. 1992. The Myth of Progress: Pitfalls of the Term Post-colonialism. *Social Text* 31/32: 84–98.

————. 1995. *Imperial Leather: Race, Gender, and Sexuality in the Colonial Conquest*. London: Routledge.

Meier, G. 1937–39. Die Ritualtafel der serie Mundwaschung. *Archiv für Orientforschung* 12: 40–45.

Mengue, P. 1994. *Gilles Deleuze ou le système du multiple*. Paris: Éditions Kimé.

Meuris, Jacques. 1994. *René Magritte, 1898–1967*. Cologne: Benedikt Taschen.

Michalowski, Piotr. 1992. Early Mesopotamian Communicative Systems: Art, Literature, and Writing. In *Investigating Artistic Environments in the Ancient Near East*, ed. A. Gunter. Pp. 53–69. Smithsonian Institution.

————. 1995. Sumerian Literature: An Overview. In *Civilizations of the Ancient Near East*, ed. J. Sasson. Pp. 2270–91. New York: Scribners.

Mitchell, Timothy. 1988. *Colonizing Egypt*. Berkeley and Los Angeles: University of California Press.

————. 1989. The World as Exhibition. *Comparative Studies in Society and History* 31: 217–36.

Mitchell, W. J. T. 1983. *The Politics of Interpretation*. Chicago: University of Chicago Press.

————. 1986. *Iconology: Image, Text, Ideology*. Chicago: University of Chicago Press.

————. 1992. Postcolonial Culture, Postimperial Criticism. *Chronicle of Higher Education* 19. Reprinted in *The Post-colonial Studies Reader*, ed. Bill Ashcroft, Gareth Griffiths, and Helen Tiffin. Pp. 475–79. London: Routledge.

————. 1994. *Picture Theory: Essays on Verbal and Visual Representation*. Chicago: University of Chicago Press.

Mitter, Partha. 1992. *Much Maligned Monsters: A History of European Reactions to Indian Art*. Chicago: University of Chicago Press.

———. 1994. Decadence in India: Reflections on a Much-Used Word in Studies of Indian Art and Society. In *Sight and Insight: Essays on Art and Culture in Honour of E. H. Gombrich at 85*, ed. John Onians. Pp. 379–97. London: Phaidon.

Monk, Daniel Bertrand. 1993. Orientalism and the Ornament of Mediation. *Design Book Reviews* (Summer/Fall): 32–34.

Moore-Gilbert, Bart. 1997. *Postcolonial Theory*. London: Verso.

Morandi, D. 1988. Stele e statue reali assire: diffusione e implicazione ideologiche. *Mesopotamia* 23: 105–56.

Morgan, Lewis Henry. 1877. *Ancient Society: Researches in the Lines of Human Progress from Savagery through Barbarism to Civilization*. New York: Meridian Books.

Morris, Sarah. 1992. *Daidalos and the Origins of Greek Art*. Princeton, N.J.: Princeton University Press.

Mouffe, Chantal and Ernesto Laclau. 1985. *Hegemony and Socialist Strategy: Towards a Radical Democratic Politics*. London: Verso.

Moxey, Keith. 1986. Panofsky's Concept of "Iconology" and the Problem of Interpretation in the History of Art. *New Literary History* 17: 265–74.

———. 1991. Semiotics and the Social History of Art. *New Literary History*. 22: 985–99.

———. 1994. *The Practice of Theory: Poststructuralism, Cultural Politics, and Art History*. Ithaca, N.Y.: Cornell University Press.

———. 1995. Motivating Art History. *Art Bulletin* 77 (3): 392–401.

———. 2001. *The Practice of Persuasion: Paradox and Power in Art History*. Ithaca, N.Y.: Cornell University Press.

Muscarella, Oscar White. 1995. Cult Pedestal of the God Nusku. In *Assyrian Origins: Discoveries at Ashur on the Tigris*, ed. P. O. Harper et al. Pp. 112–13. New York: Metropolitan Museum of Art.

Nelson, Robert. 1997. The Map of Art History. *Art Bulletin* 79 (1): 28–40.

Nochlin, Linda. 1983. The Imaginary Orient. *Art in America* 71 (5): 119–91.

Nötscher, Friedrich. 1928. Die Omen-Serie šumma âlu ina mêlê šakin. *Orientalia* 31.

———. 1929. Die Omen-Serie šumma âlu ina mêlê šakin. *Orientalia* 39–42.

———. 1930. Die Omen-Serie šumma âlu ina mêlê šakin. *Orientalia* 51–54.

Nylander, Carl. 1980. Earless in Nineveh. *American Journal of Archaeology*, 48: 329–33.

———. 1997. The Mutilated Image. In *World Views of Prehistoric Man*, ed. L. Larsson. Pp. 235–59. Stockholm: Kungl.vitterhets, historie och antikvitets akademien

———. 1999. Breaking the Cup of Kingship. *Iranica Antiqua* 34: 71–83.

Oguibe, Olu. 1993. In the Heart of Darkness. *Third Text* 23: 3–8.

Oppenheim, A. Leo. 1956. *The Interpretation of Dreams in the Ancient Near East*. Transactions of the American Philosophical Society. Vol. 46. Philadelphia: American Philosophical Society.

————. 1974. A Babylonian Diviner's Manual. *Journal of Near Eastern Studies* 33: 197–220.

————. 1977. *Mesopotamia, Portrait of a Dead Civilization.* Chicago: University of Chicago Press.

Parpola, Simo. 1993a. *Letters From Assyrian and Babylonian Scholars.* SAS vol. 10. Helsinki: Helsinki University Press.

————. 1993b. Mesopotamian Astrology and Astronomy as Domains of Mesopotamian Wisdom. In *Die Rolle der Astronomie in den Kulturen Mesopotamiens,* ed. H. Galter. Pp. 47–60. Graz: Grazer Morgenländische Studien 3.

————. 1997. *Assyrian Prophecies.* SAS vol. 9. Helsinki: Helsinki University Press.

Parpola, S., and R. Whiting, eds. 1997. *Assyria 1995.* Helsinki: The Neo-Assyrian Text Corpus Project. University of Helsinki.

Pausanias. 1977. *Description of Greece.* Trans. W. H. Jones. Cambridge, Mass.: Harvard University Press.

Peirce, Charles Sanders. 1931–58. *Collected Works.* Ed. C. Hartshorne and P. Weiss. Cambridge, Mass.: Harvard University Press.

————. 1940. Logic as Semiotic: The Theory of Signs. In T*he Philosophy of Peirce: Selected Writings,* ed. J. Buchler. London: Routledge.

————. 1991. *Peirce on Signs: Writings on Semiotics by Charles Sanders Peirce.* Ed. J. Hoopes. Chapel Hill: University of North Carolina Press.

Piaget, Jean. 1973. *The Child and Reality: Problems of Genetic Psychology.* Trans. A. Rosin. New York: Grossman.

Pittman, Holly. 1996. The White Obelisk and the Problem of Historical Narrative in the Art of Assyria. *Art Bulletin* 78 (2): 334–55.

Plato. 1867. *Sophists.* Trans. L. Campbell. Oxford: Clarendon.

————. 1892. *Menexenus: Dialogues.* Trans. B. Jowett. Oxford: Clarendon Press.

————. 1926. *Cratylus.* Trans. N. Fowler. Cambridge, Mass.: Harvard University Press.

————. 1960. *Laws.* Trans. J. Tate. London: Dent.

Postgate, J. Nicholas. 1992. *Early Mesopotamia: Society and Economy at the Dawn of History.* London: Routledge.

————. 1994. Text and Figure in Ancient Mesopotamia: Match and Mismatch. In *The Ancient Mind: Elements of Cognitive Archaeology,* ed. Colin Renfrew. Pp. 176–84. Cambridge: Cambridge University Press.

Potts, Alex. 1994. *Flesh and the Ideal: Winckelmann and the Origins of Art History.* New Haven, Conn.: Yale University Press.

Potts, Daniel. 1997. *Mesopotamian Civilization: The Material Foundations.* Ithaca, N.Y.: Cornell University Press.

Pratt, Marylouise. 1992. *Imperial Eyes: Travel Writing and Transculturation.* London: Routledge.

Preziosi, Donald. 1989. *Rethinking Art History.* New Haven, Conn.: Yale University Press.

————. 1998. *The Art of Art History.* Oxford: Oxford University Press.

Price, Sally. 1989. *Primitive Art in Civilized Places.* Chicago: University of Chicago Press.

Prichard, James Cowler. 1813. *Researches on the Physical History of Man.* London: Arch.

Pritchard, James B. 1969. *Ancient Near Eastern Texts Relating to the Old Testament.* Princeton, N.J.: Princeton University Press.

Reiner, Erica. 1966. La Magie babylonienne: Le Monde du Sorcier. *Sources Orientales* 7: 69–98.

Reiner, Erica and Miguel Civil. 1967. Another Volume of Sultantepe Tablets. *Journal of Near Eastern Studies* 26: 177–211.

Renan, Ernest. 1968. La Réforme intellectuelle et morale de la France. Oeuvres complètes I. Cambridge: Cambridge University Press.

Renfrew, Colin, ed. 1994. *The Ancient Mind: Elements in Cognitive Archaeology.* Cambridge: Cambridge University Press.

Renger, Johannes, and Ursula Seidl. 1980–83. Kultbild. In *RLA* 6: 307–19.

Ricoeur, Paul. 1984 *Time and Narrative.* Trans. K. McLaughlin and D. Pellauer. Chicago: University of Chicago Press.

Roaf, Michael. 1990a. *Cultural Atlas of Mesopotamia.* Oxford: Equinox.

———. 1990b. Sculptors and Designers at Persepolis. In *Investigating Artistic Environments in the Ancient Near East,* ed. A. Gunter. Pp. 105–14. Washington, D.C.: Smithsonian Institution.

Rodowick, D. N. 1994. Impure Mimesis, or the Ends of the Aesthetic. In *Deconstruction and the Visual Arts,* ed. P. Burnette and D. Wills. Pp. 96–117. Cambridge: Cambridge University Press.

Rorty, Richard. 1979. *Philosophy and the Mirror of Nature.* Princeton, N.J.: Princeton University Press.

Russell, John M. 1991. *Sennacherib's* Palace without Rival *at Nineveh.* Chicago: University of Chicago Press.

Sachs, A. 1969. Akkadian Rituals. In *Ancient Near Eastern Texts Relating to the Old Testament,* ed. J. B. Pritchard. Pp. 331–45. Princeton, N.J.: Princeton University.

Saggs, H. W. F. 1995. *The Babylonians.* London: British Museum.

Said, Edward W. 1978. *Orientalism.* New York: Vintage Books.

———. 1983. Opponents, Audiences, Constituencies and Community. In *The Politics of Interpretation,* ed. W. J. T. Mitchell. Pp. 7–32. Chicago: University of Chicago Press.

———. 1993. *Culture and Imperialism.* New York: Vintage Books.

———. 1996. *Peace and Its Discontents.* New York: Vintage Books.

Sartre, Jean-Paul. 1963. Preface. In *The Wretched of the Earth* by F. Fanon. Trans. C. Farrington. New York: Grove Press.

Sasson, J., et al., eds. 1995. *Civilizations of the Ancient Near East.* New York: Scribners.

Schäfer, Heinrich. 1974. *The Principles of Egyptian Art.* Trans. J. Baines. Oxford: Clarendon Press.

Schapiro, Meyer. 1969. On Some Problems in the Semiotics of Visual Art: Field and Vehicle in Image-Signs. *Semiotica* 1 (3): 223–62.

Scheil, Vincent. 1900. Textes élamites-sémitiques, première série. Mémoires de la Délégation en Perse II. Paris.

———. 1901. Textes élamites-anzanites, première série. Mémoires de la Délégation en Perse III. Paris.

Schele, Linda. 1986. *The Blood of Kings: Dynasty and Ritual in Maya Art.* Fort Worth, Tex.: Kimbell Art Museum.

Schlegel, August Wilhelm von. [1801] 1963. Die Kunstlehre. *Vorlesungen über schöne Literatur und Kunst.* Vol. I. Stuttgart: W. Kohlhammer.

Schmandt-Besserat, Denise. 1992, *Before Writing.* Austin: University of Texas Press.

Schnapp, Alain. 1994. Are Images Animated? The Psychology of Status in Ancient Greece. In *The Ancient Mind: Elements in Cognitive Archaeology,* ed. C. Renfrew. Pp. 40–44. Cambridge: Cambridge University Press.

Schwartzer, Mitchell. 1995. Origins of the Art History Survey Text. *Art Journal* 54 (3): 24–29.

Seeden, Helga. 1994. Western Archaeology and the History of Archaeological Sites. In *The East and the Meaning of History.* Pp. 53–72. Studi Orientali 13. Rome: Bardi.

Shanks, Michael. 1996. *Classical Archaeology of Greece.* London: Routledge.

———. 1999. *Art and the Greek City State: An Interpretive Archaeology.* Cambridge: Cambridge University Press.

Shanks, Michael and Christopher Tilley, eds. 1987. *Re-Constructing Archaeology: Theory and Practice.* London: Routledge.

Shohat, Ella. 1992. Notes on the Postcolonial. *Social Text* 31/32: 99–113.

Slemon, Stephen. 1994. The Scramble for Post-colonialism. In *De-Scribing Empire: Post-colonialism and Textuality,* ed. C. Tiffin and A. Lawson. London: Routledge.

Speiser, E. A. 1969. Akkadian Myths and Epics. In *Ancient Near Eastern Texts Relating to the Old Testament,* ed. J. B. Prichard. Pp. 60–119. Princeton, N.J.: Princeton University Press.

Spivak, Gayatri Chakravorty. 1974. Introduction. In *Of Grammatology,* by Jacques Derrida. Baltimore: Johns Hopkins University Press.

———. 1985. The Rani of Simur: An Essay in Reading the Archives. *History and Theory* 24 (3): 247–72.

———. 1987. *In Other Worlds: Essays in Cultural Politics.* New York and London: Routledge.

———. 1988. Can the Subaltern Speak? In *Marxism and the Interpretation of Culture,* ed. Cary Nelson and Larry Grossberg. Pp. 271–313. Urbana: University of Illinois Press.

———. 1993. *Outside in the Teaching Machine.* London: Routledge.

Spivey, Nigel. 1996. *Understanding Greek Sculpture.* London: Thames and Hudson.

Spycket, Agnes. 1968. Les statues de culte dans les textes mésopotamiens des origines à la Ire dynastie de Babylone. Paris.

———.1981. *La statuaire du proche-Orient ancien*. *Handbuch der Orientalistik 7*. Vol. 1. Leiden: E. J. Brill.

Stocking, George W. 1982. *Race, Culture and Evolution: Essays in the History of Anthropology*. Chicago: University of Chicago Press.

———. 1987. *Victorian Anthropology*. New York: Free Press.

Stolper, Matthew. 1992. On Why and How. In *The Construction of the Ancient Near East*, ed. A. Gunter. Pp. 13–22. Culture and History 11. Copenhagen: Academic Press.

Strommenger, Eva. 1964. *The Art of Mesopotamia*. London: Thames and Hudson.

Summers, David. 1991. Real Metaphor: Towards a Redefining of the Conceptual Image. In *Visual Theory*, ed. N. Bryson, M. A. Holly, and K. Moxey. Pp. 231–59. Oxford: Polity and Blackwell.

Taussig, Michael. 1993. *Mimesis and Alterity: A Particular History of the Senses*. London: Routledge.

Thomas, Nicholas. 1994. *Colonialism's Culture: Anthropology, Travel and Government*. Cambridge: Polity Press.

Tiffin, Chris, and Alan Lawson, eds. 1994. *Describing Empire: Postcolonialism and Textuality*. London: Routledge.

Todorov, Tzvetan. 1982. *Theories of the Symbol*. Trans. C. Porter. Ithaca, N.Y.: Cornell University Press.

———. 1992. *The Conquest of America: The Question of the Other*. Trans. R. Howard. New York: Harper-Collins.

———. 1993. *On Human Diversity*. Trans. C. Porter. Cambridge, Mass: Harvard University Press.

Turner, F. M. 1981. *The Greek Heritage in Victorian Britain*. New Haven, Conn.: Yale University Press.

Usher, S. 1988. Greek Historiography and Biography. In *Civilizations of the Ancient Mediterranean: Greece and Rome*, ed. M. Grant and R. Kitzinger. Pp. 1525–40. New York: Scribners.

van der Veer, Peter. 2001. *Imperial Encounters: Religion and Modernity in India and Britain*. Princeton, N.J.: Princeton University Press.

Vernant, Jean-Pierre. 1974. *Divination et Rationalité*. Paris: Éditions du Seuil.

Volney, C. F. 1822. *Les ruines, ou méditations sur le révolutions des empires*. Paris: Bossange frères.

———. 1959 [1787]. *Voyage en Égypte et en Syrie*. Ed. J. Gaulmier. Paris: Mouton.

von Soden, Wolfram. 1972. *Akkadisches Handwörterbuch*. Wiesbaden: Otto Harrassowitz.

White, Hayden. 1973. *Metahistory*. Baltimore, Md.: Johns Hopkins University Press.

———. 1978. *Tropics of Discourse*. Baltimore, Md.: Johns Hopkins University Press.

Whitfield, Peter. 1994. *The Image of the World*. London: The British Library.

Wiggerman, F. A. M. 1992. *Mesopotamian Protective Spirits: The Ritual Texts*. Groningen: Styx and PP.

Wilcke, Claus. 2000. *Wer las und schrieb in Babylonien und Assyrien: Überlegungen zur Literalität im alten Zweistromland*. Munich: C. H. Beck.

Williams, Raymond. 1958. *Culture and Society, 1780–1850*. London: Chatto and Windus.

———. 1973. Base and Superstructure in Marxist Cultural Theory. *New Left Review* 82: 3–16.

———. 1983 [1976]. *Keywords: A Vocabulary of Culture and Society*. Rev. ed. London: Fontana Press.

Winckelmann, Johann Joachim. 1872. *The History of Ancient Art*. Trans. G. H. Lodge. Boston: James R. Osgood and Co.

Winter, Irene J. 1981. Royal Rhetoric and the Development of Historical Narrative in Neo-Assyrian Reliefs. *Studies in Visual Communication* 7: 2–38.

———. 1989. The Body of the Able Ruler: Toward an Understanding of the Statues of Gudea. In *DUMU-E2-DUB-BA-A: Studies in Honor of Åke Sjöberg*, ed. H. Behrens. Pp. 573–83. Philadelphia: University Museum.

———. 1992. Idols of the King: Royal Images as Recipients of Ritual Action in Ancient Mesopotamia. *Journal of Ritual Studies* 6 (1): 13–42.

———. 1997. Art in Empire: The Royal Image and the Visual Dimensions of Assyrian Ideology. In *Assyria 1995*, ed. S. Parpola and R. M. Whiting. Pp. 359–82. Helsinki: The Neo-Assyrian Text Corpus Project, University of Helsinki.

Young, R. J. C. 1990. *White Mythologies: Writing History and the West*. London: Routledge.

———. 1995. *Colonial Desire: Hybridity in Theory, Culture and Race*. London: Routledge.

Zimansky, Paul. 1993. Review of *Before Writing*, by Denise Schmandt-Besserat. *Journal of Field Archaeology* 20: 513–17.

Žižek, Slavoj. 1989. *The Sublime Object of Ideology*. London: Verso.

———. 1991. *Looking Awry: An Introduction to Jacques Lacan through Popular Culture*. Cambridge, Mass.: MIT Press.

———. 1993. *Tarrying with the Negative: Kant, Hegel and the Critique of Ideology*. Durham, N.C.: Duke University Press.

———. 1994. *Mapping Ideology*. London: Verso.

Index

Acknowledgments

I would first like to thank John Baines and Stephanie Dalley for their invitation to present these ideas in their earliest form at the Oriental Institute, Oxford University, in 1994. Many of the discussions I had with colleagues in Oxford that year became incorporated into Chapter 6 and filtered into other chapters also, so that this first opportunity to discuss the project became the foundation for much of my subsequent thinking on the issues of image making and the dialectical relationship between texts and images.

An earlier version of Chapter 6 appeared in *Art History* (1995, vol. 18, no. 3) under the title "Assault and Abduction: The Fate of the Royal Image in the Ancient Near East." I am grateful to the Association of Art Historians and Blackwell publishers for permission to include it here. A short version of Chapter 2 was delivered to the Rencontre Assyriologique Internationale at Fondazione Cini, Venice, in the summer of 1997. I am grateful for the many valuable comments and the tremendous encouragement I received from the participants there. That paper appears as "The Extraterrestrial Orient Colonizing Mesopotamia in Space and Time" in *Landscapes, Territories, Frontiers and Horizons in the Ancient Near East*, ed. L. Milano (Venice: Università Ca Foscari, 2000) and was published in Arabic in *al Hayat* (August 1998). Another summary version appears as "Conjuring Mesopotamia: Imaginative Geography and a World Past" in *Archaeology Matters: Culture and Politics in the Eastern Mediterranean*, ed. L. Meskell (London: Routledge, 1998). I thank Routledge for permission to include it here. I am also grateful for comments made on this subject by Hamid Dabashi and the members of the Iranian Studies Seminar at Columbia University, where I presented this paper in the spring of 1998.

I thank Joan Aruz and Ron Wallenfels of the Metropolitan Museum of Art for kindly providing photographs and permission to publish figures 4 and 21, Doris Nicholson of the Bodleian Library, Oxford, for helpful information on the al Idrisi map (figure 3), and Ulla Kasten of the Yale Babylonian Collection for kindly providing the image and permission to publish the Assyrian Dream Book tablet (figure 6). I am especially grateful to Hans Nissen for his assistance in finding and providing an appropriate image of an Uruk IV tablet (figure 5).

My sincere thanks to the following friends and colleagues, who, each in his or her own way, encouraged and inspired the project, offered advice and assistance, or read and commented on the text: Qais al Awqati, John Baines, Jeremy Black, Frederick Bohrer, Norman Bryson, Jerry Cooper, Barbara Frank, Lamia al Gailani, Ann Gibson, Jack Goody, Donald Hansen, Tomas Hlobil, Tara Jaff, Mario Liverani, Clemente Marconi, Bojana Mojsov, Barbara A. Porter, Manoj Pradhan, Martin Powers, Selma al Radhi, Julian Reade, Julian Reilly, Michael Roaf, Jack Sasson, Elizabeth Stone, Marc Van De Mieroop, Franz Wiggerman, Irene Winter, and Norman Yoffee. I would like to express my admiration of and offer special thanks here to Carl Nylander for his gracious and diligent response to my writings and for taking my criticisms as an opportunity and a means of opening a dialogue and continuing the discussion on iconoclasm in Near Eastern antiquity. The title of this book is borrowed from the great Sumerologist Thorkild Jacobsen (Jacobsen 1987), whose work has been an inspiration also in many other ways.

In the end I offer my deepest thanks to Keith Moxey, above all others, for his staunch support of this project and to Ian Hodder and Robert Preucel, who gave me the space to present this work.